SELECTED PLAYS
OF
RUTHERFORD MAYNE

Irish Drama Selections

General Editors
Joseph Ronsley
Ann Saddlemyer

IRISH DRAMA SELECTIONS

ISSN 0260–7962

SELECTED PLAYS
OF
RUTHERFORD MAYNE

Chosen and with an Introduction by

Wolfgang Zach

Irish Drama Selections 13

2000
COLIN SMYTHE
Gerrards Cross, Bucks.

THE CATHOLIC UNIVERSITY
OF AMERICA PRESS
Washington, D.C.

First published in Great Britain in 2000
by Colin Smythe Limited, Gerrards Cross, Buckinghamshire SL9 8XA

British Library Cataloguing in Publication Data
A catalogue record for this book is available from the British Library
ISBN 0-86140-292-8
ISBN 0-86140-293-6 pbk

*

First published in North America in 2000 by
The Catholic University of America Press, Washington D.C.

Library of Congress Cataloguing-in-Publication Data

Mayne, Rutherford, 1878–1967.
[Plays. Selections]
Selected plays of Rutherford Mayne / chosen and with an introduction by
Wolfgang Zach.
p. cm.—(Irish drama selections : 13)
Includes bibliographical references (p.).
ISBN 0-8132-0978-1 (alk. paper).—ISBN 0-8132-0979-X (pbk. : alk. paper)
1. Ulster (Northern Ireland and Ireland)—Drama. 2. Ireland— Drama. I. Zach,
Wolfgang. II. Series.

PR6025.A965 A6 2000
822'.914—dc21
99-049786

Produced in Great Britain
Typeset by Art Photoset Ltd., Beaconsfield, Buckinghamshire
Printed and bound by T.J. International Ltd., Padstow, Cornwall

CONTENTS

INTRODUCTION

Samuel John Waddell, who took the stage-name Rutherford Mayne when he embarked on a theatrical career, was the most prolific, versatile, and successful playwright that the Irish Literary Revival in Ulster brought forth. In the course of his career as a dramatist, from 1906 to 1934, he wrote thirteen plays – ten plays for the Ulster Literary Theatre, one for the Dublin-based Theatre of Ireland, and two for the Abbey Theatre. His early realistic Ulster 'peasant plays' were especially successful, among them *The Drone* (1908), the most popular Irish folk comedy of the first half of the twentieth century. From 1904 onwards until late in his life he also performed a great number of major roles in plays of his own and of other writers, usually to great acclaim, mainly in Belfast and Dublin but also on tours to England and Scotland. His plays disappeared from the stage in the 1950s and when he died at the age of eighty-nine, in 1967, his artistic achievements were almost forgotten. Unfortunately, he did not write an autobiography, and, in spite of his importance to the development of Irish theatre, substantial studies of his life and work still wait to be written.[1] Seven of his eight published plays – his most important ones – have been included in this edition. With one exception, Mayne's five unpublished plays were also his least successful and Mayne may not have wanted to see them in print. In any case, they share the fate of the majority of the forty-seven plays written by authors for the Ulster Literary Theatre (1904-1934) which have remained unpublished and are no longer accessible even in manuscript form.[2] Two important prose pieces (one of Mayne's essays and an interview), have been included as they provide direct insight into his personality, views, and career.

*   *   *

Samuel John Waddell was born in Tokyo in 1878 and got his early education in Japan under the tutorship of his Irish parents, the Rev. Hugh Waddell, a Presbyterian missionary, originally from Glenarm, Co. Antrim, and his wife Jane, née Martin, of Tullyallen. Hugh Waddell, also the son of a Presbyterian minister, had left Ireland

vii

immediately after graduating from Queen's College Belfast and being licensed to preach the Gospel. After missionary work in China and Spain he accepted a call from the United Presbyterian Church of Scotland to set up a mission in Tokyo after Japan's legalization of Christianity in 1873. The fourth of the Waddells' ten children, eight boys and two girls, Samuel left Japan for the first time at the age of fourteen, in 1892, when his father sent his ailing wife to Belfast with their children. Soon after, in the same year, Jane Waddell died from typhoid fever which she must have contracted in Japan when the disease reached epidemic proportions, killing people by the hundreds. In 1893, Hugh Waddell married his cousin, Martha, returned to Tokyo, and his second wife and his four younger children followed him soon after. The six elder children of the Waddells, among them Samuel, remained in Belfast to receive their further education there, while their father stayed in Tokyo until 1900 when his mission was closed and he was forced to leave Japan with his remaining family. They all returned to Belfast where Hugh Waddell died only a year later, leaving his family in precarious financial circumstances.[3]

At first sight, it appears unlikely that Samuel Waddell and his youngest sister Helen,[4] two of the most significant Ulster writers of their age, should come from this Irish-Japanese Presbyterian missionary background. However, several factors were greatly conducive to the development of their artistic, literary and linguistic talents. Most importantly, their home was not dominated by a stereotyped staunch and hard art- and pleasure-shunning Puritan; from the existing documents their father emerges as a humorous and loving man, a dedicated Christian missionary as well as a liberal educator. He was interested not only in religious but also secular literature so that the reading of both the St. James Bible and of authors from Shakespeare and Scott to Tennyson and Beecher-Stowe was the daily fare in the Waddells' family circle. In addition, Samuel was exposed to a multilingual and multicultural environment where the new and small outposts of Western Christianity competed with the age-old and fascinating culture of Japanese Buddhism. Their father not only switched from one language to another with ease (Helen Waddell describes his reading aloud the Psalms in Hebrew, the New Testament in Greek, the Lord's Prayer in Japanese); he was also an eager student of the colloquial language and traditional imagery of the Japanese peasants, which he used in his sermons, preached in Japanese. His children consequently were familiar with different ideological and artistic views and observant of the difference between linguistic registers and idioms. Like his sister, Samuel Waddell learned to speak Japanese and was also greatly impressed by Japanese art; we do not know to what extent he was familiar with Japanese drama, which does not appear to have exerted an influence on his works. Another aspect of Japanese life did, for the older Waddell children grew up in the most turbulent time of social upheavals. Living in rather poor circumstances themselves, only thinly clad and barefoot, or at most sandalled, they were proud of being Japanese 'born and bred', and they not only heard of, but were also directly confronted with, the precarious situation of the peasants (which was similar to and perhaps even worse than that in Ireland), their suffering and dying from want and diseases as well as their despair and rioting. In fact, it was the land question which dominated politics in the early Meiji period of the 1870s and '80s when the end of the feudalistic absolute power of the daimyos, the Japanese landlords, and the redistribution of the land, for some time, went hand in hand with the economic plight of the peasants before the new order brought real change for the farmers.[5] It is with these impressions that Samuel came to Ireland where he found that the land question also dominated politics and was still in need of being settled. It is probably more than a coincidence that he should become centrally concerned with 'the land' in his future life.

Samuel Waddell's education in Belfast did not lead in an artistic direction. In 1892 he attended the Royal Belfast Academical Institute and after his father's death in 1901 he and his elder brothers had to take on bread-winning jobs in order to support themselves and their younger brothers and sisters. While working for a Belfast building company, Samuel Waddell studied engineering (partly in night classes) at Belfast Mercantile College, graduated from the Royal University of Ireland in 1907, and took up work as a surveyor. In 1909 he joined the Irish Land Commission and got involved in solving the great land problem, which busied him all his remaining life. In 1911, he was sent to the West of Ireland to help with dividing and redistributing the land of the big estates and later went to live in Dublin; but he still travelled extensively around Ireland and retired as chief inspector of the Commission in 1950, one of the most important government civil servants of the Irish Republic.

Waddell's great energy and huge vitality, reflected in his portrait in the Abbey Theatre and the article in *The Bell* reproduced here, explain how but not why he managed to combine his successful career as an engineer and government official with that of artist – a playwright, who wrote more than a dozen plays, and an amateur actor, who acted main roles in dozens of plays. As he actually led a 'double life', it is particularly apt that he should have taken a *nom de plume* (Rutherford and Mayne were the second Christian names of the two brothers he was closest to) when he embarked upon his parallel career as an actor-playwright for the Ulster Literary Theatre (later renamed the Ulster Theatre) in 1905. This kept him active until late in his life although the members of the group were and remained amateurs. He may also have considered becoming a professional actor performing with Mollison's Company in England and Ireland in 1908, shortly before he took his job with the Irish Land Commission.

How important the Ulster Theatre was to him can be seen from the fact that – although he had left Belfast in 1911 for the West of Ireland and later to Dublin – he kept his close affiliation with it not only as a playwright but also as an active Board member until 1930 and as an actor up to its dissolution in 1934 when, in his own words, the Ulster Theatre 'died as it lived – in penury'. The seasons of the Ulster Theatre were brief (one to two weeks or even shorter) making it possible for him to go to Belfast or to Dublin where the group performed regularly, or occasionally to other cities in Ireland or England. When he moved to the South, he also acted at the Abbey and the Gaiety Theatre from the 1920s on. He was still active as an actor in his late sixties and in 1944 at the Gaiety Theatre managed to repeat his great success as Brutus Jones in O'Neill's *Emperor Jones*, first performed at the Abbey Theatre in January 1927. He lived to see his plays disappear from the Irish stage in the 1940s and '50s, but towards the end of his life one late achievement must have given him much satisfaction: when Belfast gained a permanent theatre-building, something that he had dreamed of from the beginning of his theatrical career. As a member of the Ulster Theatre Mayne had always hoped that the group would not have to be merely a guest at some Belfast institution, usually the Grand Opera House, but that it would have a theatre of its own. Early attempts at fund-raising failed and in 1930 he also had to give up his hope that the troupe would remain an amateur company and use their accumulated profits to this purpose. It was thirty years later, in 1960, when he got involved in a renewed attempt at building a theatre in Belfast. In this year, Mayne became a trustee of Belfast's Lyric Players' Theatre, in connection with a drive for funds to build a real theatre, and he lived to see the laying of its cornerstone in 1965. The Lyric Players' Theatre was opened in 1968.

In his private life, Samuel Waddell's affiliation with the Ulster Literary Theatre had important consequences. In 1902 he met the members of the group for the first time, among them Joseph

Campbell, the poet, John Campbell, the artist, and their sister Josephine Campbell. He admired their acting, acted with them from 1905 on, moved in their circle, and fell in love with Josephine. In 1909, he dedicated *The Drone* to 'Seveen' (as an actress Josephine appeared under the name of Seveen Canmer), and he married her, a Roman Catholic, in 1910. This marriage of a descendant of two old Presbyterian families, with many ministers among his ancestors, and the son of a Presbyterian missionary, to a Roman Catholic, was certainly unusal, especially considering the time they lived in, and is perhaps only understandable in view of his early liberal, muticultural education in Japan.[6] His wife kept acting for the Ulster Theatre, under the name Josephine Mayne, mostly in her husband's plays, at least to the end of the 1920s. They had a daughter, Ginette. Two years after Josephine's death in 1941, he married her sister Frances, who survived him. After his death at Our Lady's Manor, Dalkey, on 25 February 1967, his lying-in-state took place at the Church of Our Lady of Perpetual Succour, Foxrock, and he was buried at Dean's Grange Cemetery.[7]

*   *   *

Mayne's involvement with the theatre began in 1902 when his school-fellow and friend David Parkhill introduced him to a group of young Belfast theatrical enthusiasts who wanted Ulster to play a role in the Irish Literary Revival and stage Irish plays. Waddell, aged twenty-four, saw their first production, was fascinated by AE's *Deirdre,* though less so by Yeats's *Cathleen ni Houlihan,* and by the acting of John and Joseph Campbell, and joined this artistic circle. After a row with W. B. Yeats over performance rights, the group decided to write and stage their own plays with a definite Ulster dimension. When in 1904 this group formally established the Ulster Literary Theatre, Samuel Waddell (from now on Rutherford Mayne) was among its founding members, as were the Campbells and other artistically-minded people from various professional backgrounds who turned to acting and/or writing. Among them there were the young architect David Parkhill (who wrote under the pen-name Lewis Purcell), the politician Bulmer Hobson, and the talented Morrow brothers, who ran a painting and decoration business; Harry Morrow, under the name of Gerald MacNamara became the other important playwright-actor of the Ulster Theatre, and Fred Morrow directed most of Mayne's plays. The group also edited a short-lived journal, *Uladh* (1905/6) in which they discussed their principles and printed their first plays. One of these early plays, Purcell's *Enthusiast* (1905), gave Mayne the opportunity of acting his first part, the servant man Rab, and influenced him in writing his first play, *The Turn of the Road*.

The Turn of the Road was first produced at Queen's University, Belfast, in December 1906 with Rutherford Mayne as Samuel James and his future wife, Josephine Campbell, as Jane Graeme. It was the first in a series of six realistic folk plays which Mayne wrote over the next eight years, all of them entirely set in a farmer's kitchen, and it had an important subject at its centre: the age-long enmity towards the arts in the puritanical Ulster society. Some years later, Mayne defined his purpose not as an attack on puritanism as such but as 'an assault against . . . a pervasive evil in Ireland, philistinism'.[8] It is hard to see what made Mayne write a play about Ulster peasant life in the Co. Down dialect; he had insight into the hard life of Japanese peasants but had little opportunity of experiencing the life and speech of Ulster farmers, apart from some contact when he stayed with relatives in the Banbridge area of Co. Down. This is not to deny the play another autobiographical dimension as, at that time, Mayne himself encountered a conflict similar to that experienced by his hero Robbie John: both were made to face the painful choice between the traditional 'respectable' bread-winning profession (farm life/ engineering) and the 'unrespected' insecurity of an artist (fiddling/ acting). Mayne's convincing realistic technique, which he later explained as a specifically Ulster 'appalling sense of reality', should not blind one to the fact that the play owes most to Mayne's imagination and to literary influence, especially to the realistic peasant plays written by Lewis Purcell and Padraic Colum. To Purcell's Enthusiast (1905) he owes the Ulster dialect as well as the theme of a character's dedication to an idea and his love of books which he defends against the prejudiced opposition of narrow-minded farmers; in Colum's *Broken Soil* (1903) he found the character of a fiddler who leaves his farm and follows the call of music. These concrete influences also did not go unnoticed by the early reviewers of *The Turn of the Road*, although *The Freeman's Journal* (16 December) and *The Northern Whig* (15 December) appreciated Mayne's originality, especially his depiction of characters and situations from Ulster peasant life. The Belfast reviews though predominantly positive were less enthusiastic than the critics and the audience at the Abbey when the Ulster Literary Theatre produced the play in March 1907. Joseph Holloway wrote in his diary:

I have not enjoyed myself so much at a theatre for a very long time as at the

Abbey tonight in witnessing the first performance in Dublin of the Ulster Literary Theatre. . . . Rutherford Mayne's . . . *The Turn of the Road* was full of human nature and clever telling dialogue. The struggle of an artistic soul amongst uncongenial surroundings is set forth convincingly by the dramatist . . . Mr Waddell was capital as 'Samuel James'. . . . The play was splendidly received, and the author bowed his thanks to the enthusiastic audience, which was the largest I have seen at the Abbey since *The Playboy* row.[9]

W. B. Yeats was also present and, recalling the performance in November 1908, he criticized the 'mechanism' of the play but praised its 'sincere observation' and focus on 'the details of life'. In fact, so impressed was he that he described the Ulster Players as 'the only dramatic society, apart from our own, which is doing serious artistic work'.[10] The reviewers of the play for *Sinn Féin* (6 April 1907) and *The Lady of the House* (15 April 1907)were equally fascinated by the play's 'fidelity to reality' and 'artistic realism', which they contrasted favourably with the artificiality of the Abbey plays, especially Synge's. *The Turn of the Road* was praised as 'delightful and successful', 'brilliantly written', 'delightful and natural'. The critic of the *Irish Times* even called it 'beyond question one of the most sterling productions of the Irish literary revival ever seen at the Abbey Theatre'. *The Turn of the Road* became one of the most popular plays in the repertoire of the Ulster Theatre, was regularly staged in Belfast and Dublin for more than two decades, and was immediately printed. It was also produced by other companies in Ireland and England, taken on tours of England and Scotland by William Mollison's and Whitford Kane's companies in 1908 and 1911. The Ulster actor Whitford Kane claimed in his autobiography *Are We All Met?* that he discovered his Irish identity through *The Turn of the Road*.

Mayne's great success with *The Turn of the Road* was eclipsed by the reception of his next play *The Drone*, which not only became the most successful of all the plays staged by the Ulster Theatre but one of the most popular Irish plays of the first half of the twentieth century. The play is centred on a likeable, good-natured and witty 'parasite' who manages to avoid work and survive in a work- and wealth-addicted farm environment by using his wits and by playing upon people's hope of future wealth. The play may also be taken as a commentary upon the inhumanity of the dominant Ulster work ethic and the necessity of family solidarity and brotherly love to counteract it. Originally, Mayne wrote his comedy in two acts, leaving it to the audience to imagine how the 'drone' would extricate his brother from his fix, his breach of promise of marriage, and it was in this form that the play was first produced at the Abbey Theatre on 24 April 1908. The immediate reviews were mixed but most of them were full of praise. While *The Evening Herald* thought that *The Drone* was 'in no sense an ambitious venture', S. Connolly in *Sinn Féin* called it a 'masterpiece of comedy of life and manners, the finest of its kind', *The Irish Independent* hailed the 'genius' which makes the 'audience . . . gape with astonishment', and the *Irish Times* critic emphasized its innovative artistic potential when he wrote: 'no more significant production has been seen in Dublin in our day. We seem to be on the verge of a revolution in dramatic art, and remarkably enough, it has been left to Ulster to lead the way.'

In its expanded, three-act form the play was probably premièred at Belfast in May 1909, before being staged at the Abbey on 26 November 1909. 'C.A.' in The Dublin *Evening Mail* (27 November) conceded that it was 'a successful comedy, as witness the continuous laughter of the audience' but did not accept it as 'drama in any true sense', while 'Jacques' in *The Irish Independent* of the same date voiced what made Irish theatre-goers almost addicted to *The Drone* in the next two decades:

> As for *The Drone*. To say anything of this most droll of droll stage pictures would be to mention laughter in every sentence. A third act dealing with a breach of promise action has been added. The continuous laughter of the audience paid tribute to play, players, and authors. What really excellent artistes all those Ulster players are!

In its three-act version, *The Drone* was printed and reprinted, translated into Irish, and staged by the Ulster Theatre at Belfast and Dublin year after year, in almost all its seasons, taken to other cities in Ireland and England, and also produced by almost every other dramatic society in Ireland up to the 1940s. Whitford Kane took it to London where it was a success at the Royalty Theatre in February 1912. There, an American manager saw it and took it to the United States where, after trials at Washington and Baltimore, it failed miserably at Daly's Theatre, New York, on 30 December 1912, was damned by the critics and had to close after two performances. This reception in America, which might have been expected of a play with 'a drone' as its hero, was the only exception to its stunning run of successful productions; for example, on a tour of the Ulster Theatre to Scotland and England in 1923 the play, with Mayne as John Murray, was again very well received. A London reviewer wrote enthusiastically: 'There has been nothing in London quite like *The*

Drone . . . since Lennox Robinson's *The White Headed Boy*.'[11] In Ireland, the play actually passed into folklore; Sam Hanna Bell recalls that when John McBride, the Ulster actor, first appeared in The Drone, he expressed an uneasiness about his lines to his producer, Fred Morrow. 'Don't worry,' Morrow reassured him, 'if you need a prompt the audience will prompt you.'[12]

When Mayne was on tour in England acting professionally with the Mollison Company, his next dramatic effort, *The Troth*, a tragedy in one act, was premièred in October 1908 at the Crown Theatre, Peckham, London, with Whitford Kane in the cast. This was Mayne's first attempt at the popular Irish genre of a one-act play, his first tragedy, and his first historical play. Set in the mid-19th century, it deals with the Irish land problem in the form of a pact between two starving tenants, a Catholic and a Protestant, who cross over their religious barriers, assassinate their cruel landlord and show solidarity even beyond the grave. When the play was produced by the Uster Literary Theatre in Belfast and Dublin in the following year, its critical reception in the North was remarkably different from that in the South. Belfast critics reviewed the play favourably. *The Belfast Telegraph* stated, '*The Troth* grips like great music',[13] and *The Northern Whig* observed that Mayne handled his 'tragic motive . . . with power, directness, and refreshing realism. The characters owe nothing to tradition.'[14] In Dublin, the reviews were negative, and the critic of the *Dublin Evening Mail* described it as 'Mid-Victorian melodrama . . . deserving no place in the literature of Irish life' as Mayne's picture of 'the distressful Irish peasant' in his play was 'completely irrelevant to Irish life at present'.[15] This drew a spirited defence from Padraic Colum, who also lectured the reviewer on the central importance of the period of evictions in 19th-century Ireland, but did not comment upon what I see as the implied relevance of the play's theme to the time. In *The Troth*, Mayne reminds his fellow-Irishmen of the hardship and deprivation suffered by the mass of the peasants before the Land Acts passed between 1881 and 1903 brought some relief but did not really solve the land problem by abolishing the landlord system. What Mayne implicitly pleads for is non-denominational solidarity among the Irish population in achieving a just distribution of the land in Ireland. What cannot be overlooked is again the autobiographical dimension of the play, the fact that, soon after having written *The Troth*, Samuel Waddell himself broke down the religious barrier between Protestants and Catholics in Ulster in real life by marrying a Catholic and that he devoted half of his future 'double life' to settling the Irish land problem by joining the Irish Land Commission.

Despite its mixed critical reception, *The Troth* proved to be quite popular, was taken into the repertoire of the Ulster Theatre and often staged, usually as a curtain raiser for *The Drone* or *The Turn of the Road*, at least into the 1920s. Whitford Kane staged it at the Maiden Lane Theatre, London, in 1910, where Mayne met Galsworthy, Pinero, Barrie, and Granville-Barker who were all present at this special matinee performance, and in 1911 Kane also took the play, together with *The Drone* and *The Turn of the Road*, to Liverpool and Manchester where the plays were also well received and Mayne regularly had to make speeches at curtain calls.

Rutherford Mayne's first three peasant plays, *The Drone*, *The Turn of the Road*, and *The Troth,* were by far the most successful pieces that he wrote for the Ulster Literary Theatre. His following plays in the same vein, *The Gomeril* (1909), *Red Turf* (1911) and *Evening* (1914) met with an unfavourable reception. *The Gomeril, A Farcical Comedy in One Act* was his only play written at that time for a company other than the Ulster Literary Theatre. The recently-founded Dublin-based Theatre of Ireland performed it at the Rotunda, in April 1909. This play, about a farmer and a spinster, went almost unnoticed and was dismissed by Susan Mitchell in the 8 May issue of *Sinn Féin* as 'much less than a play and hardly an incident', which only 'made a good vehicle for some northern accents, and that bitter jesting that sharpens here and there to a point in the somewhat amorphous humour of the north'. Mayne did not attempt to stage a performance in Belfast or to have it published.

His next one-act peasant play, *Red Turf*, was received with critical acclaim in Belfast when it was premièred in a production by the Ulster Literary Theatre at the Grand Opera House on 5 December 1911. A clear-sighted review, which one can still subscribe to today, appeared in *The Northern Whig* the following day:

The author tried for the same style of effect in *The Troth*, but since then his handling has become surer, and he knows how to get the most out of his material. The story develops swiftly and inevitably, and there is an intensity that one missed in the earlier work. It deals with the grimmest side of Irish land-hunger, the passionate hate that possession of a piece of land can breed between neighbour and neighbour, and no concessions at all are made to the sugar-and-milk-school.

Red Turf is, in fact, Mayne's most intense, compact, emotionally charged play concentrating its focus on the value of the land, with utterly convincing motivation, fine characterization and realistic speech. However, in its outspoken bitterness and disillusionment it was in conflict with the mood of his time, and the play failed both with the Belfast audience and the audience in Dublin where it was performed by the Abbey School of Acting in December 1911. The Dublin audience, relishing more homely fare, was shocked, and the Dublin critics damned it. The reviewer for *The Irish Independent* (8 December 1911) described it as a 'by-product of Abbey theatricality', with swearwords and blaspheming added to the usual 'peasant quality'. He disqualified it as literature, art, and drama and his critique culminated in his calling the play 'fifteen minutes of preposterous piffle' and 'redolent rubbish'. He found himself in complete agreement with his colleague from the *Evening Herald* who dismissed it as 'nothing more than a squalid row in a Galway kitchen between two farmers over a strip of bog' (8 December 1911). In view of the discrepancy between the artistic quality of the play and its miserable reception, one can only sadly think of the positive commentary that had appeared in *The Northern Whig* two days earlier: 'The sordid bitterness of *Red Turf* may irritate some people, but on others and on those who know Ireland best it will have a tonic effect.' The play actually proved to be too irritating to become part of the repertoire and, despite of – or, rather, because of – its merits, disappeared from the stage. Fortunately for us, Mayne did not refrain from having the play published so that we can still study it (including Mayne's attempt at reproducing Galway speech) and can also hope to see it revived some day.

Mayne's *Evening, A Co. Down Playlet in One Act* (1914) is the last of his six folk plays wholly set in a farmer's kitchen, and it is also his shortest play, a kind of microdrama. In the twilight of a summer evening Hans Mullen, an old farmer, struggles with acknowledging that his strength has gone and, through the intervention of his gentle wife, eventually accepts that he has to make his strong son, John, 'master of the house'. Again, as in *Troth*, Mayne deals with the problem of land ownership but seems to have been intent on writing a contrasting companion piece, as *Evening* is characterized by subdued tone, benevolent atmosphere, reasonable speech, and peaceful solution. Psychological realism in the characterization suffers, however, and the serious conflict of generations among the farm-owning country people is sentimentally covered up instead of artistically revealed. The play disappeared from the stage after a private performance by the Iona Players in Dublin on 31 December 1913 and one by the Ulster Theatre in Belfast on 2 March 1914.

In 1910, Mayne began expanding his dramatic scope experimenting with other forms of drama and, until 1923, produced five plays in different genres for the Ulster Theatre: *Captain of the Hosts* (1910), reworked as *Neil Gallina* (1916), a tragedy in three acts; *If* (1914), a political farce, again in three acts; *Industry* (1917), a melodramatic play in two acts; and *Phantoms* (1923), a one-act play which he called 'a comedy or tragedy'. With the exception of *Industry*, which kept the stage for a decade, the plays written in Mayne's 'middle period' were not successful and disappeared after a season or two. Apart from *Phantoms* (1923) and his 'Prologue' to *Industry*, they remained unpublished.

In *Captain of the Hosts*, Mayne broke new ground in several ways: it is his first full-length tragedy, it is set in the suburban city instead of the country, and he also deals with a new theme, religion and love. In this Shavian drama of ideas, Neil Gallina knows that he is dying from tuberculosis and has turned to alcohol and dissipation. Falling in love with Barbara, an evangelical missionary, he turns into a fiery evangelist himself, but under the impression that she does not love him and has left the mission, he reverts to his old ways and succumbs to Death, 'the Captain of the Hosts'. *The Northern Whig* (9 March 1910) called the play 'the most ambitious bit of work Rutherford Mayne has yet attempted and . . . the biggest undertaking the Ulster Literary Theatre has tackled,' and goes on to praise Mayne's portrayal of Neil as well as his 'city types, from prize-fighters to religious frauds' and the 'strong dash of satire' in the play. The reviewer however adds that although Mayne 'got hold of a good central idea . . . it tends to evaporate in words . . . instead of becoming crystallized in action' and that particularly Barbara was 'more a mouthpiece for theories than a living figure'. Mayne saw weaknesses in the play himself, rewrote it and had it performed by the Ulster Theatre on 13 December 1916, under the new title *Neil Gallina*. According to critics, Mayne made the play more compact, cut out digressions and made the dialogue less weighty, but he did not change the basic features of his original play. The reviewer in *The Belfast News-Letter* (14 December 1916) summarized its contents, praised the realistic portrayal of some of the characters but criticized the alleged conventionality of its plot. The play also failed with the audience in this version and was not taken into the repertoire of the Ulster Theatre. Like *Red Turf,* it may have been too courageous a play for its time. It also seems to have an autobiographical dimension and, in any case, might have been too daring again, this time in showing the shaky basis of religious and missionary zeal.

In his next play, *If* (1913), Mayne switched his genre from tragedy to farce, his theme from religion to politics, and his setting from the streets of Belfast to a hotel at an Irish seaport. On 17 December 1914, *The Irish Times* described the plot:

> Mr Mayne pokes much harmless fun at the people of Portahoy, a seaport in Ulster, which is in the throes of a political election. He depicts the fervour of the Orangemen of the town in their devotion to the cause and to Colonel Sylvester, an excitable gentleman, who is the Unionist candidate. The Colonel promises a sum of £2,000 to build an Orange hall if a free site is obtained. Tom, a waiter in the local hotel, is the fortunate owner of a desirable site, and . . . is induced to hand it over to the Orangemen on the condition that Colonel Sylvester wins. Tom in his heart is very anxious for the Colonel's defeat, but despite the machinations of the 'suffragettes' in poisoning the water supply and making many voters ill, the Colonel wins.

The critic goes on to praise Mayne's power of characterization and dialogue as well as his performance as Colonel Sylvester but calls the story 'jagged' and 'tiresome', criticizes the play as 'rather uneven' and recommends 'some judicious pruning before it can be regarded as finished'. The play was premièred by the Ulster Theatre in Belfast on 5 December 1913, it was again performed in Belfast and at the Gaiety Theatre in Dublin in December 1914 but then fell into oblivion. It is Mayne's only play dealing with party politics and is also interesting for its satire of the fervour of the 'Orangemen' and of political over-enthusiasm as well as for its dealing with material (hotel life at the seaport of Portahoy, Tom the waiter, and an irascible Colonel) which he recycled in his later play, *Peter*.

In February 1915, Rutherford Mayne acted the title-role in Helen Waddell's *The Spoiled Buddha*, his sister's only play, when it was staged by the Ulster Theatre in Belfast, with great applause for his acting. The play itself, partly set in Japan and taking a somewhat irreverent look at Buddha and his disciples, was a daring experiment in writing a philosophical play and was clearly above the heads of the audience and the critics. It shared the fate of most of her brother's plays of that time in not being revived. To us, it is also of interest as it clearly shows the difference between Helen and Samuel Waddell's treatment of Japan in their works: while she put it at the centre, he did not openly refer to his youthful Japanese experience in most of his plays and wanted to make his plays appear as realistically Irish as possible.

On 6 December 1917, *Industry*, Mayne's only play of this period which held the stage for some years, was premièred, as had become usual, at the Grand Opera House in Belfast. Again, he chose a new dramatic form, that of a melodramatic play, a new setting, the sleepy small Ulster town of Tubbermurray, and a new and important theme, the impact of industrialisation on the traditional agricultural Irish society. It describes the opening of a factory in Tubbermurray by C. J. M'Loughlin, an American entrepreneur, and the resulting conflict with the gentry as well as with his workers. Lady Loftus, the owner of the neighbouring estate, hates the new factory atmosphere with its dirt and noise, declines to sell part of her land to him, and attempts to get rid of him. She incites McNamee, a discontented mechanic, to engineer a strike among the workers, who hate M'Loughlin's tyranny, to blow up the works and maybe to kill its owner. The factory is destroyed, but miraculously M'Loughlin escapes unhurt, with his will-power unbroken and his loss covered by insurance. Although he leaves the small town of Tubbermurray, which reverts to its old state of quiet country life, as shown both in the Prologue and Epilogue of the play, the message is that M'Loughlin will try elsewhere and that industrialisation cannot be stopped. In his play, Mayne deals with the conflict between modernity and tradition, industrialisation and agriculture, land-owners and factory-owners, capital and labour, factory work and farm life. His theme was topical and Mayne's melodramatic treatment of his subject was such that the audience's reaction justified the inclusion of the play in the repertoire of the Ulster Theatre for the next decade. The critics, however, were less kind. In *The Belfast News-Letter* of the following day, Mayne's power of creating impressive characters was acknowledged, but the reviewer remarked that 'the play would be all the better for the sharp application of the pruning knife'. The reviewer spoke positively about Mayne's performance of M'Loughlin and of the acting generally as did the critic of *The Evening Herald* on 13 December, who was also critical of the play itself: 'The players have to work on rather poor material, but they made the most of the occasionally good patches of comedy.' From the existing material, it is impossible to assess the aesthetic quality of the play.

For the next six years, which were dominated by the hardship, terror and suffering of the Irish fight for independence and civil war, Mayne did not have a new play staged. In 1923 *Phantoms*, his last play written for the Ulster Theatre, was produced at the Gaiety Theatre in Dublin, with his wife, Josephine Mayne, playing the part of HagU. Critical reception of the play was mixed, with an emphasis on the obscurity of the play's meaning, and, although one critic accorded it a permanent place in the theatre, it failed with the audience and was not not even tried out in Belfast. It is another of Mayne's middle-period plays that failed, but it is of genuine interest both formally and thematically. *Phantoms* is a historical play based on a folk legend, ironically set 'in the Bronze Age or thereabouts', and clearly characterized as an experiment by Mayne's calling it 'a Comedy or Tragedy'. It is an anti-war play in which the old generation is depicted as evil and responsible for the brutal warfare that is described in the play. Gnu and HagU governed by a murderous spirit, hatred, and lust, sell the spear-heads and battle-axes they manufacture to their equally dehumanized primitive customers, Seeki, a tribal chief, and The Gowlan, an outlaw, who attempt to kill each other, their follows and families, and take delight in plundering, killing and even burning their enemies, including their children. Eventually, Gnu and HagU murder each other, too, which may be regarded as a kind of poetic justice. At the end of the play, however, the hope is expressed that the future will eventually bring peace, not through Seeki's victory over the Gowlan, but through the surviving young generation: Danon turns from spear-making to flute-making and is united with the innocent Seeva, the Gowlan's daughter. In symbolic form, Mayne displays the horrors of the recent war in Ireland and expresses the hope of a new beginning. At the same time, he also satirizes the heroicization of the Irish past and of its central figures in Revivalist drama as well as the homely atmosphere and dialogue of the traditional peasant kitchen plays. In their primitive kitchen, Gnu and HagU have a pot and a fire but they brew poison instead of tea, and in their world it is only the superior power of weapons, not the individual's valour, which decides battles. Comic humour is replaced by malicious laughter and snarling, and while the language is still recognizably stage Irish-English in its syntax and idiom here it is depoeticized, often deliberately crude and reduced to a minimum. Like *Red Turf, Phantoms* makes no concession to the 'sugar-and-milk-school' although it does not match the earlier play artistically.

In the 1920s Mayne remained active as an actor, appearing at the Abbey Theatre in his greatest success as Brutus Jones in O'Neille's *Emperor Jones* in 1927. In her *Journal*, Lady Gregory makes special mention of Mayne's 'wonderful performance'. She invited him and Lennox Robinson to dinner where they discussed the languishing state of the Ulster Theatre as well as, understandably, Samuel Waddell's work with the Land Commission and his involvement in dividing up the land of the big estates, with the pragmatic and sometimes questionable decisions that had to be taken.[16] Mayne's extensive contacts with Lennox Robinson influenced him in offering his new three-act play, *Peter*, to the Abbey Theatre. This was also welcomed by W. B. Yeats, who ascribed to it 'great capacity for managing the stage, for keeping it vivid and amusing', called it a 'godsend' and, like Lennox Robinson, expected a great success for the play.[17]

Produced by Robinson, *Peter* was premièred on 28 January 1930, with a great success for the author, the producer, and the actors, especially for F. J. McCormick as Sam Partridge. The reviewer for *The Evening Herald* on the following day called the play 'abundantly rich in humour' and was particularly impressed by its 'witty dialogue'. He claimed that *Peter* would further enhance Mayne's well-established reputation as a playwright and concluded from the enthusiastic reception at its first night that it should become extremely popular. Lady Gregory recorded in her *Journals* for 9 February 1930, 'At the Abbey *Peter* continues his triumphant career – really less than a play than an 'Entertainment' – but a very lively one and beautifully acted to full houses'. In a letter to George Shiels she was kinder regarding *Peter*'s dramatic form and expressed her hope that Mayne 'opened up a new seam, as they say in mining', and that he 'should be a great acquisition to the Abbey'.[18] The play was not only printed and reprinted but also translated into Irish. It was revived at the Abbey several times from the 1930s to the 1950s, with a memorable production in 1955 directed by Tomás MacAnna, with Vincent Dowling as Peter. In fact, the play was Mayne's greatest theatrical success since *The Drone*, more than twenty years earlier. The play is experimental in its use of Prologue and Epilogue to define the contents of the play itself as *Peter*'s dream. This may owe something to Lennox Robinson's dramatic experimentation, although it should be added that Mayne remained true to his characteristic realistic technique in the main body of his play.

Early reviews of the play remarked upon its great comic potential in situations, characters, and dialogue, but the themes dramatized in the play were not discussed. Mayne's central concern here is with the problematic role of art and the artist in an Irish society dominated by a new inartistic moneyed class, which has taken the place of the peasant's philistinism as depicted in *The Turn of the Road*. A comparison between the two plays shows that Mayne has completely reversed his position towards the place of art and the life of an artist. *Peter*'s artistic gifts are similar to those of Robbie John, but *Peter* becomes an artist by necessity, not by inclination, and the call of the fiddle's tune has been replaced by the call of the harbour's siren at the new port. *Peter* is drawn to engineering just as Robbie John was drawn to fiddling. One cannot overlook the autobiographical dimension in the depiction and evaluation of *Peter*'s 'double life' as an artist and engineer but, more importantly, this new reversed position also serves to criticize the precarious role of the arts and the artist in Ireland: they are seen as being at the mercy of the nouveau riche and managers (*Peter*'s monetary problems force him to sell his artistic talent to Sam Partridge who reduces him to a 'clown', a 'pièrrot', and a 'gigolo', and Mr McCleery, the would-be Ulster poet, whose imitative Yeatsian nature poems appear strangely out of place in the luxurious hotel environment, suffers a writer's block when confronted with his clientèle's literary ignorance as represented by Colonel Blake). In contrast to *The Turn of the Road* and *The Drone* where Mayne attacked traditional work ethics, a 'respectable' money-earning employment is fully endorsed in *Peter*. Scott insists that whatever *Peter* decides to do, he should 'do everything thoroughly', and *Peter* is greatly relieved when he finds out that he has passed his exam and can begin working as an engineer and will not have to make a living by using his artistic talent professionally. Other themes – the victory of love over money, the criticism of the entrepreneurial class that subordinates everything to its commerical interests, and the satire of the persistent Irish cringe to the English aristocracy – also make us see that *Peter* is more than just an 'entertainment'. The play comes close to matching *The Drone* in comic power and is certainly the most modern of Mayne's plays in its cinematic quality.

Spurred on by his success with *Peter*, Mayne wrote one more full-length play, *Bridge Head*, which was staged at the Abbey on 18 June 1934, directed by Lennox Robinson with F. J. McCormick as Stephen Moore. As mentioned by Joseph Holloway and others, the play met with an enthusiastic reception and the audience at the première gave Mayne a standing ovation. As emphasized by Mayne himself in his 'Author's Note' and by critics of the première, his central theme is the cutting up of the old estates and the redistribution of the land in Western Ireland to small farmers by the officers of the Land Commission as a result of the Irish Land Acts.[19] In the words of the Irish Press on the following day :

It is a saga of the Land Commission and its heroes – the official sent down from Dublin to take away the land from some and to give it to others. . . . *Bridge Head* breaks new ground and the making of government officials into heroes is surely a feat in itself.

The play won the Casement Prize for the best Irish play of 1934/35. The Scottish playwright James Bridie called it 'a noble piece of work;

stirring to the imagination and uplifting to the heart. It is a credit to the theatre and to mankind. It is hard to find any flaw in this good play.'[20] It was revived at the Abbey, and also produced at the Westminster Theatre, London, in 1939, its significance being compared by some critics to Synge's Playboy. However, unlike *Peter* the play did not become a lasting stage success, although in the 1960s BBC Northern Ireland contemplated a performance, and a television production in Italy was also considered.

Bridge Head is certainly of great historical interest as Mayne deals with one of the most important aspects of social life after the 'Troubles' in Ireland, one that was central to the aims of the new Republic and made possible by the Land Act of 1923: the transfer of landownership from the old gentry to new smallholders by putting the machinery for making tenants their own landlords, and for expropriating land for relieving congestion, on a compulsory basis. Mayne made this redistribution of 'the land' in Ireland his central theme in his last play. As the reviewer of *Bridge Head* in the *Leader* on 30 June 1934 reflected,

Ah, the land, the land. The eternal theme of Irish drama. Fountain of love and hatred and greed, and annuities and bounties, and economic wars and life and death. The play portrays the trials of the Land Commissioner, the land hunger and jealousies of landless and near landless men . . . [and] the heart-burnings of the landed gentry, whose land is being compulsorily acquired.

Bridge Head also has a strong autobiographical dimension, which is more overt than it is in *Peter,* as Mayne essentially deals with his work for the Land Commission, and with the part he himself played in the division and redistribution of the land in Western Ireland. Another, more hidden autobiographical aspect should also be mentioned: Mayne's last play is the only one among his works in which his youthful experience of Japan and his continued interest in it are reflected. His creation of the character of Inari (Japanese for 'fox') Gosuki, a member of the Japanese Parliament, who comes to Ireland to study the land problem and the work of the Irish Land Commission, could not be explained without our knowing about Mayne's Japanese background and his early confrontation with the problem of land ownership in Japan. Gosuki's broken English, his interspersed Japanese phrases and his courteous behaviour are certainly comic but his main function is that of an intelligent and critical foreign commentator who compares the situation in Ireland with that of Japan. He is also made to pinpoint the weaknesses in the reaction of the Irish people whenever 'the land' is concerned, their greed, hatred, envy, and use of violence which, as he observes, is in conflict with the Christian doctrine of love and the brotherhood of man. Gosuki's Japanese expressions and imagery as well as the information that we get from him about Japanese life and institutions show not only Mayne's great knowledge but also his high esteem of Japanese culture.

The play also contains other well-portrayed characters and striking situations that illustrate the Irish 'land hunger' and the problem of establishing a new social order in the Irish Republic. Nevertheless, *Bridge Head* is less perfect as a drama than has been suggested by some early commentators and more recent critics. The play's artistic and ideological problem is not so much Mayne's alleged siding with the old order, the Barringtons, whose entire property is taken away from them and who are left only with their family grave, or his omission in showing any decent small farmer, as the reviewer of the *Irish Press* complained. The text allows another reading, and Mayne's portrayal of the conflict between the landlord and the new farmers as well as his character sketches, especially that of Dan Dolan, are the most memorable features of his play. I believe the problem lies elsewhere, in Mayne's unqualified heroicization of the land commissioner, Stephen Moore, who is idealized in his complete impartiality, sole service to the cause, and unflinching sense of duty. The audience is meant to admire Moore's doctrine of self-denial and work ethic although it robs his assistant, O'Neill, who is forced to accept Moore's value system, of his love and of any happiness in his private life. Especially in view of Mayne's work for the Land Commission, this idealization of the land commissioner among realistically flawed characters takes on a self-congratulatory and self-justifying tone, and, to critical recipients, Mayne's advocacy of the priority of work at all costs appears in all its inhumanity. Mayne also continued what we have already observed in *Peter*, the reversal of the position taken in his early plays, especially in *The Turn of the Road* and *The Drone*, where he had fought against the social pressures towards conformity and the stifling Protestant work ethic of his time in the name of individual self-fulfilment. By taking his non-artistic professional life in idealized form as the subject of *Bridge Head*, Mayne did not keep the necessary aesthetic distance from his material – with artistically and ideologically questionable results. Nevertheless, by writing about the work of the Irish Land Commission in *Bridge Head*, he finally managed to merge the two selves of his 'double life' – Samuel J. Waddell, land commissioner, and Rutherford Mayne, playwright. This was the logical end of his career as a playwright.

Wolfgang Zach

NOTES

1   John Killen's 'Introduction' to his selection of Mayne's plays (*Selected Plays*, Belfast: Institute of Irish Studies, 1997, pp. 1-18), is the only account of some length, but his aim is different and he deals with only a few of Mayne's plays. However, in recent years he was the first to take an interest in Mayne and has unearthed new information, to which I am indebted here.

2   I have managed to find mss. of only two of his published plays, *The Turn of the Road* and *Bridge Head*, which are now in the holdings of Queen's University, Belfast. I am most grateful to Prof. John Cronin for his help in locating these mss. and to Dr John Killen for his search among the Rutherford Mayne papers recently acquired by the Linen Hall Library, Belfast.

3   I am greatly indebted to Prof. Hiroshi Suzuki of Waseda University, Tokyo, for his help with finding information on the Rev. Hugh Waddell and Samuel Waddell's Japanese background as well as for his translation of Japanese texts. Information on the Waddell family was also kindly given me by the Presbyterian Church in Ireland and the Belfast Royal Academy.

4   Helen Jane Waddell (1889-1965), was a writer, scholar, and translator. She was the first woman to be elected to the Irish Academy of Letters (see D. Felicitas Corrigan, *Helen Waddell. A Biography*, London: Gollancz, 1986). The book is also the best published source for the life of the Waddell family, including Samuel, in Japan and Ireland.

5   See Mikisa Hane, *Peasants, Rebels, and Outcasts*, New York: Pantheon, 1982.

6   A great interest in Roman Catholicism can also be observed in his sister Helen Waddell's writings.

7   *The Irish Times*, 27 February 1967. I have not been able to locate any obituaries in Belfast and other Dublin papers.

8   As reported by Sam Hanna Bell, *The Theatre in Ulster*. Dublin: Gill and Macmillan 1972, p. 27.

9   *Joseph Holloway's Abbey Theatre. A Selection from his Unpublished Journal, Impressions of a Dublin Playgoer*, ed. Robert Hogan and Michael J. O'Neill. Carbondale, Ill.: Southern Illinois University Press; London and Amsterdam: Feffer & Simons, Inc., 1967, pp. 91-92.

10   *Samhain*, November 1908, p. 5.

11   John Killen, 'Introduction' to *Selected Plays*, ed. John Killen, Belfast: Institute of Irish Studies, 1997, p. 9.

12   *The Theatre in Ulster*, p. 34.

13   *Ibid.*, p. 35.

14   *Ibid.*

15   *Ibid.*

16   *Lady Gregory's Journals*, Volume 2, Books Thirty to Forty-Four, 21 February 1925 – 9 May 1932, ed. Daniel J. Murphy, with an Afterword by Colin Smythe. Gerrards Cross: Colin Smythe, and New York: Oxford University Press, 1987, pp. 164-65, 167-68.

17   Killen, 'Introduction' to *Selected Plays*, p. 13; see also *Letters to W. B. Yeats*, eds. Richard J. Finneran, George Mills Harper, William M. Murphy, NewYork: Columbia University Press; London & Basingstoke: Macmillan Press, 1977, 2 vols., pp. 500, 502.

18   *Lady Gregory's Journals*, Vol. 2, pp. 500, 503.

19   Samuel Waddell also talked about his work in the Irish Land Commission in his Thomas Davis lecture, quoted in Killen, 'Introduction,' pp. 13-14. A general survey of the land legislation and the work of the Land Commission is provided in C. K.

Kolbert and T. O'Brien, *Land Reform in Ireland*. Cambridge: Cambridge University Dept. of Land Economy, Occasional Papers No. 3, 1975.

20 Quoted on the inside front flap of *Bridge Head*, London: Constable, 1939.

THE TURN OF THE ROAD

A PLAY IN TWO SCENES AND
AN EPILOGUE

TO

LEWIS PURCELL

In remembrance of his kindly aid and criticism

CHARACTERS

WILLIAM JOHN GRANAHAN, a farmer
MRS GRANAHAN, his wife
SAMUEL JAMES, ⎫ their sons
ROBBIE JOHN, ⎭
ELLEN, their daughter
THOMAS GRANAHAN, father of Wm. John Granahan
JOHN GRAEME, a farmer
JANE, his daughter
MR TAYLOR, a creamery manager
A TRAMP FIDDLER

The action takes place throughout in the Kitchen of William John Granahan's house in the County of Down.

TIME – the present day (1906)

A month elapses between Scenes I and II

This play was first produced on 4 December 1906, privately, at the Examination Hall of the Queen's University, Belfast, by the Ulster Literary Theatre; repeated 17–19 December 1906, in public performance, at the Ulster Minor Hall, Belfast, with the following cast:

WILLIAM JOHN GRANAHAN	W. R. Gordon
MRS GRANAHAN	Brigid O'Farrell
SAMUEL JAMES	Rutherford Mayne
ROBBIE JOHN	S. Bullock
ELLEN	Lily Coates
THOMAS GRANAHAN	Arthur Gilmore
JOHN GRAEME	Gerald MacNamara
	(Harry Morrow)
JANE	Edith Lilburn
MR TAYLOR	John Field Magee
A TRAMP FIDDLER	James Story

Directed by Fred Morrow

2

THE TURN OF THE ROAD

SCENE I

A farm kitchen of the present day. Door at back, opening to yard, and window with deal table on which are lying dishes and drying cloths with basin of water. A large crock under table. A dresser with crockery, etc., stands near to another door which opens into living rooms. Opposite there is a fireplace with protecting breasts, in which a turf fire is glowing. About eight of a summer evening in July. MRS GRANAHAN *and* ELLEN *are engaged at a table washing and drying the plates after the supper.* THOMAS GRANAHAN, *the grandfather, is seated at fireplace, and has evidently just finished his stirabout. The strains of a quaint folk-air played on violin sound faintly from the inner room.*

MRS GRANAHAN. Is that the whole of them now, Ellen?

ELLEN. Yes, that's all now but one. (*She goes across to grandfather and lifts the plate.*) Have you finished, grand-da?

GRANDFATHER. Yes, dearie, I have done. (*He pauses and fumbles for his pipe, etc.*) Isn't that a fiddle I'm hearing?

ELLEN. Yes. Robbie is playing the fiddle in the low room.

MRS GRANAHAN (*arranging plates on dresser and turning round*). I wish some one would stop that boy's fool nonsense wi' his fiddle. He's far too fond of playing. It would stand him better to mind his work. (*Calls.*) Robbie! (*Louder.*) D'you hear me, Robbie?

ELLEN. Oh, let the boy be, mother. It's the first time I've heard him at it this week.

GRANDFATHER. Och, aye! Let the boy enjoy himself. You're only young wanst you know, Mary.

ELLEN. I think it must be a great thing to be a great musician. Sometimes I believe Robbie should try his luck with that fiddle of his. Somehow I know – I feel he *is* a genius at it.

MRS GRANAHAN. What notions you do have to be sure. To think of a big grown man like Robbie John spending his lifetime at an old fiddle. (*Sharply.*) Blathers and nonsense! It's time that boy was out looking at the cattle. (*Calls.*) Are you there, Robbie? (*Louder.*) Robbie John.

3

ROBBIE JOHN (*the fiddle ceases suddenly and he comes out and stands with it in his hand at the door*). Aye?

MRS GRANAHAN. You'd better go down to the low field and see the cattle haven't broken through into Aura Boyd's corn. You couldn't keep them beasts in when the flies get at them.

ROBBIE JOHN. Just one second till I try this again.

MRS GRANAHAN. Now, will you go when I tell you. You and your ould fiddle. It'll be the death of you yet. Mind what I say.

ROBBIE JOHN (*coming through door and standing there*). Bad cess to the cattle and Aura Boyd.

GRANDFATHER. He's a tarr'ble unneighbourly man.

MRS GRANAHAN. He's a cross-grained man right enough, but it wouldn't do to have the cattle tramping and eating his corn.

ROBBIE JOHN. I was down there only ten minutes ago when you sent me, and they were eating there quite peaceable.

MRS GRANAHAN. Now, will you go Robbie John, when your mother wants you. Aura Boyd sent over here this forenoon to say if that Kerry cow broke into his field again he'd have the law agin us.

ROBBIE JOHN. Och, he's a cross ould cratur. Sure, she had only one foot through the hedge when he turned her. (*Seeing his mother is impatient.*) All right; I'm away. (*He goes back into room, leaves fiddle there, comes into kitchen again and goes out by door to yard.*)

MRS GRANAHAN. He's as ill to drive as the ould mare to meeting a Sundays. (*She goes and looks through door into room.*) Look at the time it is and your father and Samuel James never back yet, Ellen. They're terrible late of coming.

ELLEN. Och, I suppose they've met some dealer at the fair and are driving a hard bargain as usual.

GRANDFATHER. I wonner if they got that foal red off their hands yet. It'll be a job I'm thinking. He was a miserable baste, and tarr'ble broken in the wind.

ELLEN. Och, trust father to make that all right. I heard Mr Taylor, of the creamery, say that father could sell ou skim milk for cream better than any man he knew.

MRS GRANAHAN (*seating herself at chair beside table at back*). Oh, aye. It's easy for him to talk, but money's hard of making, and if people's soft it's their own fault. Only I hope they've no taken any drink.

GRANDFATHER. It's no fault in a good man if he does take a half-un.

MRS GRANAHAN. Now, don't you be starting to talk that way. It's always the way with them dailers. Muddle the good man's head

4

with whiskey, and then *do* him.

ELLEN. They'll not muddle father much, I'm thinking. Besides, Samuel James is with him.

GRANDFATHER. Samuel James is a cunning rascal.

MRS GRANAHAN. Don't you miscall my son, Mr Granahan. He's a canny good son and works hard, and is worth more than half-a-dozen men like Robbie John. They'll not put their finger in his eye. (*Going to the window.*) Bless my heart, there's that sow among the kale. Shoo! (*She goes out and is heard shouting.*)

ELLEN (*laughing*). That poor sow! It has the times of it!

(ROBBIE JOHN *enters and sits down near his grandfather.*)

GRANDFATHER. Well, son, what about the cattle?

ROBBIE JOHN (*weariedly*). Och, they're all right. I know they'd be all right. It's always the way.

GRANDFATHER (*soothingly*). They are a terrible newsance, indeed, Robbie.

ROBBIE JOHN. But that's not what troubles me. Why can't mother leave me alone for just a few minutes till I get some time to myself at the fiddle. I never touch it but I'm taken away and sent off somewhere.

ELLEN (*seating herself at chair beside Robbie John*). Don't be cross with her, Robbie, dear. She's anxious about the cattle.

ROBBIE JOHN. But, Ellen, look here. Any time I can get to have just a tune on that fiddle some one is sure to take me away from it. Father sends me out to mend gaps that were mended, or cut turf that was cut, or fodder horses that were foddered. And when he's away and I might have some chance, mother does the same. Here I've been working for the past week, day in and day out, and the very first chance I get I must run after the cattle or something. (*Despondently.*) Nobody has any feeling for me here at all.

GRANDFATHER. Now, now, Robbie. It's all for your own good, son, she does it.

ELLEN. And we feel for him, don't we, grand-da? You mustn't look so cross, Robbie. You know that they think you're too much wrapped up in that fiddle of yours, and they want to break you off it.

ROBBIE JOHN (*determinedly*). That they never will. Never.

GRANDFATHER (*gazing amusedly at Robbie John*). Sowl, Robbie, you look like one of them prize fighting men ye see up in the town.

ELLEN. I wish Jennie Graeme seen you with that face. You wouldn't get your arm round her so easy then; would he, grand-da?

GRANDFATHER. A bonny wee girl she is, and has a fine farm and land

5

coming till her. (*Aside.*) Boys a dear, but them musicians gets the fine weemin.

ROBBIE JOHN. Aye. Creamery managers gets them too, grand-da, an odd time.

GRANDFATHER. Indeed, that Taylor man will get a body can cook sowans anyway.

ELLEN (*looking through window*). Here's mother.

MRS GRANAHAN (*enters and sits down exhausted on chair at side of table next door*). That sow is a torment. I just had her out and back she doubles again. She just has me fair out of wind turning her out.

ROBBIE JOHN (*rising and making toward door into room*). I can go and have some practising now.

MRS GRANAHAN. Robbie John, I seen the carts coming up the loaning. Your father will be in in no time. He'll no be pleased to see you han'ling that (*pointing to the fiddle*) just when he comes back. (*Starts up as if suddenly reminded.*) I must go and get them eggs counted. (*Goes out again through door to yard.*)

ELLEN. Aye, Robbie, don't take it. He'll just think you've been playing it all the time he was away. And he's always that cross after markets you couldn't stand him.

ROBBIE JOHN (*sitting down again*). You're right. I don't want another talking to like the last one; but it's hard. (*He takes up a stick from fuel beside fireplace and starts whittling it. The rattle of carts is heard. SAMUEL JAMES passes the window and walks in. He has the appearance of a man partly drunk and inclined to be talkative.*)

ELLEN. Well, how did the fair go off? (SAMUEL JAMES *takes off his overcoat, flings it on back of chair beside dresser, reels, and sits down heavily.*) Ah, you've been taking a drop as usual.

SAMUEL JAMES (*smiling cheerfully*). The fair? Oh, it was great value. Sure, grand-da, he sould the foal for thirty pounds!

GRANDFATHER (*delightedly*). Boys a dear, but William John Granahan bates the devil. And who took her?

SAMUEL JAMES. There was a cavalryman bought her. Boys, but da is the hard man to plaze! We stopped at MucAlanan's on the way home and met William John McKillop there, and he tould the ould man he was a fool to let a good horse go at that price, for he was looking all roads to give him thirty pounds for it, only he couldn't get in time for the sale.

GRANDFATHER (*incredulously*). Who did you say? McKillop?

SAMUEL JAMES (*laughing*). Aye.

ROBBIE JOHN (*smiling*). Sure McKillop hasn't two sov'rins in the wide world. He was only taking a rise out of da.

SAMUEL JAMES. Sure I knowed the ould yahoo hadn't the price of a nanny-goat. But of course da took it all in for gospel. And me sitting listening to him telling ould McKillop what a grand action the foal had and the shoulders the baste had, and the way it could draw thirty hundred up Killainey hill without a pech.

GRANDFATHER (*chuckling*). William John Granahan makes a tarr'ble fine Sunday school teacher.

SAMUEL JAMES (*grinning*). But to see ould McKillop sitting there as solemn as a judge, drinking it all in as if gospel and winking at me on the sly, the ould rascal, and cursing his luck at losing such a bargain.

(*The voice of* WILLIAM JOHN GRANAHAN *can be heard inviting some one to come on. The strains of a fiddle played by uncertain but unmistakeably professional hands, sound without.*)

ELLEN (*looking out through window into yard*). Who's that father has got with him, Samuel James? Such a dirty-looking rascal!

SAMUEL JAMES (*chuckling*). Da got a hoult of him at Buckna cross roads, and right or wrong he'd have him home wi' him to show Robbie John what fiddling brings a man till.

ELLEN (*severely*). It's my mind that you and father have stayed too long in the public-house, Samuel James. (WILLIAM JOHN GRANAHAN *and* TRAMP *fiddler can be seen outside window.*) Look at them – coming in! Wait till mother sees the pair of them!

(WILLIAM JOHN GRANAHAN *comes in leading a ragged-looking bearded tramp with an old fiddle tucked under his arm.*)

WILLIAM JOHN GRANAHAN. Now we're hame, and we'll get a drop to drink and a bite to eat, Mr Fiddler. (*He goes over to fireplace and stands with his back to the fire.*) Take a seat at the fire and warm yourself. (*No one offers a seat to the tramp, who stands puzzled looking and swaying in a drunken manner in the kitchen.*) Ellen, get a drop of tay and give this poor misguided cratur something to eat.

(ELLEN *evidently disapproves of the tramp and does not offer to obey. The* GRANDFATHER *rises in disgust and moves his chair nearer the fireplace away from the tramp.*)

TRAMP (*to* ELLEN). Your pardon, noble lady, I intrude. Your pardon, signor, I incommode you. Times change and so do men. Ladies and gentlemen, behold in me the one time famous leader of the Blue Bohemian Wind and String Band, that had the honour of appearing before all the crowned heads of Europe.

7

WILLIAM JOHN GRANAHAN. God bless me, d'you say so, mister? D'ye hear that, Robbie John? There's a fiddler for you and see what comes of it.

TRAMP. Perhaps with your permission I may venture to play you a few extracts from my repertoire. I can play to suit all tastes from a simple country ballad to a concerto by Brahms or the great Russian composer Tschaikouski.

WILLIAM JOHN GRANAHAN (*open-mouthed*). Them Rooshians has the tarr'ble names!

TRAMP. Firstly I shall play that touching little ballad I heard Monsieur here warble so sweetly as we rolled homeward on his chariot. If I play, he accompanies me with voice. N'est ce pas, Monsieur?

WILLIAM JOHN GRANAHAN (*nervously*). Is your mother out, Ellen?

ELLEN. She's looking after the hens, I think. She won't hear you.

(WILLIAM JOHN GRANAHAN *starts singing two verses of a folk song, the tramp accompanying meanwhile with fiddle, always putting in an extra flourish. The rest all join, even the grandfather beats time with a stick. The door opens and* MRS GRANAHAN *appears seemingly astonished at the uproar. All suddenly cease singing except the tramp, who goes on playing. He suddenly notices the cessation.*)

TRAMP. Bravo. A most exquisite little air and beautifully rendered. (*He stops short on seeing* MRS GRANAHAN, *who stands glaring at him.*) Your pardon, madam. You are the mistress, I take it, of this most noble and hospitable house.

MRS GRANAHAN (*ignoring him, and going to centre, where she looks angrily at* WILLIAM JOHN GRANAHAN). You should be well ashamed of yourself, William John Granahan. What will they say about you in the Session I wonder next Sabbath Day. D'you think my house is a home for all the dirt and scum of the countryside?

TRAMP. Your pardon, madam. You owe me an apology. Appearances belie me, but scum I am not. I was at one time the well known and justly famous leader of the Blue Bohemian Wind and String—

MRS GRANAHAN. Wind and string fiddlesticks. Out you go. Out you will go. I want no tramps in here upsetting my house and making it the talk of the neighbours. Out you go at once.

TRAMP (*with drunken pride*). I thrust my company on no man or woman uninvited.

MRS GRANAHAN. Out you go. I want no excuses. Put him out of this, Samuel James. The drunken wretch coming in here. A nice place you'd have it, William Granahan, with your fine company.

WILLIAM JOHN GRANAHAN. I brought home here as a tarr'ble and

8

awful warning to Robbie John what this sort of an occupation brings a man till. You see him, Robbie John. There's you're great fiddling for you. Be warned in time.

ROBBIE JOHN (*the* TRAMP *moves to the door.* ROBBIE JOHN *rises and goes across to him and taps him on the shoulder*). Here. (*Slips him money.*) God be with you, poor wandering soul.

TRAMP. Sir, I thank you. (*With a drunken confidence.*) Perhaps I could yet please your ears with a romanza which I composed myself—

MRS GRANAHAN. Away with you out of this. We want none of your music here.

SAMUEL JAMES (*to* TRAMP). Why don't you give up playing that fiddle of yours and turn your hand to honest work?

TRAMP (*proudly*). Desert my fiddle. The fiddle presented to me at Vienna by my orchestra! A genuine old Cremona 200 years old! Rather would I wander in Hades for ever. Never! Though cruel words stab and wound me. (*Half sobbing*). Farewell. (*He blunders out.*)

(*A silence. Then the strains of a melancholy air like a serenade come from outside. It slowly dies away in the distance.* ROBBIE JOHN *moves forward as if to go out.*)

MRS GRANAHAN (*sharply*). Robbie John. Where are you going? Don't dare to leave the house. My son going out to keep company with the likes of that dirty rapscallion.

ROBBIE JOHN. Ah, mother, pity the poor wretch. Did you not see the tears in his eyes for all his fine talk? I should like to know more about him.

SAMUEL JAMES. If you went to the sergeant at the barrack, I warrant ye he could tell you more about him. (*He bends down as if to catch the sound of the fiddling which grows very faint.*) Listen! (ROBBIE JOHN *moves to door and opens it.*)

MRS GRANAHAN (*angrily*). Where are you going?

ROBBIE JOHN (*raptly*). Listen. (*The fiddling ceases and he quickly goes out.*)

WILLIAM JOHN GRANAHAN (*good naturedly*). Well, Mary, the foal's sould at last.

MRS GRANAHAN. I've a crow to pluck with you over that same foal, William Granahan. I suppose they did you as usual.

WILLIAM JOHN GRANAHAN (*angrily*). Nine and thirty year ha'e I gone till market, and no man, woman, child, dog or divil ever got the better of me in a bargain yet, and right well you know it. (*With pride.*) I sould the foal for thirty pounds, not a ha'penny less.

MRS GRANAHAN (*doubtfully*). I hope you have it all with you.

WILLIAM JOHN GRANAHAN. I have it all but two shillings and wan penny.

MRS GRANAHAN. And can you account for them?

WILLIAM JOHN GRANAHAN. Woman dear, would you ha'e me go and come to market without a ha'penny in my pocket? Have some gumption about ye. (*In a loud angry voice.*) I'm danged but the next time I make a good bargain I'll go and have a week to myself in Newcastle or Belfast. I'm young enow yet.

MRS GRANAHAN. There. Stop your fool talk in front of the childre and go and change your clothes.

GRANDFATHER. It was a good price indeed.

SAMUEL JAMES (*slyly*). Yes. He sold it for thirty pounds and William John McKillop looking all roads to give him forty for it.

WILLIAM JOHN GRANAHAN (*angrily, and stamping his foot*). Will you hould your tongue, you blathering idiot. Bad scran to ye for a meddle— (*He goes forward to go into room and aims a box on the ears at* SAMUEL JAMES, *who retreats to table and watches him go through door followed by* MRS GRANAHAN. *A noise of voices in angry argument is heard.*)

SAMUEL JAMES. Now he'll catch it. If I had been da I would have kept back five pound and tould her I sold it for twenty-five, but the ould man's that honest he knows no better. (ROBBIE JOHN *enters. He crosses over and seats himself near the table.*) Well, Robbie, and what d'ye think of his great object lesson till ye. It was me put it intil da's head. I thought there might be a bit of value.

ELLEN. There, I just thought it was you did it. You're a schemer, that's what you are.

GRANDFATHER. Aye. There's a dale of the crook in ye Samuel James. You're deeper nor one would think.

SAMUEL JAMES (*suddenly to* ROBBIE JOHN). I see Jenny Graeme at the market to-day, Robbie. (*A pause.*) Oh, well maybe you're no interested in her. (*To* ELLEN.) Man, there was a fine lock of cattle at the fair, Ellen.

ELLEN. I'm sure there was. Who was with Jenny Graeme. (*She nudges* SAMUEL JAMES *slyly.*) Who left her home?

SAMUEL JAMES (*slyly at* ELLEN, *winking*). Young M'Donnell of the Hill Head was looking after her pretty close.

ELLEN (*glancing at* ROBBIE *and then at* SAMUEL JAMES, *and smiling*). He's a very nice young man.

ROBBIE JOHN (*savagely.*) I wish her luck with yon booby.

SAMUEL JAMES. There's nothing the matter with him. He has a nice place and a fine farm forbye.

ROBBIE JOHN. Farms and cattle and crops don't make a fine man.

GRANDFATHER. Deed, now, Robbie, they goes a long ways.

SAMUEL JAMES. Better nor bows and fiddles and such trash. (*To* ROBBIE JOHN.) I heerd up at Bann to-day that ye won three pounds at the Feis at Newcastle a Monday.

ELLEN. I knew that on Tuesday. It was fine of Robbie, wasn't it?

SAMUEL JAMES. It all depends. Da heerd it for the first time to-day, and I can tell you it didn't seem fine to him. Coorse a pound or two would ha'e made a differ of opinion same as it done with you, I expect.

ELLEN. You needn't sneer at me. It was me told Robbie to keep it. He was going to give it all up. I wouldn't be so mean to take it off him.

SAMUEL JAMES. Oh, you're an unusual sort of young woman, I know, but if Robbie John takes my advice he better choose quick between playing the fiddle and staying on here. Of course, Robbie, you can plaze yourself. I suppose you could make as much by fiddling as if you stayed on here and waited till we had the place divided among the three of us.

ELLEN. Why I heard from Mr Taylor that father was worth four or five hundred pounds, and then the two farms besides.

GRANDFATHER. Aye. You'd be a long time, Robbie John, 'arning that wi' your fiddle. Don't heed his fool talk, son. Stay at home and never mind the musicianers.

ELLEN. I'm sure Mr Graeme would never let his daughter marry a penniless fiddler – even if she would herself. I don't know. She might and she – mightn't.

SAMUEL JAMES (*rising from table and stretching himself.*) Coorse, if he made a name for himself he could marry the landlord's daughter. I heerd the quality go mad after the musicianers. (*Goes out to yard.*)

GRANDFATHER. Robbie. Come here.

ROBBIE JOHN. Aye. What is it?

GRANDFATHER. Take heed till yourself. I know what's going on better nor you. Take an ould man's advice. Settle yourself down and give up that string instrument. Coorse, I dare say you may go and become a great man with it, but you are more likely to become a cratur like thon that was in as not. There's no good running risks. And your father, I heerd him say himself, if you make your bed you'll lie on it, for he'll never help you out once you take to the fiddling.

11

ELLEN. Aye, Robbie. It's far better not to run the risk of becoming a beggar man.

ROBBIE JOHN. Well, I'll think over it, Ellen. I'll think over it.

GRANDFATHER. Robbie, come out with me. (*The two go out by door into yard.* WILLIAM JOHN *and* MRS GRANAHAN *come in arguing excitedly.*)

MRS GRANAHAN. Well, you can ha'e the pound if you like, but I can tell you it's a sore pinch to make things do. What with the price of the sugar riz up and the flour.

(SAMUEL JAMES *comes in again, apparently having overheard the squabbling, and seats himself expectantly at the table.*)

WILLIAM JOHN GRANAHAN. There. That's enough to do about it. (*He goes over to the fireplace and faces* MRS GRANAHAN.) Twenty-nine pound you'll get and no more. (*Emphatically.*) Mind that.

MRS GRANAHAN. I'll mind it, right enough, William Granahan. And it's a sore time I have trying to keep in with one hand what you lavish out with the other.

SAMUEL JAMES (*nudging* ELLEN *shyly*). I was talking by the way to Mrs McCrum, the milliner, mother, to-day, and she said to give you word she'd have your new tay gown ready for you a Tuesday week.

WILLIAM JOHN GRANAHAN (*triumphantly*). There you are, ma'am. There you are. Keeping it in wi' one hand, were you? Faith if I know anything you lather it out with both hands and feet. You want to rob me of me one pound, do ye? And all for an ould tay gown? (*Contemptuously*). A tay gown!

ELLEN (*maliciously*). A tay gown's not expensive.

WILLIAM JOHN GRANAHAN. Oh, indeed now. Hach. You'll be wanting one next, I suppose. A nice house this is, where a man couldn't get keeping as much as would buy him an ounce of tobaccy. (*Viciously.*) Man, I do hate this hypockerisy.

MRS GRANAHAN. I'll not talk any more till ye, William Granahan. You're full of drink and bad tongued.

WILLIAM JOHN GRANAHAN (*wildly*). If you say any more till me, I'll smash all the crockery in the house.

MRS GRANAHAN. Come out, Ellen, to the creamery, and maybe when we come in again he'll be a bit cooler in the head. (*She hurries out, followed by* ELLEN, *through door to yard.*)

WILLIAM JOHN GRANAHAN (*to* SAMUEL JAMES). She's a tarr'ble woman, your mother, when she's started. But I'm much obliged to you, Samuel James, for the mention of that tay gown. By me sang but that turned the enemy's flank. (*Laughs.*) I'm danged but you're the boy. (*Gratefully.*) Heth you saved me a pound anyway.

SAMUEL JAMES (*rising and going over sheepishly to him*). You'll not forget me, da? Will you?

WILLIAM JOHN GRANAHAN (*suspiciously*). Na.

SAMUEL JAMES. Well, ye might gie us a part of it.

WILLIAM JOHN GRANAHAN. How much d'ye want?

SAMUEL JAMES. Twelve shillings.

WILLIAM JOHN GRANAHAN. Would you take the very boots off my feet. Where would I get ye twelve shillings?

SAMUEL JAMES. Out of the pound of coorse. Where else?

WILLIAM JOHN GRANAHAN (*grumblingly*). You're asking ower much. If it was a saxpence (SAMUEL JAMES *shrugs his shoulders*), or a shilling (SAMUEL JAMES *shrugs more emphatically*), or two shillings.

SAMUEL JAMES. No.

WILLIAM JOHN GRANAHAN. Or half a crown?

SAMUEL JAMES. No.

WILLIAM JOHN GRANAHAN. I'd think nothing of lending them till ye. But twelve shillings. Would three shillings no do?

SAMUEL JAMES. No. It won't. Either give me the twelve shillings or I'll tell her about your conduct—

WILLIAM JOHN GRANAHAN. There. There it is, an bad scran to ye. To think of me walking ten mile to the fair and back and arguing wi' dailers and cheats of all kinds and getting thirty pounds for a baste I wouldn't buy myself for thirty shillings, and only getting eight shillings out of it.

SAMUEL JAMES (*whistling and counting the money delightedly*). Aye. It's a hard world and no mistake.

WILLIAM JOHN GRANAHAN (*excitedly*). I'll go down to the shough and drown myself, I will.

SAMUEL JAMES. Na. Go to MucAlanan's and drown yerself.

WILLIAM JOHN GRANAHAN. I'm danged but you're right. Na. Na. She'll hear me going out by the gate.

SAMUEL JAMES. Boys, but you're the poor hearted man. Well, I'm away. (*He makes to door.*)

WILLIAM JOHN GRANAHAN. Where now?

SAMUEL JAMES. To Courdy Williamson's for the loan of a monkey wrinch for the new machine. The hay's for cutting the morrow.

WILLIAM JOHN GRANAHAN. Oh, aye. An, you'll be for coorting that young imp of a daughter of his, I warrant ye. Were you there yesterday forenoon?

SAMUEL JAMES (*somewhat taken aback*). Yes. Why d'ye ask?

13

WILLIAM JOHN GRANAHAN (*sarcastically*). Oh, nothing. Only I hadn't a sowl to help me wi' them cattle.

SAMUEL JAMES. Well, wasn't Robbie John at home? What ailed him, he couldn't help ye?

WILLIAM JOHN GRANAHAN. Look you here, Samuel James. I've been worried with that boy this long time. (SAMUEL JAMES *nods approvingly.*) I've made up my mind to-day after seeing yon scarecrow we met at Buckna cross roads, Robbie John aither mends himself or he goes out of this.

SAMUEL JAMES. You're right, da. You ha'e stood his goings on a long time. I think ye do well to stop him. It's only doing him a kindness.

WILLIAM JOHN GRANAHAN. I'll just ask him to burn it when he comes in. If he won't he can just plaze himself. I'll ha'e no more to do with him. (*Suddenly.*) I wonder what his mother would say to that?

SAMUEL JAMES. She's just as tired of it as you are. Wait; I'll call her in. (*Going to the door and shouting.*) Are you there, ma'am?

MRS GRANAHAN (*without*). Aye. (*She comes in and stands looking inquiringly at both of them.*) What bee ha'e you got now in your bonnet?

SAMUEL JAMES. Da's just been talking about Robbie John, and he wants you to hear what he says.

WILLIAM JOHN GRANAHAN. Robbie John's an idle useless bauchle. He'll aither mend himself or go out of this.

MRS GRANAHAN (*sharply*). Mend yourself first, me good man.

WILLIAM JOHN GRANAHAN. It's not like as if he took a drop o'drink or fell in with bad company for you'll get quet of drink and bad company if you ha'e no money.

SAMUEL JAMES (*slyly*). It was mother and I larnt you that.

WILLIAM JOHN GRANAHAN (*snappishly*). Will you hould your tongue. (*To* MRS GRANAHAN.) When he might ha' been looking after the cattle or the pigs or something else, where is he? Up in the loft playing that damnation fiddle of his. Night and morning he's at it.

MRS GRANAHAN. Deed and he's doin' badly by it, and no mistake. He's not been worth a ha'penny till us, this last six months. I think you do right just to stop him.

SAMUEL JAMES. I heerd he won three pound at the Feis last Monday at Newcastle.

WILLIAM JOHN GRANAHAN. There you are. And he never offered me one ha'penny of it. Me that brought him up and reared and fed him. Them that plays the fiddle comes to no good end, I can tell

14

ye. (*Reminiscently and with a sort of shame-faced pride.*) Not but I wasn't the great man at it myself wanst. And you were the girl that could have danced to it, Mary. But, thank God, I quet it.

SAMUEL JAMES (*curiously*). Why?

WILLIAM JOHN GRANAHAN. I might have took to drink and bad company and the like.

MRS GRANAHAN. You're no rid of that yet, William Granahan. Ye mind what way ye come home last Bann Fair on top of the bread cart.

SAMUEL JAMES (*slyly*). Aye. And the way the Scarva man done him out of the price of the two pigs.

MRS GRANAHAN. That's one thing I can't get over. Was it in a public-house ye met him?

WILLIAM JOHN GRANAHAN. There. There. That's enough to do about it. I hear enough about drinking from John Graeme every session day without you etarnally at it. Call Robbie John in for me. (SAMUEL JAMES *goes out.*) Now, do you hear what I say, woman. I'll ha'e no more of this casting up about Bann Fair or those pigs. So forever hould your peace about it. For I'm deeved listening to you. (SAMUEL JAMES *re-enters, followed by* ROBBIE JOHN *and the* GRANDFATHER.) Where's that fiddle of yours, Robbie John? Bring it to me. (ROBBIE JOHN *looks curiously at him and then at* SAMUEL JAMES. *He goes into room and brings it out. He holds it in his hands and looks suspiciously at the father.*) Now, Robbie John, listen to what I and your mother have thought about this. For our sake and your own we want you to give up that accursed thing and put it from you.

ROBBIE JOHN. Why? What harm does it do you or me?

WILLIAM JOHN GRANAHAN. It makes you negleck your work. It makes you think of things you shouldn't think of. It makes you lose sleep at nights sitting up and playing, and then you can't rise in the morning. When you should be polishing the harness or mending a ditch, or watching the cattle, or feeding the poultry, you've got this thing in your hand and practising on it.

ROBBIE JOHN (*indignantly*). It's not true. I don't do these things. I—

WILLIAM JOHN GRANAHAN. Now will you attend to your duties and give up this playing. What good will it ever do ye? Ye seen what it brought yon man till that was in here. It's a tarr'ble warning till ye.

ROBBIE JOHN. The fiddle didn't make him what he is. The drink did that.

15

WILLIAM JOHN GRANAHAN (*scornfully*). Aye. The leader of an ould circus band or something like. (*Getting excited.*) I'd just do with that as I'd do with a sarpint. Trample it under my heels.

ROBBIE JOHN (*threateningly*). I'll kill the first man dares to put a hand on it.

WILLIAM JOHN GRANAHAN (*angrily*). You dare talk that way to your father.

MRS GRANAHAN. Now, Robbie, dear. Don't be getting on that way.

GRANDFATHER. Robbie, my son, mind what I was telling you. It's better to bear it if you can, my son. It's a hard thing, but you can take my word for it, you'll no regret it.

WILLIAM JOHN GRANAHAN (*sadly*). I had of coorse a will drawn up and signed by 'torney McAllan, and was for laving ye nice and comfortable when I was to be taken away. (*He breaks down.*) Robbie, Robbie, my son, sure it's not my heart you're for breaking.

SAMUEL JAMES. Coorse I heerd from one of the judges, Robbie, at the Feis that you had the touch of a master, and all that sort of thing; but I advise ye— (*Here the* GRANDFATHER *shakes his stick at him threateningly.*) I advise ye – of coorse it's hard to know.

GRANDFATHER (*looking angrily at* SAMUEL JAMES). Don't think of that, Robbie. Sure every man that plays a fiddle thinks he's a genius. Don't be led astray, son.

WILLIAM JOHN GRANAHAN (*coaxingly*). Aye. Your grand-da has sense with him, Robbie. After all what about it. Man, there's that bonny wee lass waiting for you at Graemes. To the fire with it. (ROBBIE JOHN *hesitates, then, with head bowed, he goes forward to place it on the fire.*)

(CURTAIN.)

16

SCENE II

The same scene. ELLEN *and* MRS GRANAHAN *seated near fire.*

ELLEN. So Mr Graeme is coming over here to settle matters with father to-day, do you say?

MRS GRANAHAN. Yes, child, he's coming to-day.

ELLEN. What is it all about?

MRS GRANAHAN. Well, I suppose he's anxious to see what money is coming to Robbie John. He doesn't want to throw his daughter away without asking questions. I expect she's well enough to do to marry anyone she likes, but he's a canny man.

ELLEN. Well, I suppose he's right. He must be anxious to see her well married.

MRS GRANAHAN. Oh, now between the two of them, Robbie John will be a sight better off nor your father and I, Ellen, when we married.

ELLEN. Robbie's a lucky man too. I never seen anyone as fond of him as she is. I wonder when father will be going to see anyone about me?

MRS GRANAHAN (*rising and and going to look out of the window*). Whist, child, you're time enough. (*After a look*). Aye. I thought we might see him soon. Tell me now (*resuming her seat*), Who was it left ye home from John Graeme's temperance lecture?

ELLEN. Why?

MRS GRANAHAN (*knowingly*). He's a brave body anyway.

ELLEN. Who?

MRS GRANAHAN. Now you're the soft lassie. Who's the manager of the creamery up beyont?

ELLEN (*unsuspectingly*). Tom Taylor, of course.

MRS GRANAHAN. And, of coorse, it was Tom Taylor left ye home, and is coming in here this minute. (*Knock at the door.*) Come in. Come in. (TAYLOR *enters.*) Why, speak of the divil – how d'ye do, Mr Taylor.

TAYLOR (*he comes in, stands rather awkwardly looking at* ELLEN, *and*

17

then goes over near them). Very well, thank you, ma'am.

MRS GRANAHAN. This is my daughter Ellen. (*Slyly.*) I think ye met her afore.

TAYLOR (*shaking hands with* ELLEN, *he detains her hand for a second and then drops it*). We did, I think, didn't we?

MRS GRANAHAN (*knowingly*). I just thought as much. (*Aside.*) Oh, well, he's a brave body, and would do rightly if the creamery does the same. (*Suddenly to* TAYLOR.) Are ye courting any this weather, Mr Taylor?

TAYLOR (*taken aback, then decides to laugh it off*). Well – eh – no. I'm not doing much that way.

MRS GRANAHAN (*incredulously*). Oh, indeed. Well I heerd otherwise. It's full time ye were looking about for a wife. You'll be getting well on past thirty soon.

TAYLOR (*fidgeting uneasily*). Oh I'm time enough for a couple of years or more. I want to look around me a bit.

MRS GRANAHAN. Well, ye better look sharp, for you'll soon be getting too ould for getting any sort of a decent girl. (*Inquisitively.*) Have ye anyone in your eye yet?

TAYLOR. I have an account to pay your good man, Mrs Granahan.

MRS GRANAHAN. Two pound ten is due. (*Thinking.*) Aye. But I suppose you'll be now in what I would call a good way of doing?

TAYLOR. There was a five per cent dividend this half year. The creamery is going on well. (*Searching in pocket and getting out account.*) Two pounds nine and six, ma'am, begging your pardon.

MRS GRANAHAN. Ach sure sixpence is naither here nor there to a creamery. (*Pauses.*) If that's the way you are, you could be married in a year's time and—

TAYLOR (*evidently desirous to lead conversation off this topic.*) Here's the money, ma'am. (*He lays it down on the table and counts it out.*) You'll do as well as Mr Granahan, I suppose. You take all to do with the money part, I think.

MRS GRANAHAN. Yes, I do. You were at the lecture last Monday?

TAYLOR (*alarmed*). What the devil— (*Suddenly to* MRS GRANAHAN, *and genially.*) Yes. Could you oblige me with a receipt, ma'am?

MRS GRANAHAN. Surely, Here, Ellen, get me the pen and ink. (ELLEN *goes into room.*) I suppose now there were some nice young weemen there – eh, Mr Taylor?

TAYLOR (*uneasily*). Yes. And don't forget the stamp, ma'am.

MRS GRANAHAN. Ach, sure a penny stamp's what you always carry with ye. (*Confidently.*) I think shame on ye, Mr Taylor, trifling with the poor girls. There's no excuse for a man of your age.

18

TAYLOR (*fidgeting*). Well, well, I— Here's a stamp ma'am. (*Impatiently.*) I'm young enough yet. I don't want to marry yet awhile.

MRS GRANAHAN. Well now, I think ye'd be better of some one to look after ye. There's William John Granahan. He's never done being thankful since he married. He says he doesn't know what he mightn't have been if he hadn't married me.

TAYLOR (*slyly*). I can quite believe that.

MRS GRANAHAN. It was a good job for him, I can tell ye. For what with going to dances and the like and public-houses, he was for making a nice mess of himself. (*Confidentially.*) And between you and me, Ellen will no be so badly off aither when he goes. (ELLEN *comes in and puts paper, etc., on table.*)

TAYLOR. Here's the stamp, ma'am.

MRS GRANAHAN (*not noticing*). And there's a girl for you, Mr Taylor, that we spent a deal of time over, and was brought up most careful. She's none of your or'nary girls.

ELLEN (*sharply*). Mother! (*She looks at* TAYLOR, *smiles, and shrugs her shoulders.*)

MRS GRANAHAN (*motioning silence.*) There's too many girls running about and all they can do is – sing a song or two, and dress themselves up like play actresses, and run about at bazaars and the like trying to get ahoult of young men.

TAYLOR. You're quite right, ma'am.

MRS GRANAHAN. Now, there's Ellen was four years at a boarding school that Mr Graeme recommended till us, and I can tell you she got the proper schooling, and let alone that, she can bake, sew or knit, and knows all about the managing of a house.

ELLEN. Oh quit! (*She looks differently across at* TAYLOR, *who grins*).

MRS GRANAHAN (*counting money.*) Here. It's sixpence short of the count.

TAYLOR. Let me see. (*He goes to table and counts money.*) Two and two's four, and two's six, and two and six is eight and six, and one shilling – nine and six.

MRS GRANAHAN (*thinking*). Nine and six. I thought it was – oh, yes, it was nine and six.

TAYLOR. Yes. Nine and six.

MRS GRANAHAN. Very good. I'll write you a receipt. (*Takes pen and paper.*)

ELLEN (*to* TAYLOR, *who stands looking over at her*). You haven't been round this way for a long time, Mr Taylor. What ailed you, you didn't call?

19

TAYLOR. Oh, I was very busy. (*He looks at* MRS GRANAHAN, *who is writing laboriously. Then goes and examines a fiddle that hangs on the wall*). Why! I thought Robbie John had burnt his fiddle and promised to play no more!

MRS GRANAHAN. Aye, so he did, but there's a strange story with that thing you're looking at. There was a tramp come here one day I was out, and when I come back I found him playing away on that thing, and the house in an uproar.

TAYLOR. Aye? He left it here then?

MRS GRANAHAN. No, wait till I tell ye. I packed him out of this, and the next thing I heerd about him was when a wheen of weeks ago he was got half dead with wet and cold in the Flough Moss. John McKillop was down for cutting turf and found him in a peat hole with his hands on the brew, and the ould fiddle beside him.

ELLEN. Yes. The poor soul died the next day, and just before he died he asked McKillop to bring over his fiddle to give to Robbie John. Robbie had been kind to him some time or other, and the poor being never forgot it.

TAYLOR. Ach, aye. I do remember hearing something about it. They said he had been a big man in his day I think.

MRS GRANAHAN. Aye. He was blathering the day he was here about being the leader of an ould band or something like, now that I call to mind. But, indeed, I paid no heed till him, for he was part drunk.

TAYLOR (*curiously*). You didn't get Robbie to burn this one, I see.

MRS GRANAHAN. Well, you see, Samuel James said it was a very valuable one, and worth fifty pounds or more maybe. There's an inscription on it somewhere if you look.

TAYLOR (*taking down fiddle and examining it*). Aye, so I see. "To Nicholas Werner, as a token of esteem from his orchestra. Vienna, 1878."

ELLEN. Yes, poor soul. He was telling the truth, and no one believing.

TAYLOR. And does Robbie never play it?

ELLEN. Not since he promised that I know of. But all the same it must tempt him, for I see his eyes fixed on it often enough when he thinks no one's looking.

TAYLOR (*he looks over at* MRS GRANAHAN, *who appears to be engrossed in her writing. He is just slipping his arm around* ELLEN *when* MRS GRANAHAN *looks up. He instantly drops his arm.*)

MRS GRANAHAN. Have you that stamp, Mr Taylor?

TAYLOR. It's usual, Mrs Granahan, for whoever signs the receipt to supply the stamp; however, there you are. (MRS GRANAHAN *licks*

20

the stamp and signs the receipt.) The writing doesn't come easy to you, ma'am.

MRS GRANAHAN. Now, it's not very courteous making fun of poor ould weemen, Mr Taylor. I thought better of you nor that.

TAYLOR. Ould weemen? Talk sense, Mrs Granahan. I only wish my old woman, if ever I have one, looks as well as you do.

MRS GRANAHAN. There, there, none of your fool nonsense. You don't go blarneying me, like you do the likes of Ellen there.

ELLEN. Ach, mother!

MRS GRANAHAN. I'm much obliged to ye for the money, Mr Taylor. I must put it by me. (*Goes into room.*)

ELLEN. I suppose you've heard about Robbie?

TAYLOR (*coming near her*). No. What happened?

ELLEN. He's to be married to Jane Graeme at Christmas, and Mr Graeme's coming over here to-day to settle about the money.

TAYLOR (*slyly*). I wonder whom your father will be settling matters with, Ellen, when you get engaged?

ELLEN. Why, of course – whoever gets me, I suppose.

TAYLOR. Well there's one thing I wouldn't haggle with him over.

ELLEN. And what would that be?

TAYLOR. Yourself, of course. (*He draws her to him and makes to kiss her.* ROBBIE JOHN *and* SAMUEL JAMES *pass by the window and* ELLEN *immediately slips away from him. When they come in she lifts a can and goes out by door to yard.* ROBBIE JOHN *and* SAMUEL JAMES *seat themselves at the table. Leaning against table and nodding to both.*) Well, how's the corn doing?

SAMUEL JAMES. Oh, fairly well the year. How's the cream market?

TAYLOR. Much the same. Nothing new with you, I suppose?

SAMUEL JAMES. Well, they're going to settle Robbie the day, that's all. He's a lucky boy.

TAYLOR. I wish you joy, Robbie.

ROBBIE JOHN. Thank ye. Thank ye kindly. She's a nice wee girl.

SAMUEL JAMES. You don't seem as gay hearted as I would expect, does he, Mr Taylor? You'd think he was for getting hung or something. I suppose ye heard all about him giving up the fiddle playing? And the luck of it. To burn his old fiddle, and then get another a few days after. You'd think there was some sort of a strange warning or advice or something in it.

TAYLOR. It is very strange.

ROBBIE JOHN. Samuel James, do ye remember the time that ould tramp was playing on his fiddle as he went out that day down the loney? (SAMUEL JAMES *nods.*) Well, it seemed to me as if he were

21

playing to bring me out after him. D'ye mind the story, Mr Taylor, about the piper that went off with all the children, and was never heard tell of again.

TAYLOR. Aye.

ROBBIE JOHN. Well, I could feel him drawing me out after him the very same way. And last night, as sure as death, I heard the same uncanny air singing in my ears, and it seemed to be calling me to come out of this.

TAYLOR (*exchanges startled looks with* SAMUEL JAMES.) Och, I suppose the wind or something outside. But there's no doubt, Robbie, you have a genius for the fiddle. There was a German professor of music at Newcastle the day you won the prize and he was— But it's not right of me to make you vexed, now you've stopped playing.

SAMUEL JAMES. Ach, he doesn't mind you telling. Do ye, Robbie? Tell and hearten him up a wee bit.

TAYLOR. This German was so struck with your playing that he was looking for you all roads, but you were nowhere to be found.

ROBBIE JOHN (*interested*). Aye? I went straight home. I wonder what he wanted?

SAMUEL JAMES. Perhaps he could have given him a lift, eh, Mr Taylor?

TAYLOR. He was talking to me afterwards, and by the way, I had clean forgot. (*Fumbling in his pocket.*) He gave me his card to give you. I have it on me somewhere I think. (*Producing it.*) Aye, there it is. (*Reading.*) Professor— something or other, Royal College of Music.

ROBBIE JOHN. Keep it. If I had it, it would only tempt me.

TAYLOR (*looking significantly at* SAMUEL JAMES, *who indicates by shaking his head that he considers* ROBBIE JOHN *hopeless.*) You're a queer character. All right. But you can have it any time. (*To* SAMUEL JAMES.) I wish I had said nothing about it. Where's the old man?

SAMUEL JAMES. The two old men are out in the haggard, but (*slyly*) Ellen's in the cream-house. (TAYLOR *goes out through door at back.* SAMUEL JAMES *looks over at* ROBBIE JOHN, *who sits in deep thought near the fire.*) You can no hoodwink me, Robbie. You're no happy.

ROBBIE JOHN. I'm happy enough. (*Angrily.*) Don't be tormenting me.

SAMUEL JAMES. Faith you look happy. (*Drawing closer.*) I seen you last night at it.

ROBBIE JOHN (*looks round startled.*) I couldn't keep from it. There's a

22

spell or something on it.

SAMUEL JAMES. Na. Na. But every fiddle has its spell for you. You broke your promise.

ROBBIE JOHN. You followed me then?

SAMUEL JAMES. Yes. Ye crept on your stocking soles to the back of the forth ditch, and played there for two mortal hours, till I was heart feared they'd miss us out of bed, and raise a cry.

ROBBIE JOHN. And you stood two hours in the night listening to me.

SAMUEL JAMES. I 'clare to God there's something out of common with you or that fiddle, for I had to stop and listen, and me teeth chattering with could.

ROBBIE JOHN. I did wrong, I know, but look here, Samuel James, as long as I see that thing hanging there, my hands are itching to hold it, and the tunes I could play – they keep running in my head. (*Suddenly rising.*) I'll destroy it.

SAMUEL JAMES (*quieting him down*). Na. Na. It's a valuable fiddle.

ROBBIE JOHN. It is. Ach, man, but it does tempt me sorely.

SAMUEL JAMES. Aye. You might make a fortune, the dear knows. Man, I know what I would do if I could play like you. (*Sarcastically.*) That was if ye had the heart.

ROBBIE JOHN (*excited*). Ach quit! Quit talking to me that way. (*Goes out by door at back.*)

SAMUEL JAMES (*getting off seat and standing about centre of room*). He'll take to it yet. (*He goes over nearer fireplace.*) I can see it working in him. Sure his hands are trembling and his fingers twitching all the times he's looking at it. (*The* GRANDFATHER *enters softly by door at back. He stands looking at* SAMUEL JAMES, *who does not observe him.*) Maybe it's no right of me to let it hang there. Ach. He maybe could make money plenty. I want till have a fine place and a lock of money. And I'll build a bigger house.

GRANDFATHER (*hobbling over to his seat*). Aye. Aye. Ye could do a heap with money, Samuel James.

SAMUEL JAMES (*alarmed, but endeavouring to bluff with a show of geniality*). Money's the thing, grand-da.

GRANDFATHER. It's a tarr'ble fine thing, there's no doubt. Food and drink and fine clothes and fine houses ye can get.

SAMUEL JAMES. And tobaccy and cigars, and the front seat at a consart.

GRANDFATHER. Here. Don't be tempting Robbie John about playing on that fiddle. You've upset the boy.

SAMUEL JAMES (*sharply*). I don't tempt him.

GRANDFATHER. You're always reminding him of it. I can see what you're working for Samuel James. Ye want all the money for yourself.

SAMUEL JAMES. Have sense, grand-da. Sure they're settling the matter to-day, and he's to be married at Christmas. He wouldn't do anything rash now.

GRANDFATHER. The clock has no struck the hour yet, Samuel James. Ye could no tell what's working in his mind.

SAMUEL JAMES. Well, he'd be a fool, and what's more, he knows himself to be one if he goes. He'll lose all the money from da if he goes, and I'm sure Jennie Graeme's father wouldn't turn his head to look at a fiddler.

GRANDFATHER. Aye. He's tarr'ble proud of his family.

MRS GRANAHAN (*opens door of room and comes in*). Here. I seen Mr Graeme and your da coming up the loney from the window in the low room.

SAMUEL JAMES. Well, they'll be coming in here and we're only in the road. Come and twist a wheen of ropes for me. (SAMUEL JAMES *and* GRANDFATHER *go out by door at back.*)

MRS GRANAHAN (*takes brush and sweeps floor. She then arranges a kettle at the fire. Then goes to door and looks out.*) Aye. Here he bees now and that good man of mine talking till him a dozen till one. And ten till one, he'll have John Graeme that angered with his arguing that there'll be nothing settled the day. (*Sound of* WILLIAM JOHN GRANAHAN'S *voice. He appears to be talking at a great rate, and most emphatically.* JOHN GRAEME *and* WILLIAM JOHN GRANAHAN *pass the window.*) Aye, to be sure. He'd rather get the better of Graeme in an argyment as settle with him over twenty sons, the ould gomeril. (JOHN GRAEME *and* WILLIAM JOHN GRANAHAN *enter.*) How dy'e do, Mr Graeme? (*She shakes hands with him warmly and warns the husband by nods not to resume the argument.*) It's the brave weather for the crops this.

JOHN GRAEME. Indeed we should be deeply thankful for the mercies vouchsafed us. (*Solemnly.*) Aye indeed.

WILLIAM JOHN GRANAHAN. Well, indeed, I would be that myself, only the half of them young chickens going off with the gapes. It was a tarr'ble to do to save what's left of them.

MRS GRANAHAN. Oh, well. It's all in the way of Providence, Mr Graeme. (*She looks disapprovingly across at* GRANAHAN. *The two men seat themselves.* JOHN GRAEME *beside table and* WILLIAM GRANAHAN *on edge of table next him.*) That was a fine lecture on the temperance ye gied us, Mr Graeme, at Ballykelly. It done some people a heap of good. (*She looks across meaningly at*

WILLIAM GRANAHAN.)

JOHN GRAEME (*apparently much pleased*). Do you say so, Mrs Granahan? I'm much pleased indeed to hear of it.

MRS GRANAHAN. I only wish more of the same kind had heerd you. (*She looks across again at* WILLIAM JOHN GRANAHAN, *who avoids her eye.*) But you'll excuse me, I'm sure. I have some things next room to look after for the evening. (*She curtsies to* GRAEME, *and with a warning look at* GRANAHAN, *goes into room.*)

JOHN GRAEME. I am very much pleased indeed to hear your good woman say she liked what I said. How did ye take to it yourself, Mr Granahan?

WILLIAM JOHN GRANAHAN (*suddenly waking up from twisting and untwisting a piece of string which he has found, and in which he appears deeply interested while his wife is talking.*) How did we like the speech you gave on temperance, d'ye say? (*Carelessly.*) Och, it was a very good and sensible discoorse, so I heerd Ellen and Mrs Graeme say.

JOHN GRAEME. Ye didn't go yourself then? (*Disappointedly.*) Man, I wanted ye there particular.

WILLIAM JOHN GRANAHAN. I have no doot if I had been there I could have got up and contradicted ye, for (*emphatically*), I did not agree with all I heerd ye said.

JOHN GRAEME (*surprised*). Not agree with what I said. (*Scornfully, with evident disgust.*) Man, ye couldn't argy with facts. What did ye disagree with in the discoorse?

WILLIAM JOHN GRANAHAN. Well, for one thing, ye said there was too many public houses in the country.

JOHN GRAEME (*scornfully*). And every right-minded man would agree with that.

WILLIAM JOHN GRANAHAN. Well, I can shew you another. You'll no argy with me that if a man wants to drink he will drink.

JOHN GRAEME (*somewhat perplexed*). Well— (*slowly*) I suppose I do agree till that.

WILLIAM JOHN GRANAHAN. And if a man will drink he's bound till get drunk.

JOHN GRAEME. Na. Na. I don't agree till that.

WILLIAM JOHN GRANAHAN (*triumphantly*). Did you ever hear tell of a man who was drunk without drinking?

JOHN GRAEME. That's not in the argyment at all.

WILLIAM JOHN GRANAHAN. But I tell you it is. A man's bound to be drinking if he gets drunk.

JOHN GRAEME. I'm no contradicting that at all. I—

25

WILLIAM JOHN GRANAHAN (*interrupting*). Now, hould your tongue till I explain till ye. If a man gets drunk when he's drinking, he's bound to be drunk of coorse.

JOHN GRAEME (*contemptuously*). Ye talk like a child.

WILLIAM JOHN GRANAHAN. Now wait till I get it hammered intil ye. Now when that man's drunk he's bound to have been drinking. (*He hesitates and is obviously confused. Then suddenly seems to grasp the idea he wants*). Aye – in a public house of coorse.

JOHN GRAEME. O'coorse. What else would he do there but drink.

WILLIAM JOHN GRANAHAN. Now that man gets drunk. (*He looks enquiringly at* GRAEME.)

JOHN GRAEME (*hopelessly*). Aye.

WILLIAM JOHN GRANAHAN. Now the public houses are that scarce that he has till walk home maybe ten mile or more.

JOHN GRAEME. Well?

WILLIAM JOHN GRANAHAN. And ten till wan he gets lost or something, and they have the whole countryside upset looking for him. Now, if he had a public house convanient in his own townland, there would be no bother at all, and he could be at his work the next morning without any interrupting of labour. D'ye see what I mean?

MRS GRANAHAN (*suddenly appearing at door evidently angry*). The more public houses the less drinking did he say? If he had *his* way of it every other house from here to Buckna would be a public house. (*To husband.*) Quit your wasting Mr Graeme's time with your argyments, and settle what he has come here to do with ye.

WILLIAM JOHN GRANAHAN. Well. Well. We'll agree till let the matter drop. You have nobody but your daughter, I suppose?

JOHN GRAEME. Well, I have a sister married up in Dublin.

WILLIAM JOHN GRANAHAN. But she's in a good way of doing, I suppose?

JOHN GRAEME. Oh yes. Purty fair. Of coorse I would like to leave her something.

WILLIAM JOHN GRANAHAN. Ach, give her a lock of your hair or something. You'll lave the place to your daughter of coorse.

JOHN GRAEME. Yes. I'll be doing that.

WILLIAM JOHN GRANAHAN. Aye. It's a purty fair farm of land. Ye bought it out of coorse?

JOHN GRAEME. Two years come March, and a good reduction.

WILLIAM JOHN GRANAHAN. Aye. So I heerd. Well if ye give her the farm and what money you have I'll give Robbie a cheque for a hunnert pound.

26

JOHN GRAEME (*impressively*). William John Granahan, d'ye think this is a horse fair? My daughter will have no man unner five hunnert pound.

WILLIAM JOHN GRANAHAN (*uneasily and walking about*). Man, you'll never get her married, John Graeme, at that way of talking. Five hunnert pound! D'ye think I'm a Rockyfellow? Have some sense about ye.

JOHN GRAEME. Aither that or no son of yours weds my daughter. Five hunnert pounds and not one ha'penny less. There's the family name to be thought of.

WILLIAM JOHN GRANAHAN. Ach! Family name! A lock of ould wives' blathers about who was married till who, till you'd have your head sore taking it all in.

JOHN GRAEME. You've heerd what I have to say. Take it or leave it. You can plaze yourself.

WILLIAM JOHN GRANAHAN. Five hunnert pound. It's a tarr'ble price. Would two hunnert do? You see I have Samuel James and Ellen to provide for.

JOHN GRAEME. A Graeme of Killainey weds no man unner five hunnert pound, William Granahan. Mind that. I want my daughter married to no beggarman.

WILLIAM JOHN GRANAHAN (*excitedly*). Beggarman! Beggarman, did ye say? Hats, John Graeme, I think ye should be proud of one of yours marrying a Granahan. Money or no money, that's a nice way of talking.

JOHN GRAEME. I suppose ye know I come of good family, Mr Granahan?

WILLIAM JOHN GRANAHAN (*sarcastically*). I heard ye were once cotter folk up by Dromara mountain.

JOHN GRAEME (*proudly*). My father and my forefathers had my farm – aye, from the time of the planting.

WILLIAM JOHN GRANAHAN. D'ye tell me? I nivir seen your lease of the farm, but if coorse if ye say so. Did ye never hear tell of Smith, Hunter, and Fargison?

JOHN GRAEME (*contemptuously*). John Smith, of Ballykelly?

WILLIAM JOHN GRANAHAN (*disgusted*). Yon cratur? Ballykelly? (*Proudly.*) Lonnon! Well, my mother was a daughter of Samuel James Smith, and a niece of Robert John Francis Fargison.

JOHN GRAEME (*contemptuously*). I never heerd tell of them.

WILLIAM JOHN GRANAHAN. I wonner at your ignorance, John Graeme. A well educated man like yourself as set yourself up to be teaching the congregation on matters of law and the temperance question (*raising voice*), and you that ignorant of common information.

MRS GRANAHAN (*opening door and coming in a few steps*). William John Granahan, didn't I tell ye not to be raising argyments. How you manage at the markets I never could understand. Get your business done, and have settled with it.

WILLIAM JOHN GRANAHAN (*soothingly*). Whist, whist woman, I was only discoorsing. Mind the tay and I'll mind the rest. There. There. I agree to your tarms, John Graeme. I'll do it, though it's leaving me tarr'ble short.

JOHN GRAEME (*impressively*). But there's one thing I'll no have, William Granahan.

WILLIAM JOHN GRANAHAN (*alarmed*). And what might that be?

JOHN GRAEME. If your son is to marry my daughter, I'll have none of his music. It's all very well for quality and the like to go strumming on instruments, but it's not meant for a sensible farmer.

WILLIAM JOHN GRANAHAN. Aye. I agree with that. But look here. Mind ye a song or two and a bit of a tune on a long winter's night keeps one from thinking long, and between you and me, it keeps you from the bottle.

JOHN GRAEME. That's where you and I differs. Supposing he starts playing a dance tune or two, and the neighbours gather in. You like to do the thing decent, and ye send out for drink, and then it goes from bad to worse. Na. Na. I'll have none of that.

WILLIAM JOHN GRANAHAN. Well. Well. Make your mind easy. `Ye know he has promised me never to play again, and I don't think you'll hear much of his fiddling.

JOHN GRAEME. I'm right glad to hear it, and I'll take your word for it.

WILLIAM JOHN GRANAHAN. Very good. (*With admiration.*) Man, you'd have made a great horsedealer, John Graeme.

JOHN GRAEME. Aye. I had an uncle in the town, a dealer, and he was always saying that.

WILLIAM JOHN GRANAHAN. And well you could have done it, if I knowed anything. I'll go to Banbridge a Friday with you to settle with the lawyers.

JOHN GRAEME. Very good. I'll call for you with the trap that day. It's time I was for going home.

WILLIAM JOHN GRANAHAN. We were expecting ye over that day, and I think Mrs Granahan has the tea laid in the low room. (*Calls.*) Mrs Granahan!

MRS GRANAHAN (*from room*). Yes. (*She comes in and stands waiting near door.*)

28

WILLIAM JOHN GRANAHAN. We're just after settling up about Robbie John and Jennie. Can you get us a drop of tea?

MRS GRANAHAN. If you could just take Mr Graeme for a turn round I could have it for you in wan second. The table's laid and the kettle's boiling. Is your daughter with you, Mr Graeme?

JOHN GRAEME. Aye. She was coming over after me. I suppose she should be here by now.

WILLIAM JOHN GRANAHAN. Well I can show you the new reaper and binder I got. That new Wexford machine, I was telling you about a Sunday in the Session.

JOHN GRAEME. Very good. I'll just go out and see it.

(WILLIAM JOHN GRANAHAN *and* JOHN GRAEME *go out by door at back*).

MRS GRANAHAN (*going over to fire and arranging kettle*). Five hunnert pound, and after me telling him to keep till four hunnert. Wait till I get ahoult of him again. I'll speak till him. Did he not hear me thumping four times on the door till remind him. He must have a soft spot in his heart for Robbie John. (*Tap at door.*) Come in. (JANE GRAEME *enters somewhat diffidently.*) Oh, it's you, Miss Graeme. (*Shakes hands.*) You're welcome, indeed. Your father's just gone out with my good man.

JANE. Yes. I know – but I thought perhaps – well that Robbie was here.

MRS GRANAHAN (*inspecting her critically.*) Deed, now, I couldn't tell you where he might be.

JANE. I'll just sit down a minute. I suppose you are all doing well here, Mrs Granahan?

MRS GRAHANAN. Ach, aye. As well as one could expect. There's nothing to make much complaint of.

JANE. I haven't seen Robbie about for some time, Mrs Granahan. I suppose he's working hard at the harvest.

MRS GRANAHAN. Aye 'deed, there's a brave press of work on now, what with the corn a cutting, and the rest of it, he's been gey busy of late.

JANE. Indeed I am sure he was. (*She looks round, sees the fiddle hanging up where* TAYLOR *has left it. Aside.*) Is that the fiddle he was telling me about, I wonder? (*To* MRS GRANAHAN.) Is that the tramp's fiddle, Mrs Granahan?

MRS GRANAHAN. Aye, that's the poor cratur's belongings. But you needn't be afeard. Robbie's indeed been very good. He's never played on it to my knowing, and keeps his promise well.

JANE. Poor Robbie. Do you not think he's unhappy about something or other, Mrs Granahan? He's got very dull and moody this last while.

MRS GRANAHAN. Deed, now, I don't see much odds in him, Miss Graeme. He never was a great boy with his tongue anyway (*slyly*), bar maybe an odd one or two he would make up to.

JANE. I think you do wrong to keep that fiddle hanging up before his eyes when he has promised never to play again.

MRS GRANAHAN. Och, blatherations. I never heard the like of the sort of talk people goes on with nowadays. Do you think my son bees only an ould ba crying for a toy? Deed now I don't think he worries hisself much about it.

JANE (*aside*). Poor Robbie. (*To* MRS GRANAHAN.) Robbie's a poor hand at the farming, Mrs Granahan.

MRS GRANAHAN (*snappishly*). Och aye. But he's greatly mended since he gave up playing.

JANE. Yes. He's a very poor farmer. But he was a wonder with his fiddle.

MRS GRANAHAN. Oh, well. It cannot be helped. He's better without.

JANE. I don't know. (*She goes over and takes down the fiddle, seats herself, and draws the bow across it as it lies on her lap.*) Robbie could make it speak to you. He used to make me cry, and then laugh after it. (*She places the strings near her ear and thumbs it wrapt in thought.*)

MRS GRANAHAN (*looking contemptuously at her and then rising*). You just stay here a second till I fix the tay. (*She goes into room.* JANE *remains seated where she is, occasionally touching the strings and seemingly deep in thought.* ROBBIE JOHN *passes window. He looks in and then goes quickly to door and enters.*)

ROBBIE JOHN. Who's that fiddling? (*Goes over to* JANE.) Why, it's you. I heard you had come.

JANE. Yes. I'm just in a minute or two. (*He sits down beside her.*) Robbie.

ROBBIE JOHN. Well?

JANE. Answer me one question. Aren't you a very poor farmer?

ROBBIE JOHN. Well – I – suppose I am.

JANE. I knew you were. You're no good for selling cattle or going to market, or looking after crops.

ROBBIE JOHN. You're very hard on me, Jane, to-night. What's put all that into your wee head?

JANE. I've been listening to this and its been telling stories on you.

ROBBIE JOHN. Aye and when it's hanging there dumb it's speaking to me, calling to me. Don't think I'm mad, Jane, but I can't stand it much longer. What makes them hang it there to tempt me? Why? Just because they think they can make a few miserable pounds they'll keep it there making me a liar, a pledge breaker, a man who can't keep his promise. I'll end it now. I'll smash it. (*He makes to take the fiddle out of her hands.*)

JANE (*resisting*). No. No. I want to say – I want to ask something, Robbie. What does it say to you?

ROBBIE JOHN. What does it – ach – I wonder would you laugh at me like the rest if I told you?

JANE (*sitting closer and putting her arm about his neck*). What does it say? Tell me. I would never laugh at you, Robbie.

ROBBIE JOHN (*hesitatingly*). Ach – about – about taking it and making a name for myself with it. (*Bitterly.*) It sounds like fools talk, doesn't it.

JANE. To my father and yours it would sound like that, and Samuel James would laugh at you, but he'd encourage you to believe in it.

ROBBIE JOHN. Let me break it then. Smash it.

JANE (*determinedly*). No. Look, Robbie, if I said it was whispering you the truth, what would you say?

ROBBIE JOHN (*surprised*). But you never would.

JANE (*determinedly*). I say it is the truth.

ROBBIE JOHN. You don't know what you are saying. If I did take to it again look what would happen. My father would turn me out, and your father would forbid me then ever looking at you again. Jane Graeme engaged to a penniless fiddler, and she the best match in the whole countryside. I need never think of you again, Jane.

JANE. I don't care what they did. If you took to that fiddle and went away, would you forget me soon?

ROBBIE JOHN. Forget you, Jane? What makes you think that? Sure you know I gave it up sooner than lose you.

JANE. Then take that fiddle and do what your heart tells you to. I wondered often and often what it was that made you so sad, and I know now. God made you a musician, and not a farmer.

ROBBIE JOHN. And you? What would you do?

JANE. I know and trust some day, God willing, you'll come back to me, rich and famous enough to have them all at your feet. I know you will.

ROBBIE JOHN. God bless you, wee girl, for you've put a heart into me. (*The embrace.* MRS GRANAHAN *comes in.*)

MRS GRANAHAN. There. There. Bide a wee. Here they're all coming in for their tea.

(WILLIAM JOHN GRANAHAN, GRAEME, TAYLOR, SAMUEL

31

JAMES, *and* GRANDFATHER *come in.* ROBBIE JOHN *goes over
to fiddle and puts it into a case.*)

WILLIAM JOHN GRANAHAN (*puzzled*). So you're at it again, are you?
Well, I suppose there's no harm in giving Miss Graeme a tune, but
I thought you were a man to your word.

ROBBIE JOHN (*determinedly*). Look here. I want you all to know I am
going to try my luck with this.

SAMUEL JAMES (*exultingly*). You're going to leave us like to make
money with it.

ROBBIE JOHN. I'm going to try.

MRS GRANAHAN. Robbie John, are you daft? What wild nonsense are
ye talking about? And you to be married at Christmas, and
everything settled about you this very day.

ROBBIE JOHN. I am determined to do it. Nothing can keep me back.

JOHN GRAEME. There. That's enough. My daughter jilted by a
Granahan! Come home out of this, Jane Graeme. (*He stamps his
foot angrily and beckons her to come.* JANE *moves past* ROBBIE
JOHN *where he is standing, and then suddenly kisses him and goes
out with her father.*)

WILLIAM JOHN GRANAHAN (*passionately*). You see what you have
done, Robert John Granahan. Broken your parents' hearts, and
made the name of the Granahans a disgrace to the countryside.

ROBBIE JOHN. My mind's made up. Give me the address of that
Professor you told me of, Mr Taylor.

TAYLOR. You're a fool, Robbie. (*Producing card and handing it to
him.*) There. That's it.

WILLIAM JOHN GRANAHAN. There's time yet, man. After John
Graeme and make it up with him. Swear you were only making
fun. (*Wildly.*) Quick d – n ye before it's too late.

ROBBIE JOHN. I stick by the fiddle.

WILLIAM JOHN GRANAHAN (*mad with anger*). Then stick by the
fiddle. And know if ever you are weary or ahungered or in want
ye need never look me for any help. (*Shouts.*) Out you go! Out!
Don't dare one of you as much as till take his hand. Out! Out the
same as the beggar man gone, with the curse of your father on
you! (ROBBIE JOHN *goes towards back and stands a moment as if
in silent appeal at the open door.* MRS GRANAHAN *rushes forward
to her husband as if to entreat mercy. He angrily puts her away.*)
Out! Out you go!

(CURTAIN.)

EPILOGUE

The same scene, about midnight. There is no light except that of one or two candles and the turf fire. GRANDFATHER *seated at fire.* WILLIAM JOHN GRANAHAN *leaning despondently on table beside which he is seated.* SAMUEL JAMES *in his favourite seat on the top of the table. Wind, storm and rain outside.*

GRANDFATHER. Aye. Aye. But it's no use talking now. Ye might have been a wee bit the less hasty.

WILLIAM JOHN GRANAHAN. And who was going to thole yon conduck. It was too bad of him and after the to-do we had over him this very day. It's a sore heartscald, Robbie John, ye've been to me this day.

SAMUEL JAMES. Ach, sure its over. It's full time we were in our beds. (*Viciously.*) You'd think he was dead and buried to hear the two of you going on. Sure for all knows he may be coming back and a great name with him.

GRANDFATHER. That's you to the ground, ye cunning rascal. Keep him out at all costs. (*Thunder and lightning.*) D'ye hear yon? To think of that poor sowl with his wee bit of a coat out in the could and wet. If any harm come till him, Samuel James, know this, you were the cause of it.

SAMUEL JAMES. It was his own choosing.

GRANDFATHER. His own choosing? Who flattered him and led him on? Who kept the fiddle hanging there and would let no one take it down, a continuing temptation till him? And you, William John Granahan, with your lust for money. Aye. Lust for money. You couldn't abide him heartening up the house with a tune or two, but ye'd break the boy's heart sending him our till work again, and him working as much as two of Samuel James there. Ye thought he was wasting time and money. D'ye think there's nothing in this life beyond making money above the rent. I tell you it's not the money alone that makes life worth living. It's the wee things you think nothing of, but that make your home a joy to

33

come back till, after a hard day's work. And you've sent out into the could and wet the one that was making your home something more than the common. D'ye think them proud city folk will listen to his poor ould ballads with the heart of the boy singing through them. It's only us – it's only us, I say, as knows the long wild nights, and the wet and the rain and the mist of nights on the boglands – it's only us I say could listen him in the right way. (*Sobbing*), and ye knowed, right well ye knowed, that every string of his fiddle was keyed to the crying of your own heart.

WILLIAM JOHN GRANAHAN (*half sobbing*). There. There. God forgive me, my poor ould boy. I did na know. Whist. Maybe if I say a word or two – Oh God forgive us this night our angry words, and have mercy on my wayward son, O Lord, and keep him safe from harm, and deliver him not unto the adversary. Amen.

GRANDFATHER. Amen. Aye. Aye. Ye done well. Let not the sun go down upon your wrath.

WILLIAM JOHN GRANAHAN (*going to door*). It's a coorse night. (*Pauses.*) I'll leave the door on the hesp. (*He unbolts the door.*)

(CURTAIN.)

THE DRONE

A COMEDY IN THREE ACTS

CHARACTERS

JOHN MURRAY, a farmer
DANIEL MURRAY, his brother
MARY MURRAY, John's daughter
ANDREW MCMINN, a farmer
SARAH MCMINN, his sister
DONAL MACKENZIE, a Scotch engineer
SAM BROWN, a labourer in John Murray's employment
KATE, a servant girl in John Murray's employment
ALICK MCCREADY, a young farmer

The action takes place throughout in the kitchen of John Murray in the County of Down.

TIME – the present day (1908)

This play was first produced at the Abbey Theatre, Dublin, by the Ulster Literary Theatre, on 24 April 1908, with the following cast:

JOHN MURRAY	G. A. Charters
	(A. Gilmer)
DANIEL MURRAY	Arthur Malcolm
	(Sam Bullock)
MARY MURRAY	Seveen Canmer
	(Josephine Campbell)
KATE	Máire Crothers
	(Edith Lilburn)
SAM BROWN	Rutherford Mayne
ANDREW MCMINN	John Field
	(John Field Màgee)
SARAH MCMINN	Bridget O'Gorman
ALICK MCCREADY	Ross Canmer
	(J. P. Campbell)
DONAL MACKENZIE	Robert Henry
	(R. H. Leighton)

36

THE DRONE

ACT I

The farm kitchen of JOHN MURRAY. *It is large and spacious, with a wide open fire-place to the right. At the back is one door leading to the parlour and other rooms in the house, also a large window overlooking the yard outside. To the left of this window is the door leading into the yard. Opposite to the fire-place on the left side is another door leading into* DANIEL MURRAY'S *workshop, and beside this door is a large dresser with crockery, etc. At the back beneath the window is a table near which* KATE, *the servant, a slatternly dressed girl of some thirty years of age or more, is seated. She is carefully examining some cakes of soda bread, and has a bucket beside her into which she throws the rejected pieces.*

KATE. That one's stale. It would break your teeth to eat it. (*She throws the cake into the bucket.*) And the mice have nibbled that one. And there's another as bad. (*She throws both pieces into the bucket.*)
>   (BROWN, *the servant man, opens the door from yard and enters. He is elderly, and with a pessimistic expression of face, relieved somewhat by the sly humour that is in his eyes. He walks slowly to the centre of the kitchen, looks at Kate, and then turns his eyes, with a disgusted shake of the head, towards the dresser as if searching for something.*)

BROWN. Well! Well! Pigs get fat and men get lean in this house.

KATE. It's you again, is it? And what are you looking now?

BROWN. I'm looking a spanner for the boss. The feedboard to the threshing machine got jammed just when halfway through the first stack, and he is in a lamentable temper.

KATE (*uneasily*). Is he?

BROWN (*watching her slyly to see what effect his words have*). And he's been grumbling all morning about the way things is going on in this house. *Bread* and things wasted and destroyed altogether.

KATE. Well, it's all Miss Mary's fault. I told her about this bread yesterday forenoon, and she never took any heed to me.

BROWN. Miss Mary? (*With a deprecatory shake of his head.*) What does a slip of a girl like that know about housekeeping and her not home a year from the school in the big town, and no mother or anybody to train her. (*He stares in a puzzled way at the dresser.*) I don't see that spanner at all. Did you see it, Kate?

KATE. No. I've more to do than look for spanners.

BROWN (*gazing reproachfully at her and then shaking his head*). It's a nice house, right enough. (*Lowering his voice.*) And I suppose old Mr Dan is never up yet. I was told by Johnny McAndless, he was terrible full last night at McArns and talking – ach – the greatest blethers about this new invention of his.

KATE. Do you say so?

BROWN. Aye. No wonder he's taking a lie this morning. (*He peeps into the door of the workshop.*) He's not in his wee workshop?

KATE. No. Miss Mary is just after taking up his breakfast to him.

BROWN. Some people get living easy in this world. (*He gives a last look at the dresser.*) Well divil a spanner can I see. I'll tell the master that. (*He goes out again through the yard door, and as he does so,* MARY MURRAY *comes through the door from the inner rooms, carrying a tray with teacups, etc. on it. She is a pretty, vivacious girl about eighteen years of age.*)

MARY. Who was that?

KATE. It's the servant man looking for a spanner for your father, Miss Mary. There's something gone wrong with the threshing machine.

MARY (*taking the tray to the table and starting to get ready to wash up the cups*). I do believe sometimes that Uncle Dan's a lazy man.

KATE (*assisting her at the washing and stopping as if astonished at the statement*). And it is only now you're after finding that out! Sure the whole countryside knowed it this years and years.

MARY (*sharply*). The whole countryside has no business to talk about what doesn't concern it.

KATE. Oh, well, people are bound to talk, Miss.

MARY. But then Uncle Dan is awfully clever. He's got the whole brains of the Murrays, so father says, and then, besides that, he is a grand talker.

KATE. Aye. He can talk plenty. Sure Sarah McMinn, that lives up the Cut, says it's a shame the way he's going on this twenty years and more, never doing a hand's turn from morning to night, and she says she wonders your poor father stands him and his nonsense.

MARY. Who said that?

KATE. Sarah McMinn told Johnny McAndless that yesterday.

MARY. Sarah McMinn? Pooh! That hard, mean, old thing. No. I

38

believe in Uncle Dan and so does father. He'll make a name for himself yet.

KATE. Well, it's getting near time he done it.

MARY. They say that Sarah McMinn just keeps her brother in starvation, and she just says nasty things like that about Uncle Dan because he doesn't like her.

KATE. Aye. He never did like people as seen through him, not but she is a mean old skin-a-louse. (*The voice of* DANIEL MURRAY *is heard calling from within.*) He's up, Miss.

MARY. Are you up, uncle?

(DAN MURRAY *opens the door from the inner apartments and comes into the kitchen. He is carelessly dressed and sleepy-looking as if just out of bed, wears a muffler and glasses, and appears to be some fifty years old.*)

DANIEL. Yes. Did the *Whig* come yet?

MARY. Yes. I put it in your workshop.

DANIEL (*glancing at the clock.*) Bless my heart, it's half-past one!

MARY (*reproachfully*). It is, indeed, uncle.

DANIEL. Well! Well! Time goes round, Mary. Time goes round. (KATE *picks up the bucket and goes out by the yard door.*) Where's your father? (*He crosses over to the workshop door.*)

MARY. He's out working with Sam Brown at the threshing all morning since seven o'clock.

DANIEL. Well! Well! A very industrious man is John Murray. Very. But lacking in brains, my dear – lacking in brains. Kind, good-hearted, easy-going, but – ah! well, one can't help these things. (*He goes into the workshop and brings out the paper and crosses back to sit down at the fire-place.*)

MARY. You were very late coming in last night, uncle.

DANIEL (*uneasily*). Eh! (*He settles down in an arm-chair and opens out the paper.*)

MARY. I heard you coming in, and the clock was just after striking two.

DANIEL. Well – I met a few friends last night. Appreciative friends I could talk to, and I was explaining that new idea of mine that I've been working at so long – that new idea for a fan-bellows. It's a great thing. Oh yes. It should be. I sat up quite a while last night, thinking it over, and I believe I've got more ideas about it – better ones.

MARY. Do you think you'll make money off it, uncle?

DANIEL. Mary – if it comes off – if I can get someone to take it up, I believe 'twill make our fortune, I do.

MARY. Oh, uncle, it would be lovely if you did, and I would just die to see that nasty McMinn woman's face when she hears about you making such a hit.

DANIEL. McMinn? Has that woman been sneering about me again? That's one woman, Mary, I can't stand. I can never do myself justice explaining ideas in company when that woman is present.

MARY. Never mind her, uncle. (*Coming close beside him.*) Do you mind this time last year, uncle, when you went up to Belfast for a week to see about that patent for – what's this the patent was, uncle?

DANIEL (*uncomfortably*). Last year? This time?

MARY. Yes. Don't you remember you said you knew of an awfully nice boy that you met, and you were going to bring him down here.

DANIEL. Upon my soul, I had clean forgotten. Yes, yes. I think I did say something about a young fellow I met.

MARY. Was he nice, uncle?

DANIEL (*becoming absorbed in the newspaper*). Eh? I think so. Oh. He was – very nice chap.

MARY. Well, you said he was coming here to see me, and he never turned up yet.

DANIEL. Did I? Very possibly. I suppose he must have forgotten.

MARY (*walking away to the left and then back again pouting*). I'm sick of the boys here. There's only Alick McCready that's anyway passable. When will you see him again, uncle?

DANIEL. Well – possibly, when I go up to town again. Very soon, perhaps. That is if your father, Mary, can spare the money.

MARY (*thoughtfully*). I don't know, uncle. You see that would be five times now, and somehow you never seem to get anything done. That's what he said, mind you, uncle.

DANIEL (*mournfully*). Well! Well! To think of me toiling and moiling away in that workshop of mine, day after day, and week after week, and year after year – and there's all the thanks you get for it.

MARY. Uncle?

DANIEL (*somewhat irritably as he gets engrossed reading*). Well?

MARY. Look, if you went up to Belfast again soon, won't you see that boy? I wonder what he's like. (*She gets close beside her uncle and nestles beside him*). Is he dark or fair?

DANIEL. Yes, yes. I think so.

MARY. Dark?

DANIEL. Yes. I believe he is dark.

MARY. And tall?

DANIEL (*trying vainly to read in spite of the interruptions*). Very tall.

MARY. Oh, how nice! And uncle, is he good-looking?

DANIEL. Very. Fine looking fellow.

MARY. That's grand; and uncle, is he well to do?

DANIEL. He has ever appearance of it.

MARY. Oh you dear old uncle! (*She nestles closer to him.*) But maybe he wouldn't look at me when he has a whole lot of town girls to go with.

DANIEL. My dear niece, you don't know what a very good-looking young lady you are, and besides he saw your photograph.

MARY. Which photograph?

DANIEL (*perplexed*). Which photograph? Your own of course!

MARY. The one I got taken at Lurgan?

DANIEL. Yes. I think so.

MARY. Oh uncle! That horrid thing! Why didn't you show him the one I got taken at Newcastle?

DANIEL. My mistake. Very sorry, indeed, Mary, I assure you. But I tell you, I'll take the album with me next time. Will that do?

MARY (*laughing*). There. Now you're joking. (*Suddenly.*) What do you do all the time you stay in Belfast, uncle?

DANIEL (*uneasily*). Um – um – Business, my dear girl, business. See engineers and all that sort of thing, and talk things over. It takes time, you know, Mary, time.

MARY. You've been an awful long time inventing, uncle, haven't you?

DANIEL. Well, you know, Mary dear – time – it takes time. You can't rush an inventor.

MARY. Well look, uncle. You know I can just wheedle father round my wee finger, can't I?

DANIEL. You can indeed.

MARY. Well, look: if you promise to bring down this boy you are talking about, I'll get father to give you enough to have two weeks in Belfast. There. It's a bargain.

DANIEL. Um – well – he may not be there you know.

MARY (*disappointed*). O uncle!

DANIEL. You see he travels a lot and he may be away. He may be in London. In fact I think – yes. He said he would be going to London.

MARY. Then why not go to London?

DANIEL (*starting up and speaking as if struck with delight at the possibility*). Eh? I never thought of that! (*He collapses again.*) But no. Your father, Mary. He would never give me the money. No.

41

MARY. But you're more likely to meet people there who'd take it up, aren't you, uncle?

DANIEL. It's *the place* for an inventor to go, Mary. *The place.* (*Pauses.*) But I'm afraid when John hears about it – (*he becomes very dubious and shakes his head*).

MARY. Well, look here, uncle. Do you mind the last time when he would not give you money to go up to Belfast about your patent.

DANIEL (*sadly*). I do.

MARY. You remember you got a letter a few days after asking you to come up at once and you had to go then. Hadn't you?

DANIEL. I had.

MARY. Well, couldn't we do the same this time?

DANIEL (*looking at her uneasily*). Eh?

MARY. Couldn't we get someone to send a letter. (*Pauses and thinking, then suddenly.*) Oh, the very thing! You know that silly Alick McCready that comes running after me. Well, look, I'll get him to send a letter.

DANIEL. No good, my dear. I did it before – I mean letters on plain notepaper don't carry much weight. No.

MARY. What about – oh, I know! Uncle, a telegram!

DANIEL. Great idea! It is in soul!

MARY. And we'll put something on it like "come to London at once to see about the patent," or something like that. And he'd have to let you go then.

DANIEL. Mary, you're really a cleverer girl than your father thinks. (*Musingly.*) Two weeks in London.

MARY. And don't forget the nice boy, uncle, when you go.

DANIEL. I'll do my best to get hold of him.

MARY. No. I want a good definite promise. Promise, uncle.

DANIEL. Well, really you know, my dear, he –

MARY. Uncle, promise.

DANIEL. Um – well, I promise.

MARY. You're a dear old thing. You see, uncle, I don't want to marry Alick McCready or Jim McDowell or any of those boys, unless there's nobody else.

DANIEL. Quite right, my dear, quite right. Two weeks in London. Splendid! But it's time I was going into my workshop. (*He rises and takes the paper with him.*) I must really try and do something this morning. (*Exit by workshop door.*)

MARY (*calling after him*). You won't forget, uncle? Will you?

DANIEL. No, certainly not.

MARY. I do hope uncle brings that nice boy. Dark – tall – well set up –

well to do.

(KATE *comes in again through the yard door, and looks at* MARY, *who is gazing vacantly into space.*)

KATE. Well? What notion have you got now?

MARY. Oh! just think, Kate! How would you like a boy who was dark and tall, and well set up and well to do?

KATE. I'd just leap at him.

MARY (*laughing*). I think I will – if he comes.

KATE. I think you've plenty on hand to manage. (BROWN *opens the yard door and resumes his old position from which he stares at the dresser.*) You're back again, are you?

BROWN. Aye.

KATE. What ails you now?

BROWN. I'm looking the spanner.

MARY. The spanner?

BROWN. The spanner, Miss Mary. It's for turning the nuts like.

KATE. Have you never got it yet?

BROWN. Do you think I've got eyes in the back of my head? Underneath the seat, beside the salt-box, on the right near the wee crock in the left hand corner. (*He makes a movement to open one of the drawers of the dresser.*)

KATE. Will you get out of that, ignorance. It's not there.

BROWN (*with an appealing look at* MARY). Maybe its in the parlour?

MARY. Well, I'll take a look around. (*She goes through the door to the living rooms.*)

BROWN (*mysteriously*). Did you hear the news?

KATE. No. (*Very much interested.*) What?

BROWN. Ach! You women never know anything.

KATE. What's the news? Somebody killed?

BROWN. No. More serious.

KATE (*alarmed*). God bless me! What is it?

BROWN. Andy McMinn has a sister.

KATE (*disappointed*). Ach! Sure I knowed that years ago.

BROWN. And she's trying to get a man.

KATE. Well. I knowed that this years.

BROWN. And Mr John Murray is a widow man.

KATE. You mean to be telling me that Mr John Murray has a notion of that old thing? Go long with you!

BROWN. Did you ever hear tell of a widow man that never got married again.

KATE. Plenty. Don't come in here talking blethers.

BROWN. Whist. There's more in what I'm telling you than you think.

43

And I'll hold you to a shilling that Sarah McMinn will be Mrs John Murray before one month.

KATE. Who told you?

BROWN. Ach! You've no more head than a yellow yorling. Where has Mr John been going to these wheen of nights?

KATE (*thinking*). Andy McMinns!

BROWN. Aye. Do you think it is to see old Andy? And sure he's been talking to me all morning about the way the house is being kept. No hand to save the waste; bread and things destroyed; hens laying away; eggs ate up by the dozen and chickens lost and one thing and another. And hinting about what money a good saving woman would bring him. And Mr Daniel—.

KATE. Sh – he's in there working.

BROWN. Working? Ah, God save us! Him working! The last man that seen Mr Dan working is in his grave this twenty years. (*He goes over next workshop door.*) I'll just peep in at him through the keyhole. (*He goes over and does so, and then beckons* KATE *over. She peeps in and grins. As they are thus occupied* ALICK MCCREADY *opens the door and stands gazing at them. He is a type of the young well-to-do farmer, respectably dressed and good-looking.*)

ALICK. Well! Well! Some people earn their money easy!

BROWN. Aye. In soul. Just look in there to see it. (MCCREADY *looks in and bursts into a loud hearty laugh.* BROWN *hurriedly goes out by the yard door and* KATE *by door to inner rooms.*)

DANIEL (*opening door and standing there, perplexed looking*). What's the matter?

ALICK. Ah. I was just laughing at a wee joke, Mr Murray.

DANIEL. It must have been very funny.

ALICK. Aye. It was. (*Coming close to* DANIEL, *who walks slowly to the middle of the kitchen.*) I say. Were you at McArn's publichouse last night?

DANIEL (*looking round cautiously to see that no one else can hear him*). Well, just a minute or two. Why?

ALICK. There was someone there told Andy McMinn this morning, I believe, that you'd been talking of a great invention altogether, and he was that much curious to see it that him and his sister Sarah are coming over this day to have a look at it.

DANIEL. Who? Sarah McMinn?

ALICK. Aye. She's very anxious to see it, I believe.

DANIEL. Um. Rather awkward this. She's not a woman that, plainly speaking, I care very much to talk about my ideas to.

ALICK. But have you got something struck out?

DANIEL. McCready, come here. (ALICK *goes closer to him.*) It is really a great idea. Splendid. But I've a great deal of trouble over it. In fact I've been thinking out details of a particular gear all morning.

ALICK. Aye. (*He looks at* DANIEL *and then endeavours to restrain unsuccessfully a burst of laughter.*)

DANIEL (*angrily*). You were always an ignorant fellow anyway and be d – d to you. (*He turns to go towards his workshop.*)

ALICK. Ah, Mr Murray, I beg your pardon. It's another thing altogether I'm thinking about. I just wanted a talk with you this morning. You have a nice wee girl for a niece, Mr Murray.

DANIEL (*somewhat mollified*). Well?

ALICK (*bashfully*). And I was wondering if you could put in a good word for me now and again with her.

DANIEL. Now, look here, Alick. We can all work nice and comfortably together, can't we?

ALICK. Aye.

DANIEL. Well, if you behave yourself like a man with some manners, and not like an ignorant clodhopper, I can do a great deal for you.

ALICK. Thank you, sir. You know, Mr Murray, I have as nice a wee farm, and as good stock on it as well, as any man in the county, and if I'm lucky enough to get that niece of yours, you'll always be welcome to come and pass a day or two and have a chat.

DANIEL. I think you and I will get along all right, Alick. There's one or two little things I need badly sometimes in this house. I mean I want help often, you know, Alick, to carry my points with John; points about going to see people and that sort of thing, and it's really very hard to manage John on points like that, unless we resort to certain means to convince him they are absolutely necessary.

ALICK (*uneasily*). Yes. I sort of follow you.

DANIEL. You know what I mean. John's a little dense, you know. He can't see the point of an argument very well unless you sort of knock him down with it. Now, if a thing is fair and reasonable, and a man is so dense that he can't see it, you are quite justified – at least, I take it so – to manufacture a way – it doesn't matter how – so long as you make that dense man accept the thing, whatever it is, as right. Do you follow me?

ALICK. I'm just beginning to see a kind of way.

MARY (*appearing at door from inner rooms*). I can't see that thing anywhere. (*She suddenly sees* ALICK.) Oh Alick! You here!

ALICK. Yes. It's a nice morning, and you're looking beautiful!

MARY. Oh, bother. (*She seems to suddenly recollect something.*) Oh, I say! uncle! You remember? Uncle!

DANIEL (*somewhat perplexed*). Eh?

MARY (*motioning towards* ALICK). Telegram to come to London.

DANIEL. Ah – Oh, yes, yes.

MARY. Let's go into your workshop and tell Alick what we want. Come on.

ALICK. I'll do anything in the world you want.

> (*They all go into the workshop. As they disappear,* JOHN MURRAY, *sweating and angry looking, comes through from the yard followed by* BROWN. JOHN *is a tall, stout man, with a rather dour countenance and somewhat stolid expression. He is a year or so the elder of Dan in age. He goes to the dresser, puts his hand on the top shelf, takes down a spanner and throws it down angrily on the table.*)

JOHN. There. There you are, you stupid-looking, good for nothing, dunder-headed, Italian idiot you.

BROWN. You're something terrible cross this morning.

JOHN (*heatedly*). Is it any wonder? Away out at once now and put her to rights and quick about it. (BROWN *meekly goes out.*) The like of servant men nowadays, I never seen in my mortal days. A concern of ignorant bauchles, every one of them.

DANIEL (*opening door of workshop and peeping out. He sees* JOHN *and goes over to him with a genial air*). Good morning John.

JOHN (*snappishly*). Good afternoon.

DANIEL. John, what do you think, I believe I have just come on to a great idea about—

JOHN. Ach! You and your great ideas! Here you've been blundering and blethering and talking these fifteen years and more, and I've never seen anything come of them yet.

DANIEL (*soothingly*). I know, John, I know. But I'm handicapped you know. Bad place to work in and all the rest of it: but you've been kind to me, John. Keeping a brother and helping him after he has lost all his money isn't a common thing with many men, but John a day will come sometime, and you'll get it all back. (*Impressively.*) Every penny. Aye, and twice over.

JOHN (*softening*). Thank you, Daniel.

DANIEL. You will, John, you will. But don't cast up things like that about the time I've been. It hurts me. A thing like this takes time to mature, you know, John. The great and chief thing for an inventor is time. Look at Palissy, the great French potter, who found out how to make porcelain glaze. Why he worked for years and years at his invention. And there was the man who found out how to make steam drive engines. Look at the years those men spent – and no one begrudged them.

JOHN. I suppose that now.

DANIEL. Certainly, John, nothing surer. And look at the fortunes those men made. But the great difficulty is trying to get someone to take up your patent. You see these men had the eyes of the world fixed on them. People knew all about them, and had their hands stretched out ready to grab what they invented. (*Pathetically.*) I – I'm just a poor unknown man struggling in a wee dark corner.

JOHN (*touched*). Never mind, Danny. You'll make the name of the Murray's known yet, maybe.

DANIEL. I'll do my best, John. But mind you it would take me to be pushing on this thing that I have found out and bringing it before people to notice. You see I've got it all ready now except for a few small details.

JOHN (*much interested*). Have you now? I would like you sometime to explain it to me, Daniel. I didn't quite get on to it the last time you were telling me about it.

DANIEL. Some time again. Oh yes. But John – I'll have to go to some of the towns soon to see people about it. The bigger the town the better the chance, and John (*impressively*) – London's the place.

JOHN (*aghast*). London! In all the name of the world, yon place! Would Belfast not do you?

DANIEL. No. I don't like Belfast. They're a mangy, stick-in-the-mud, follow-in-the-old-ruts crowd. Never strike out anything new. It's a case of London or nothing.

JOHN (*dubiously*). It will be a terrible expense this London visiting.

DANIEL. It'll be worth it.

JOHN. Now, Danny, I would like to oblige you, but what do you think it would cost me?

DANIEL. Well, I could live cheap you know, John, and do without meals an odd day, and go steerage and third class, and that sort of thing. I would say about fifteen pounds roughly. That would let me stay more than a week.

JOHN. Fifteen pounds! God bless me, Daniel, would you break me? No, no, I couldn't afford to give you that much.

DANIEL. Maybe ten would do it. I could sleep out under the arches an odd night or two, and—

JOHN. No, no. I'll not have that. A Murray aye had a bed to go to and

47

a sup to eat. (*After a contemplative pause.*) Here, I'll give you three pounds and you can go to Belfast.

DANIEL. I don't care much about Belfast. You know I have been there five times now, and I have never got anyone to look into the thing at all proper.

JOHN. You're too backward, Daniel, when it comes to the like of that. But ten pounds! No, I would like you to get on in the world right enough, Daniel, but I couldn't afford it. You know the way this house is being kept; it's lamentable. Tea and sugar and flour and things. Man, I'm just after paying off ten pounds to the McAfees for one thing and another, and it only a running account for two months. If I had a good housekeeper now, maybe things would alter for the better.

MARY (*coming out from the workshop followed by* ALICK). O Uncle Dan! He says he'll go at once and get it – (*she stops short in confusion on seeing her father.*)

ALICK. How are you, Mr Murray?

JOHN. O! bravely. What's the news with you?

ALICK. I was just looking over some of them ideas of Daniel's, about the new fan bellows.

JOHN. Aye. Now what do you think of it?

ALICK (*warned by* DANIEL *who nudges him*). They're great altogether.

JOHN. Do you think there will be any sale for it at all?

ALICK. I think so. (*He perceives* DANIEL *motioning assent.*) I believe there would be indeed.

JOHN. Man, I wish I had the head of some of you young fellows to understand the working of them machinery and things. (DANIEL *goes back into the workshop.*) I've the worst head in the world for understanding about them sort of things. There's Daniel, a great head on him, Daniel.

ALICK (*slyly*). He has, right enough!

JOHN (*proudly*). One of the best. When he was a wee fellow, dang the one could beat him at making boats or drawing pictures, or explaining extraordinary things to him. None. Not one. A great head on him, Daniel. He'll do something yet.

ALICK. Did you know Andy McMinn's for coming over to see you this day, Mr Murray?

JOHN (*eagerly*). This day? When? Are you sure?

ALICK. Aye, so he said. About two o'clock or so. Someone told him about Daniel's great new idea, and he's very curious to hear about it.

48

MARY. He's always poking his nose into people's business.
JOHN. Whist. Andy McMinn's a very decent man. Tell me (*rather bashfully*), was Sarah to come with him?
MARY (*alarmed*). O holy prophets! I hope not.
ALICK. Aye. She's coming too. She wanted to see it as well as Andy.
JOHN. Aye. Certainly, and she's welcome too. Mary, you can get the house ready, and the table set, and a nice tea for them when they come, and I can go and get tidied up a wee bit. (*He goes off through door into inner rooms.*)
ALICK (*leaning against the table and looking across at* MARY, *who is sitting at the opposite end*). You're as nice a wee girl as ever I–
MARY. You're an awful fool. Hurry, Alick, like a decent man and get that telegram sent.
ALICK. That uncle of yours, Mary, heth he's as canny a keoghboy as I've seen. Its the queer tears he'll be taking to himself in London if I know anything.
MARY. Hold your tongue. You've no business to talk about Uncle Dan that way. He could give you tons as far as brains go anyway.
ALICK. I believe that. (*He goes to yard door, then turns back.*) I say, Mary. What name will I put on that telegram? "Come to London at once about patent. Intend purchasing." Hadn't we better have a name?
MARY. Yes. I'll just ask uncle. (*She knocks at door of workshop.*) Uncle!
DANIEL (*without*). Yes.
MARY. What name will we put to that telegram?
DANIEL (*without*). Oh, it's not particular. Wilson, or Smith, or Brown, or Gregg.
ALICK. I'll put Gregg on it.
DANIEL. Do well.
ALICK. Did you see the fluster that your father got into, Mary, when he heard that Sarah McMinn was coming over?
MARY (*alarmed*). What?
ALICK. Did you not see how he rushed off to tidy himself up when he heard Sarah McMinn was coming over?
MARY (*seating herself on chair to right of table*). Nonsense. Father wouldn't think of that woman.
ALICK. All right. But I think I know something more than you.
MARY (*anxiously*). What? Tell me.
ALICK. Come on and leave me down the loaning a pace, and I'll tell you.
MARY (*glancing at him, and then coquettishly turning her back to him*

49

as he leans against the table). Oh, I can't. Those people are coming over, and that McMinn woman will be looking at everything and telling you how to do things in front of father, and all the rest of it.

ALICK (*entreatingly*). Leave me down the loaning a pace till I tell you the news.

MARY (*teasingly*). No.

ALICK. Come on.

MARY. No. (ALICK *moves sadly towards the door.* MARY *looks round, and then laughingly skips past him out through the yard door, and he follows her.*)

JOHN (*coming through the door from inner rooms partly dressed, with a towel in his hands, evidently making much preparation to clean himself*). Daniel! (*Loudly and crossly.*) Daniel!

DANIEL (*peeping out from workshop door*). Well!

JOHN. Tidy yourself up a wee bit, man, Andy McMinn and Sarah's coming over to see you.

DANIEL (*somewhat taken back*). Me?

JOHN. Aye. They want to see about the new invention. You can have the collar I wore last Sunday, and put on your new coat that you got in Belfast. (DANIEL *goes back into the workshop.*) I wonder what tie would be the better one? Yon green or the red one that Mary gave me last Christmas. Aye. (*Seeing no sign of* DANIEL.) D – n! Is he making no shapes to dress himself. Daniel!

DANIEL (*without*). Aye.

JOHN (*loudly*). Daniel!

DANIEL (*again appearing at door*). Well!

JOHN (*impatiently*). Come on and get on you.

DANIEL. Ach. This is always the way. Just when a man has got the whole thing worked out and the plans of the apparatus just on the point of completion he has to stop.

JOHN. Never mind, Danny. You can do it again the night or the morrow morning. I want you to look decent. Come on and get on you.

DANIEL (*beginning to regard his brother with a sudden interest and suspicion*). Who did you say was coming?

JOHN (*at door to rooms*). Andy and Sarah McMinn. (*He goes out.*)

DANIEL (*suddenly realising the import of the preparations going on*). McMinn. Mc –. (*He stops short, and then in a horrified voice.*) Surely to God he hasn't a notion of that woman? (*Calling tremulously.*) John! John!

JOHN (*at door*). Hurry up, man.

DANIEL (*appealingly*). John. Tell me, John. You haven't – you're not going to – you haven't a notion of that woman?

JOHN (*hesitatingly*). Well, Daniel, you see the house needs some one to look after it proper, and I thought – well – maybe – that Sarah would be just as nice and saving a woman as I could get, but I thought I would keep it a bit secret, don't you know, because I don't know yet if she'd have me or not. And she could talk to you better nor I could about machinery and things that would interest you, for she has an agency for sewing machines, and knows something about that sort of thing, and you'd get on great with each other. Now, hurry and get on you. (*He goes out by door into rooms.*)

DANIEL (*looking after him in a helpless manner, and sinking into a chair*). If – if she'd have him! O great God! If that woman comes to this house, I – I'm a ruined man.

(CURTAIN.)

ACT II

The same scene some hours later. The curtain rises to discover KATE *seated near table at back enjoying a cup of tea which she has made, and is drinking with relish.*

KATE. I suppose they'll be wanting jam and sugar for the tea – aye – and some of them scones Miss Mary cooked yesterday, not but you couldn't eat them, and a pat or two of butter. (*She finishes off the remains of the tea.*) Now, that's a nice girl for you! Here's company coming till the house and tea and things a wanting, and she goes and leaves all to go strolling down the loaning with that fool of a McCready.

    (BROWN *opens the yard door and comes in. He replaces the spanner on the top shelf and then turns and looks at* KATE.)

KATE. Well?

BROWN. Well, yourself?

KATE. Do you see any sign of them McMinns yet?

BROWN. Aye. I see the trap coming over the Cattle Hill. There was three in it, as far as I could make out.

KATE. Who be to be the third party I wonder? Is it their servant man?

BROWN. Do you think old Andy McMinn's servant man gets leave to drive them about of an afternoon like the clergy's? Talk sense, woman.

KATE. Maybe it's yon Scotch body I heard was stopping with them.

BROWN. Aye. Yon Mackenzie. Ach, man, but yon creature would scunder you.

KATE. Aye.

BROWN. Ach! Cracking jokes and laughing that hearty at them, and I'm danged if a bat with one eye shut could make out what he was laughing at. (*Listening.*) Here they are. I hear the wheels coming up the loaning. I'll have to go and put up the horse for them I suppose. (*He goes out by yard door.*)

KATE. I wonder if the master seen them coming. (*She rapidly clears the table and then goes over to door into room.*) I better tell him.

(*She knocks at the door.*)

JOHN (*without*). Aye. (*He comes and opens the door, dressed in his best suit of clothes.*) What's the matter?

KATE. They're just come, sir.

JOHN (*excitedly*). Are they? (*Comes into kitchen.*) Is my tie right, Kate? And my clothes – is there any dirt on the back of them?

KATE (*inspecting him critically*). You'll do grand. I never seen you looking better.

JOHN. Where's Mary? Why isn't she here?

KATE. She went out about something. She'll be back in a minute.

JOHN. Right enough, it would do her all the good in the world to have a sensible woman looking after her. She just gets her own way a deal too much in this house. (*He goes to window and looks out.*) Aye. Here they are! Tell Daniel to hurry. (KATE *goes off by door to rooms.*) Sarah's looking bravely. Man, that woman could save me thirty, aye forty, pounds a year if she was here. (*Suddenly.*) Ach! Is Daniel never ready yet? (*Calls.*) Daniel! (*Louder.*) Daniel!

DANIEL (*without*). Aye.

JOHN. Hurry, man. They've come. (JOHN *goes to yard door and goes out.*)

DANIEL (*in an exasperated voice*). Ach!

(JOHN *comes in followed by* ANDREW MCMINN, *an elderly non-descript sort of man, followed by* SARAH, *a sour faced spinster of uncertain age. In the rear is* DONAL MACKENZIE. *He is wearing a tourist costume of Norfolk jacket and knickers, and is a keen faced, hard, angular looking personage.*)

JOHN. Yous are all welcome. Every one of you. You Andy and Sarah, and Mr Mackenzie. The Scotch is aye welcome, Mr Mackenzie.

MACKENZIE. Aye. That's what I said the last time I was in Ballyannis, and was verra thirsty, and went into a beer-shop to get a dram – Black and White it was. Verra guid. (*He laughs loudly at his own joke.*)

SARAH. We brought Mr Mackenzie along with us to see your brother, John. You see he's an engineer and knows a good deal about machinery and plans and things.

MACKENZIE. Aye. There's not much about machinery that I dinna ken, Mr Murray, from a forty thousand horse power quadruple expansion doon to a freewheel bicycle. (*Proudly.*) I hae done spells work at all of them, you ken.

ANDY. I suppose Daniel's at home. Is he?

JOHN. Daniel? Oh aye, Daniel's at home. He's just tidying himself up a wee bit.

53

MACKENZIE. A wee bit paint and powder gangs a lang gait to make up defects, as you ken yourself, Miss McMinn. (*He laughs loudly.*) That's a guid one.

ANDY (*looking slyly at* SARAH). He's up out of bed then?

JOHN (*innocently*). Oh aye. He sits up late of nights working out things. (*He points to the door of workshop.*) That's his workshop.

MACKENZIE. He works then?

JOHN. Aye. He works in there. (ANDY *goes over and goes into workshop.*)

MACKENZIE. Because it doesna follow always, as I have discovered in my experience, that because a man has a workshop, he works. (*He laughs, evidently much pleased at his own humour.*)

ANDY (*looking out again through door*). There's nothing much to see in this place except a lot of dirty papers.

JOHN. That's the plans of the bellows he's working at.

MACKENZIE (*going over to workshop*). Come out, Mr McMinn, till I examine. (ANDY *comes out and he passes in.*) Eh. This is the plan of the great bellows. (*He laughs loudly.*)

ANDY. Is he making much headway with it, John?

JOHN. Indeed, now, I think he's doing bravely at it. He's keeping very close at it this day or two.

ANDY. There's a terrible amount of newspapers lying in there. Has he no other plans and drawings except what's there?

JOHN. Oh aye. He has plenty of plans and drawings somewhere, for I seen them once or twice.

MACKENZIE (*coming out*). I can't say much about that contrivance. (*He laughs.*) And, I say. Look here. He does more than draw bellows. He draws corks as well. (*He produces a bottle of whiskey almost empty.*)

JOHN. Ah, well. He's not a great transgressor either in the matter of bottle. No, no.

ANDY. And the smell of smoke in the place!

SARAH. John, I think Daniel smokes far too much.

ANDY. He should be dressed by now.

JOHN. Aye. Oh, aye. He should right enough. He's a wee bit backward before women, you know, Sarah. (*Calls.*) Daniel! (*He goes over and opens door into rooms.*) Daniel!

DANIEL (*without*). Yes. (*He appears at the door struggling vainly with his collar.*)

JOHN. Why didn't you come long ago. What kept you?

DANIEL. Your collar. (*He looks across at* ANDY *and* SARAH, *who have seated themselves at the back.*) How do you do, Andy and

54

Sarah? You're very welcome. (*He looks at* MACKENZIE, *who stares curiously at him.*)

ANDY. This is a friend of ours, Daniel, that happened to be stopping with us last summer at Newcastle in the same house, and he came over for his holidays to us this time. We brought him over to see you. They calls him Mackenzie.

DANIEL (*crossing over to the left and taking a seat near the door of the workshop.*) How do you do?

MACKENZIE (*patronisingly*). I'm glad to see you at last, Mr Murray, for I've heard a good deal about you.

SARAH. You see, Daniel, Mr Mackenzie is an engineer in one of the great Scotch engineering yards. (DANIEL'S *face expresses his dismay, which he hurriedly tried to hide.*) What place was it you were in, Mr Mackenzie?

MACKENZIE. I served six years in the engine and fitting shops with Messrs. Ferguson, Hartie & Macpherson, and was two years shop foreman afterwards to Dennison, McLachlan & Co., and now I'm senior partner with the firm of Stephenson & Mackenzie. If ever you're up in Greenock direction, and want to see how we do it, just ask for Donal Mackenzie, and they'll show you the place. (*Proudly.*) We're the sole makers of the Mackenzie piston, if ever you heard of it.

DANIEL (*uneasily*). I'm sorry to say I haven't.

MACKENZIE. And you call yourself an engineer and you don't know about Donal Mackenzie's patent reciprocating piston.

JOHN (*apologetically*). You see we be a bit out of the world here, Mr Mackenzie.

DANIEL. Yes. Now that's one point. One great point that always tells against me. (*Getting courageous.*) It really needs a man to be continually visiting the great engineering centres – Greenock, London—

MACKENZIE (*scornfully*). London's not an engineering centre – Glasgow, Hartlepool, Newcastle—

DANIEL. Well, all those places. He could keep himself posted up in all the newest ideas then, and inventions.

MACKENZIE. But a man can keep himself to the fore if he reads the technical journals and follows their articles. What technical papers do you get? Do you ever get the Scottish Engineers' Monthly Handbook, price sixpence monthly? I'm the writer on the inventors' column. My articles are signed Fergus McLachlan. Perhaps you've read them?

DANIEL. I think – um – I'm not quite sure that I have.

MACKENZIE. You remember one I wrote on the new compressed air drills last July?

DANIEL (*looking across at* JOHN, *who is standing with his back to the fireplace*). I don't think I do.

JOHN. No. We don't get them sort of papers. I did buy one or two like them for Daniel, but he told me he would just as soon have the *Whig*, for there was just as much information in it.

MACKENZIE (*laughing*). O spirit of Burns! Just as much information – well, so much for that. Now, about this new patent, this new fan bellows that I hear you're working at, Mr Murray.

DANIEL. What about it?

ANDY. We both seen the drawings in there, Daniel, but I don't think either of us made much of it. Could you not explain it to him, Daniel. Give him an idea what you mean to do with it.

JOHN. Aye. Now's your chance, Daniel. You were talking of some difficulty or other. Maybe this gentleman could help you with it.

DANIEL (*shifting uneasily, and looking appealingly at* JOHN). Well. There's no great hurry. A little later on in the evening. (*He looks at* SARAH.) I'm thinking about Miss McMinn. I don't think this conversation would be very interesting to her.

SARAH. Oh, indeed now, Mr Murray, I just love to know about it. A good fan bellows would be the great thing for yon fireplace of ours, Andy.

ANDY. Aye. Soul, it would that.

DANIEL (*uncomfortably*). No. Not just yet, John. A bit later on. I'm shy, John, you know. A bit backward before company.

JOHN. You're a man to talk about going to see people in London.

SARAH. What? Was he going to London?

JOHN. Aye. He was talking about going to London, and I was half-minded to let him go.

ANDY (*who exchanges meaning glances with* SARAH). Boys, that would cost a wheen of pounds!

MACKENZIE. Who wull you go to see in London?

DANIEL (*evasively*). Oh – engineers and patent agents and people that would take an interest in that sort of thing.

MACKENZIE. Have you anyone to go to in particular?

DANIEL. Oh, yes.

SARAH. It will cost a great deal of money, Daniel. Seven or eight pounds anyway. Won't it, Mr Mackenzie?

MACKENZIE. It would, and more.

JOHN (*looking at* SARAH *with evident admiration*). Man, that's a saving woman. She can count the pounds. (*Suddenly.*) Daniel, away out and show Andy and Mr Mackenzie the thresher, and get used to the company, and then you can come in and explain the thing to them. I want Sarah to stay here and help me to make the tea. That fool of a Mary is away again somewhere.

ANDY (*after a sly glance at* SARAH). Aye. Come on, Daniel, and explain it to us. I hear there's a new kind of feedboard on her.

MACKENZIE. How is she driven, Mr Murray?

DANIEL (*uncomfortably*). How is she what?

MACKENZIE. How is she worked – steam, horse, or water power, which?

JOHN (*motioning* DANIEL *to go, which the latter does very unwillingly*). Go on out and you can show them, Daniel. (DANIEL, ANDY, *and* MACKENZIE *go out through yard door*.) He's backward, you know, Sarah, oh, aye – backward; but a great head. A great head on him, Daniel.

SARAH. I suppose he is clever in his way.

JOHN (*seating himself close beside her and talking with innocent enthusiasm*). Ah, boys, Sarah, I mind when he went to serve his time with McArthurs, of Ballygrainey, he was as clever a boy as come out of the ten townlands. And then he set up for himself, you know, and lost all, and then he came here. He's doing his best, poor creature, till pay me for what kindness I showed him, by trying to invent things that he says would maybe pay off, some time or other, all he owes to me.

SARAH (*cynically*). Poor Daniel! And he lost all his money?

JOHN. Aye. Every ha'penny; and he took a hundred pounds off me as well. And now, poor soul, he hasn't a shilling, barring an odd pound or two I give him once or twice a month.

SARAH. Well! Well! And he's been a long time this way?

JOHN. Aye. (*Reflectively.*) I suppose it's coming on now to twenty years.

SARAH. It's a wonder he wouldn't make some shapes to try and get a situation somewhere.

JOHN. Ach, well, you know, when Annie, the wife, died and left Mary a wee bit of a wain, I was lonesome, and Daniel was always a right heartsome fellow, and I never asked him about going when he came here.

SARAH. He must be rather an expense to you. Pocket money for tobacco, and whenever he goes out a night to McArn's, its a treat all round to who is in at the time. And his clothes and boots, and let alone that, his going to see people about patents and things up to Belfast three or four times in the year. If he was in a situation and doing for himself, you could save a bit of money.

JOHN (*pensively*). Aye. Heth and I never thought much of that, Sarah. I could right enough. I'll think over that now. (*He looks at her, and then begins in a bashful manner.*) You weren't at Ballyannis School fête, Sarah?

SARAH. No. But I heard you were there. Why?

JOHN (*coming still closer*). I was expecting to see you.

SARAH (*contemptuously*). I don't believe in young girls going to them things.

JOHN (*gazing at her in astonishment*). But God bless me, they wouldn't call you young! (SARAH *turns up her nose disgustedly.*) I missed you. Man, I was looking for you all roads.

SARAH. I'm not a fool sort of young girl that you can just pass an idle hour or two with, John Murray, mind that.

JOHN. I never thought that of you, Sarah.

SARAH. Some people think that.

JOHN (*astonished*). No.

SARAH. They do. There's Andy just after warning me this morning about making a fool of myself.

JOHN (*puzzled*). But you never done that, Sarah.

SARAH. Well, he was just after giving me advice about going round flirting with Tom, Dick and Harry.

JOHN. Ah no. You never done that. Sure I knowed you this years and years, and you never had a boy to my knowing.

SARAH (*offended*). Well I had, plenty. Only I just wouldn't take them. I refused more than three offers in my time.

JOHN (*incredulously*). Well! Well! And you wouldn't have them!

SARAH. No.

JOHN. Why now?

SARAH (*looking at him meaningly*). Well – I liked somebody else better.

JOHN (*piqued*). Did he – the somebody – did he never ask you?

SARAH. He might yet, maybe.

JOHN (*hopelessly to himself*). I wonder would it be any use then me asking her.

SARAH. And I'm beginning to think he is a long time thinking about it. (*Knocking at the door.*)

JOHN (*angrily*). Ach! Who's that?

BROWN (*opening yard door and looking in*). Me, sir. Mr Dan wants to know could you not come out a minute, and show the gentlemen what way you can stop the feedboard working.

JOHN. Don't you know yourself, you stupid headed lump you. Away

58

back at once. (BROWN *hurriedly closes the door after an inquiring glance at the pair.*) That's them servant men for you. He knowed rightly what way it worked, only he was just curious. (*Savagely.*) He's a stupid creature, anyway.

SARAH. I think all men is stupid. They never see things at all.

JOHN. Now, Sarah, sure women are just as bad. There's Mary. She's bright enough someways, but others – ach—

SARAH. Mary needs someone – a woman – to look after her. Somebody that knows how to manage a house and save money. She's lost running about here. Now, I had a young girl with me once was a wild useless thing when she came, and when she left me six months after, there wasn't a better trained, nor as meek a child in the whole country.

JOHN. And you can manage a house, Sarah, and well, too. Can't you?

SARAH. I ran the house for Andy there twenty years and more, and I never once had to ask him for a pound. And what's more, I put some into the bank every quarter.

JOHN. Did you now? (*He looks at her in wondering admiration.*)

SARAH. Yes. And I cleared five pounds on butter last half year.

JOHN (*with growing wonder*). Did you?

SARAH. And made a profit of ten pounds on eggs alone this year already.

JOHN (*unable to contain himself any longer*). Sarah, will you marry me?

SARAH (*coyly*). Oh, John, this is very sudden. (*Knocking at yard door.*) I will. I will. Will you tell them when they come in?

JOHN (*now that the ordeal has been passed, feeling somewhat uncomfortable*). Well, I would rather you waited a few days, and then we could let them know, canny, don't you know, Sarah. Break the news soft, so to speak. Eh?

SARAH (*disappointedly*). Well, if you want it particular that way I – (*knocking*).

JOHN (*going to door*). Aye, I'd rather you did. (*He goes to the door and opens it and* MARY *comes in.*)

MARY. I peeped through the window and I thought, perhaps, it would be better to knock first. Its a nice evening Miss McMinn. (*She takes off her hat and flings it carelessly on a chair.*) Where's Uncle Dan? I want to see him.

JOHN. He'll be in soon enough. He's out showing Andy and Mackenzie the thresher.

MARY (*laughing*). Uncle Dan! What does he know about – (*she stops short, remembering that* SARAH *is present.*) Mr Mackenzie?

SARAH. Yes. He's a gentleman, a friend of ours, engaged in the engineering business, who has a large place of his own in Scotland, and we brought him over here to see your Uncle Dan about the invention he's working at.

JOHN. You stop here, Mary, with Sarah, and get the tea ready. You should have been in the house when company was coming. Where were you?

MARY. Oh, just down the loaning.

JOHN. Who with?

MARY. Alick McCready.

JOHN (*sternly*). Aye. You're gay fond of tralloping about with the boys.

SARAH. He's not just the sort of young man I would like to see in your company, Mary.

MARY (*impertinently*). It's none of your business whose company I was in.

JOHN (*disapprovingly*). Now, Mary, remember your manners in front of your elders, and mind you must always show Miss McMinn particular respect. (*Impressively.*) Particular respect. (*Going towards yard door.*) And you can show Sarah what you have in the house, and do what she bids you. Them's my orders. (*He goes out.*)

SARAH (*looking disapprovingly at* MARY). I wonder a girl like you has no more sense than to go gallivanting about at this time of day with boys, making talk for the whole countryside.

MARY (*sharply*). I don't have to run after them to other people's houses anyway.

SARAH. And that is no way to be leaving down your hat. (*She picks it up and looks at it.*) Is that your Sunday one?

MARY (*snatching it out of her hand.*) Just find out for yourself.

SARAH. Now, you should take and put it away carefully. There's no need to waste money that way, wearing things out.

MARY (*with rising temper*). Do you know it's *my* hat? Not yours. And I can do what I like with it. (*She throws it down and stamps on it.*) I can tramp on it if I want to.

SARAH (*smiling grimly*). Oh, well, tramp away. It's no wonder your father complained of waste and this sort of conduct going on.

(KATE *comes in through door from rooms.*)

MARY Have you got the tea things ready, Kate?

KATE. Yes, Miss.

MARY. I suppose we better wet the tea.

SARAH (*looking at the fire*). Have you the kettle on?

MARY. Can't you see for yourself it's not on.

SARAH. Here, girl (*to* KATE), fill the kettle and put it on. (KATE *looks at* MARY, *and with a shrug of her shoulders, obeys the orders.*) Where's the tea till I show you how to measure?

MARY (*in a mocking voice*). Kate, get Miss McMinn the tea cannister till she shows you how to measure. (KATE *goes to the dresser and brings the teapot and cannister over to* SARAH *at the table.*)

SARAH. But it's *you* I want to show. (MARY *pays no attention but sits down idly drumming her fingers on the table.*) There now – pay particular attention to this. (*She takes the cannister from* KATE, *opens it and ladles out the tea with a spoon into the teapot.*) One spoonful for your father and uncle, one for my brother and Mr Mackenzie, one for yourself and me, and half-a-one for Kate.

MARY. Do you see that, Kate?

KATE. Yes. Miss.

MARY (*mockingly*). Now the next thing, I suppose, is to weigh out the sugar.

SARAH. No. You always ask the company first do they take sugar before you pour out the tea.

MARY. No; not in good society. You put it on the saucers.

SARAH. Put some in the bowl, Kate, and never heed her.

MARY (*almost tearfully*). You've no business to say that, Kate! Who's your mistress here?

KATE (*very promptly*). You, Miss.

MARY. Then do what I tell you. Put on the tablecloth, and lay the cups and saucers, and make everything ready, and take no orders except from me.

SARAH. Very well. I'll learn her manners when I come to this house. (*To* MARY) I want to see the china.

MARY. Well, go into the next room and look for it.

SARAH (*going towards door to rooms*). You better mind what your father told you. (*She goes in.*)

MARY (*making a face after her*). You nasty old thing. (DANIEL *appears at the door from yard. He is nervous and worried looking. He goes and sits down near the fire-place, wearily.*) Uncle Dan. (*She goes over close beside him.*) Wasn't it good of Alick? He went away to Ballyannis Post Office to get that telegram sent.

DANIEL. A very decent fellow, Alick. (*Gratefully.*) Very obliging.

MARY (*confidingly*). Do you know, uncle, when he went off to send that telegram I was nearly calling him back. I don't care so very much now whether I see that boy you were telling me about or not. Is he – do you think, uncle – is he much nicer than Alick?

DANIEL. Nicer? (*He looks at his niece, and then begins to divine the way her feelings lie.*) Well, of course we have all our opinions on these things you know, Mary, but Alick – well, after all there's many a worse fellow than Alick, isn't there? (MARY *does not answer, but puts her head close to her uncle.*) Ah, yes.

MARY (*suddenly*). Uncle! Do you know what has happened? I heard father proposing to Miss McMinn!

DANIEL (*groaning*). Oh my! I knew it would happen! I knew it would happen! When? Where?

MARY. In here. I wanted to slip in quietly after leaving Alick down the loaning when I overheard the voices. It was father and Miss McMinn. She was telling him how she had saved five pounds on butter last half year, and ten pounds on eggs this year, and then father asked her to marry him. I knocked at the door out of divilment, and she just pitched herself at him. I–I'm not going to stay in the house with that woman. I'd sooner marry Alick McCready.

DANIEL (*despairingly*). I would myself. I daren't – I couldn't face the look of that woman in the mornings.

MARY. It's all right for you to talk, uncle. You'll be working away at your inventions, and that sort of thing, and will have nothing much to do with her, but I'd be under her thumb all the time. And I hate her, and I know she hates me. (*Tearfully.*) And then the way father talks about her being such a fine housekeeper, and about the waste that goes on in this house, it nearly makes me cry, just because I have been a bit careless maybe. But I could manage a house every bit as well as she could, and I'd show father that if I only got another chance. Couldn't I uncle?

DANIEL (*soothingly*). And far better, Mary. Far better.

MARY. And you could do far more at your invention if you only got a chance. Couldn't you, uncle?

DANIEL. No doubt about it, Mary. None. I never got much of a chance here.

MARY. I wonder could we both try to get another chance. (*Suddenly, with animation.*) Uncle!

DANIEL. Well?

MARY. Aren't you going to explain that fan bellows thing you've been working at to them when they come in? (DANIEL *nods sadly.*) Well, look. That Scotchman – he understands things like that, and that's just the reason why that nasty woman brought him over. Just to trip you and show you up, and she thinks she'll make father see through you. But just you rise to the occasion and astonish them. Eh, uncle?

DANIEL (*uneasily*). Um – well, I don't know. That Scotchman's rather a dense sort of fellow. Very hard to get on with somehow.

MARY. Now, Uncle Dan, its our last chance. Let us beat that woman somehow or other.

DANIEL. It's all very well, Mary, to talk that way. (*Suddenly.*) I wonder is there a book on machinery in the house?

MARY. Machinery? Let me think. Yes, I do believe Kate was reading some book yesterday about things, and there was something about machinery in it.

DANIEL. For Heaven's sake, Mary, get it.

MARY (*calling*). Kate! Are you there, Kate? (KATE *comes in from inner rooms.*) Where's that book you were reading last night, Kate?

KATE (*surprised*). For dear's sake, Miss! Yon dirty old thing! The one with the big talk between the old fellow and the son about everything in the world you could think of?

MARY. Yes, yes. Uncle Dan wants it. (KATE *fetches a tattered volume from the dresser and hands it to* DANIEL. DANIEL *opens it, and reads while the two girls peer over his shoulder.*)

DANIEL (*reading slowly*). "The Child's Educator. A series of conversations between Charles and his father regarding the natural philosophy, as revealed to us, by the Very Reverend Ezekiel Johnston".

KATE (*much interested*). Aye. Just go on till you see Mr Dan. It's the queerest conversation between an old lad and his son ever you heard tell of.

DANIEL (*reading*). Ah! "The simple forms of machines. The lever, the wedge, the inclined plane – Father – and here we come to further consider the application of this principle, my dear Charles, to what is known as the differential wheel and axle. Um Charles – Father – Charles. Father." (*He looks up despairingly at* MARY.) No good, my dear. Out of date. (*He, however, resumes reading the book carefully.*)

KATE (*nudging* MARY, *and pointing to door into rooms*). She's going into all the cupboards and drawers, and looking at everything. (*She turns to go back and opens the door to pass through.*) I never seen such a woman.

MARY (*raising her voice so as to let* SARAH *hear her*). Just keep an eye on her, Kate, and see she doesn't take anything.

DANIEL. I might get something out of this. Atmosphere. Pressure.

MARY. Uncle Dan. (*He pays no attention, but is absorbed in the book.*) Uncle Dan, I'm going down the loaning a pace. Alick said he might be back, and I think – (*she sees he is not listening, and slips back to look over his shoulder.*)

DANIEL (*reading*). Charles. And now my dear father, after discussing in such clear and lucid terms the use of the barometer, and how it is constructed, could you tell me or explain the meaning of the word "pneumatic".

MARY (*going towards yard door*). Good luck, Uncle Danny. I'm away. (*She goes out.*)

DANIEL. There's not much here about bellows. (*Hopelessly.*) I wish I had made up this subject a little better. (KATE *comes in evidently much perturbed and angry.*)

KATE. The divil take her and them remarks of hers. Who gave her the right to go searching that way, I wonder? Where's the silver kept, and was it locked, and how many spoons was there, and why weren't they better polished; and part of the china broke.

SARAH (*coming to door and speaking. As soon as* DANIEL *hears her voice he hurriedly retreats across to the workshop.*) Where do you keep the knives and forks?

KATE. You don't want forks for the tea.

SARAH. I want to count them.

KATE (*in amazement*). Oh, God save us! You'd think there was a pross on the house! (*She follows* SARAH *in through door.* MACKENZIE *comes in, followed by* JOHN, *then* ANDY.)

MACKENZIE. And it was a great idea, you know. The steam passed through the condenser, and the exhaust was never open to the atmosphere.

JOHN (*evidently much impressed, and repeating the word in a wondering manner*). Aye. The exhaust!

MACKENZIE. Aye. The exhaust. But now I'm verra anxious to hear your brother explaining what he's made out about the bellows. It's the small things like that you ken that a man makes a fortune of, not the big ones.

JOHN (*impressed*). Do you think that now?

MACKENZIE. You know I take a particular interest in bellows myself. I tried my hand a good while working out a new kind of bellows, and I flatter myself that I know something about the subject.

JOHN. Aye. (*Looking around.*) Where's Daniel? Daniel! Are you there, Daniel? (DANIEL *comes out and stands near the door.*) You could maybe bring them plans out you're working at and explain it to them now, Daniel. Eh? And wait, Sarah wants to hear it too. (*Calling.*) Are you there, Sarah?

64

DANIEL (*seating himself sadly*). Aye. She's in there somewhere taking stock.

JOHN (*going next door to rooms*). Are you there, dear? (SARAH *comes out.*) Daniel's going to explain the thing to us, and you wanted to hear about it. Didn't you?

SARAH. I'm just dying to know all about it. (*She seats herself to the right at back.* ANDY *sits on one side of the table and* MACKENZIE *at the other, expectantly, while* JOHN *goes over to the fireplace almost opposite his brother.*) You know, Mr Daniel, that's one thing we want very bad in our house – a good fan bellows.

DANIEL. They are very useful, very.

JOHN. Aye. They are that. (*To* SARAH.) He has a good head on him, Daniel. Eh? (*To* DANIEL.) Now go on and make it very plain so that every one can follow you. Bring out the plans and show us.

DANIEL (*uneasily*). I can explain it better without them. (*After a pause.*) Well, I suppose this subject of bellows would come under the heading of pneumatics in natural philosophy.

JOHN. Oh, now, don't be going off that way. Could you not make it plainer nor that?

DANIEL (*appealingly*). Well. Could I be much plainer, Mr Mackenzie?

MACKENZIE (*cynically*). I'm here to discuss fan bellows, not pneumatics.

DANIEL (*sotto voce*). D—n him. (*He pulls himself together.*) Well. Then I suppose the first thing is – well – to know what is a bellows.

ANDY. Aye. Man, Daniel, you start off just the same as the clergy. That's the way they always goes on expounding things to you.

SARAH (*severely*). Don't be interrupting, Andy.

MACKENZIE (*sneeringly*). Well, I think everyone here knows what a bellows is.

DANIEL. Everyone here? Do you, John?

JOHN. Aye. I would like, Daniel, to hear right what a bellows is. I mean I can see the thing blowing up a fire when you use it, any man could see that – but its the workings of it. What's the arrangements and internal works of the bellows now, Daniel?

DANIEL. Well, you push the handles together in an ordinary bellows and – and the air – blows out. (*Seeing that this statement is received coldly.*) Now, why does it blow out?

JOHN (*disappointedly*). Because it's pushed out of course. There's no sense in asking that sort of a question.

DANIEL. Well, there's a flap on the bellows – a thing that moves up and down. Well, that flap has all to do with pushing the air.

JOHN. Maybe this scientifican business is uninteresting to you, Sarah, is it?

65

DANIEL (*brightening up at the suggestion*). I'm sure it is. Perhaps we better stop.

SARAH (*smiling grimly*). Oh, not at all. I want to hear more.

MACKENZIE. You're wasting a lot of my time, Mr Murray. I came here to hear about a fan bellows.

DANIEL (*confusedly*). Oh, yes. Yes. Certainly. Fan bellows. There's a difference between a fan bellows and an ordinary bellows.

MARY (*opening door from yard and coming in*). Oh, Uncle Dan, are you explaining it to them. Did I miss much of it?

MACKENZIE. I don't think it matters much what time you come in during this.

JOHN (*impatiently*). Go on, Daniel.

DANIEL. It's very hard for me to go on with these constant interruptions. Well, I was just saying there was a difference between a fan bellows and an ordinary bellows.

MACKENZIE. Now, what is a fan bellows yourself, Mr Murray?

DANIEL (*hopelessly*). A fan bellows? Ah. Why now is it called a fan bellows?

MACKENZIE (*roughly*). Don't be asking me my own questions.

DANIEL (*with a despairing effort*). Well, now we will take it for granted it is because there must be something of the nature of a fan about a fan bellows. It is because there are fans inside the casing. And the handle being turned causes these – eh – fans to turn round too. And then the air comes out with a rush.

JOHN. Aye. It must be the fans that pushes it out.

DANIEL. Exactly. Well, now, the difficulty we find here is – (*he pauses.*)

ANDY. Aye.

JOHN. Go on, Daniel.

DANIEL. You want a constant draught blowing. That's number one. Then – well – the other. You see, if we took some of these fans.

MACKENZIE. Yes.

DANIEL (*in a floundering way*). And put them in a tight-fitting case, and put more of them inside, and understood exactly what their size was, we could arrange for the way that—

JOHN (*in a puzzled way to* SARAH). I can only follow Daniel a short way too. (*Repeating slowly.*) Put them in a tight-fitting case—

BROWN (*appearing at yard door with a telegram in his hand, and speaking with suppressed excitement*). A telegram for Mr Daniel.

DANIEL (*with a gasp of relief*). Ah! (*He tears it open and proudly reads it out aloud.*) "Come to London at once to explain patent. Want to purchase. Gregg."

66

(BROWN *goes out again.*)

MACKENZIE. Who? Gregg?

DANIEL. I suppose I better go, John?

JOHN. Let's see the telegram. (*He goes over to* DANIEL, *who hands it to him.*)

MACKENZIE. If you go to London, it'll take you to explain yourself a bit better, Mr Murray.

JOHN (*who has resumed his place at the fire, and is looking carefully at the telegram*). That will mean how many pounds, Daniel, did you say?

DANIEL (*promptly*). Fifteen, John. (MARY *goes out by door to rooms.*)

MACKENZIE. Who is Gregg?

DANIEL. Gregg? Ah. He's a man lives in London. Engineer.

JOHN (*dubiously*). Well, I suppose you – (*he pauses, then hands the telegram to* SARAH, *who stretches out her hand for it.*)

MARY (*at door*). Tea's ready. (*She stands aside to let the company past.*)

SARAH. We didn't hear all about the bellows.

ANDY (*contemptuously.*) No, nor you never will. (*He rises and goes through the door.*)

MACKENZIE (*rising and stretching himself wearily*). Any more, Mr Murray?

DANIEL. I refuse to discuss the matter any further in public. (*He goes off across to tea.*)

MACKENZIE (*going over to* JOHN *and looking at him knowingly*). Do you know what it is, Mr Murray? Your brother's nothing short of an impostor.

JOHN (*much offended*). Don't dare to say that of a Murray.

MACKENZIE (*shrugging his shoulders*). Well, I'm going for some tea. (*Exit.*)

SARAH. John, I've something to say to you again about Daniel, but the company's waiting. (*She goes out to the tea room.*)

JOHN (*sitting down moodily*). Aye.

MARY. Are you not coming, father?

JOHN. Aye.

MARY. Father! Surely you aren't going to marry that woman?

JOHN. Don't talk of Sarah that ways. I am!

MARY. Well, if you are, I'm going to say yes to Alick McCready. I don't want to yet awhile, but I'm not going to stay on here if that nasty woman comes. (*She kneels close beside her father and puts her arms round his neck.*) Oh, father, if you only give me another

67

chance, I could show you I could keep house every bit as well as that woman. (DANIEL *appears at the door. He slips across to the workshop unobserved.*) Give me another chance, father. Don't marry her at all. Let me stay with you – won't you?

JOHN. You're too late. She's trothed to me now.

MARY. Pooh. I'd think nothing of that. (DANIEL *comes out of the workshop with a bag.*) Uncle Dan! What's the matter?

DANIEL. Mary, I can't eat and sit beside that Scotchman. (*He notices* JOHN *is absorbed in deep thought, and motions* MARY *to slip out. She does so, and he looks observingly at* JOHN, *and then goes to the table, and makes a noise with the bag on the table.* JOHN *watches him a moment or two in amazed silence.*)

JOHN. What are you doing, Daniel?

DANIEL. Just making a few preparations.

JOHN. Ah, but look here. I haven't settled about London yet, Daniel.

DANIEL. Oh, London, John. (*Deprecatingly.*) Let that pass. I won't worry you about that. (*Broken heartedly.*) I'm leaving your house, John.

JOHN (*astonished*). What?

DANIEL. You've been kind, John. Very kind. We always pulled well together, and never had much cross words with one another, but – well, circumstances are altered now.

JOHN. You mean because I'm going to marry Sarah.

DANIEL. Exactly. That puts an end to our long and pleasant sojourn here together. I'll have to go.

JOHN (*affected*). Oh easy, Daniel. Ah, now, Sarah always liked you. She thinks a deal of you, and I'm sure she'd miss you out of the house as much as myself.

DANIEL. John, I know better. She wants me out of this, and I would only be a source of unhappiness. I wouldn't like to cause you sorrow. She doesn't believe in me. She brought that Scotchman over to try and show me up. You all think he did. You think I mugged the thing. You don't believe in me now yourself. (*He puts a few articles of clothing, etc., into the bag.*)

JOHN (*awkwardly*). Aye. Well – to tell you the truth, Daniel, you did not make much of a hand at explaining, you—

DANIEL (*pathetically*). I thought so. Look here. One word. (*He draws* JOHN *aside.*) Do you think Mackenzie invented that patent reciprocating piston that he's so proud of?

JOHN (*looking at him in amazement*). What?

DANIEL (*impressively*). Well. I know something about that. He stole it off another man, and took all the profits. I knew that. Do you

68

think I'm going to give away the product of my brains explaining it to a man like that! No fear, John. (*He turns again to the bag.*) I'm taking details of my bellows, and my coat, and a few socks, and the pound you gave me yesterday, and I'm going to face the world alone.

JOHN (*moved*). No, no. You'll not leave me, Daniel. Ah, no. I never meant that.

DANIEL. If she's coming here I'll have to go, and may as well now.

SARAH (*without*). John Murray!

DANIEL (*retreating slowly to the workshop*). I'm going to get that other coat you gave me. It's better than this one for seeing people in. (*He goes into workshop as* SARAH *comes out into the kitchen. She is evidently displeased.*)

SARAH. Hurry up, John. The company's waiting on you, and I don't know what's keeping you. Unless it was that brother of yours, more shame to him.

JOHN. Aye. Daniel kept me. (*Looking at her.*) He's talking of leaving. You wouldn't have that, Sarah, would you?

SARAH (*sharply*). Leaving, is he? And a right good riddance say I. What has he done but ate up all your substance.

JOHN (*astonished*). You wouldn't put him out, Sarah?

SARAH (*snappishly*). I just wouldn't have him about the place. An idle, good for nothing, useless, old pull a cork.

JOHN. Do you not like him, Sarah? (*Somewhat disapprovingly.*) You told me you thought a good deal of him before.

SARAH. Aye. Until I seen through him. Him and his letters and telegrams. Just look at that. (*She shows him the telegram.*) It comes from Ballyannis.

JOHN (*scratching his head in puzzled wonder*). I don't understand that.

SARAH. He just put up someone to send it. Young McCready or someone. You couldn't watch a man like that. No. If I come here, out he goes. You expects me to come and save you money and the like of that old bauchle eating up the profits. (*She goes towards the door into the tearoom.*) Come into your tea at once. (*Exit.*)

JOHN. By me sang he was right. (DANIEL *comes out and starts brushing his coat loudly to attract* JOHN'S *attention, and then goes across towards him and holds out his hand.*)

DANIEL. I'll say good-bye, John. Maybe I'll never see you again. (*He appears much affected.*)

JOHN (*touched*). Ach. Take your time. I don't see the sense of this hurrying. Stop a week or two, man. I'll be lonesome without you.

We had many a good crack in the evenings, Daniel.

DANIEL. We had, John. And I suppose now that you'll be married I'll have to go, but many a time I'll be sitting lonely and thinking of them.

JOHN. Aye. You were always the best of company, and heartsome. You were, Daniel.

DANIEL. Well, I did my best, John, to keep – (*he half breaks down*) – to keep up a good heart.

JOHN. You did. I wouldn't like to lose you, Daniel. (*He looks at the telegram in his hand.*) But Daniel. This telegram. It comes from Ballyannis.

DANIEL (*taken aback, but recovering his self possession*). Ballyannis? Ballyannis? Ah, of course. Sure Gregg, that London man, he was to go through Ballyannis to-day. He's on a visit, you know, somewhere this way. It's him I'm going to look for now.

JOHN. Was that the way of it? (*With rising anger at the thought of the way in which his brother has been treated.*) And she was for making you out an impostor and for putting you out. I didn't like them talking of a Murray the way they done.

DANIEL (*with sudden hope*). Are you engaged to that McMinn woman, John?

JOHN. Aye. I spoke the word the day.

DANIEL. Was there anybody there when you asked her?

JOHN. There was no one.

DANIEL. Did you write her letters?

JOHN. No. Not a line.

DANIEL. And did you visit and court much at the home?

JOHN. No. I always seen Andy on business and stopped to have a word or two with her.

DANIEL (*appealingly*). Then, John, John, it's not too late yet. (*Desperately.*) Give me – ah, give wee Mary another chance.

SARAH (*at door*). Come in, John, at once. Your tea's cold waiting, and it's no way to entertain company that.

JOHN (*angrily*). D—n her. Daniel! Out of this home you will not go. I'd rather have your crack of a winter night as two hundred pounds in the bank and yon woman. (*He reaches out his hand.*) I'll break the match. (*The two men shake hands.*)

(CURTAIN.)

70

ACT III

The same scene two weeks later. The Curtain rises to discover MARY *seated near table reading a cookery book to* KATE, *who, paying but little attention, is watching a pot boiling on the fire.*

MARY. Listen, Kate, to this. "A most desirable addition to this most appetising dish from the point of view of a gourmet"—

KATE. A what, Miss?

MARY. A gourmet.

KATE. Now what kind of a thing would that be.

MARY. It's French for a cook or something – I forget – "a most desirable addition to this dish from the point of view of a" – (*The yard door opens, and* SAM BROWN *appears with letters in his hand.* MARY *immediately throws the book aside and rushes over to him.*)

MARY. Letters! Any for me, Sam?

BROWN. Aye. There's a post card for you, Miss Mary, and a registered letter for Mr John. The posty says he'll call on the road back for the account when you sign it. (*He hands the post card to* MARY *and looks carefully at the letter.*) It's like the McMinn writing that. (*He looks at* MARY, *who is reading and re-reading the post card with a puzzled expression.*) Isn't Mr Dan to be home to-day from Belfast, Miss Mary?

MARY. Eh?

BROWN. Isn't Mr Dan expected home to-day from Belfast?

MARY. Yes.

BROWN. I wonder did he get the bellows sold? There was great talking about him last night in McArns. Some said he had sold it and made a fortune. (*He breaks off abruptly on seeing that* MARY *pays no attention to him, and then peers over to see what she is reading.*) Post cards is interesting things. Picture post cards is.

KATE. Go on out of this. We're tired hearing your gabble.

BROWN (*retreating to door and eyeing* KATE *meaningly*). The master was complaining again to me yesterday evening about the dinner he got. There's no mistake he likes his meat like myself, and right

71

enough it was bad yesterday. I was chowing haws all evening to keep off the hunger.

KATE. And couldn't you have made it up with bread? There's plenty of soda bread.

BROWN. Bread? Soda bread? Aye. There's plenty of soda, God knows, but you couldn't call it bread.

MARY (*who has been listening to the latter part of the conversation, starts suddenly up, and takes a piece of soda bread off the table and bites it hastily*). Oh, Kate!

BROWN. Aye. It's soda bread, miss, and no mistake.

KATE. You would bake it yourself, you know, miss. I throwed the most of it out yesterday, and the hens wouldn't as much as look at it. (*Seeing* MARY *is almost on the point of tears.*) Ach, never mind, Miss Mary. (*She looks at* BROWN, *who is listening.*) Go on you out of this.

BROWN. That's all the news this morning. (*He makes a grimace at* KATE *and goes out into the yard.*)

MARY. I can't understand this post card. (KATE *goes over and looks at it along with* MARY.)

"O wad that God the gift wad gie us,
To see oorselves as ithers see us."

What does that mean? "How's the uncle." It's some cheeky person anyway – "from D.M." Who could that be?

KATE. It's not McCready, Miss, is it?

MARY. No. That's not his writing.

KATE. Och, Miss Mary! Do you see the picture of the Highland man dancing, and under it – "A Mackenzie Clansman." It's thon Scotch fellow sent it.

MARY. Just like the way he would do. I met him again one night we were over at the doctor's, and he was trying to make up to me all he was able.

KATE. Aye. You might do worse than take him.

MARY. I'll hand him over to you, Kate.

KATE. Ah, no, Miss. Thank you kindly all the same. Any word from Mr Dan about the boy he was to bring you?

MARY. No. I'm not going to bother any more about boys. I'm going to keep house from this on properly. But Uncle Dan said something in his last letter about a great surprise he had for all of us.

KATE. Surprise enough it will be, and he lands home with a ha'penny in his pocket. The last time he come home he borrowed a shilling of me and niver paid me back yet. Did he sell the plans of the bellows, Miss?

MARY. He didn't say. (JOHN MURRAY *comes through yard door. He has evidently been working outside and has left his work in a hurry.*) Father, there's a letter for you. (*She hands it to him.*) A registered one too.

JOHN. Aye. So Brown was telling me. Maybe its from thon McAlenan fellow that owes me two pound for the heifer. (*He tears it open. MARY and KATE watch him with interest. His face changes as he reads, and an expression of dismay comes over it.*)

MARY (*coming closer to him*). What's the matter, father?

JOHN (*fidgeting uneasily*). Nothing, child. Nothing. (*He looks at the letter again.*) Well I'm – (*He stops short on remembering MARY is there.*) She's a caution.

MARY. Father. Tell me. Is it from the McMinns?

JOHN. Aye. (*Pacing up and down.*) I knowed she'd do it. I knowed she'd do it.

MARY. What?

JOHN. Sarah's taking an action against me.

MARY. An action?

JOHN. Aye. (*Consulting the letter.*) For a thousand pounds.

MARY (*awestruck*). A thousand pounds!

JOHN. Aye. Now the fat's in the fire. She says I promised to marry her and broke it off. At least, it's Andy that writes the letter, but it's her that put him up to it. I know that too well. (*Reading.*) "To Mr John Murray. Dear Sir, – You have acted to my sister in a most ungentlemanly way, and done her much wrong, and I have put the case intil the hands of Mr McAllen, the solicitor, who will bring it forward at the coming Assizes. If you wish, however, to avoid a scandal, we are open to settle the matter by private arrangement. Yours truly, Andrew McMinn."

MARY. That's awful, father, isn't it? (*She sits down pensively.*)

JOHN (*going over to fireplace and standing there irresolutely*). Aye. It's a terrible mess, right enough.

MARY (*brightening up*). Sure she wouldn't get a thousand off you, father?

KATE. There's John McArdle up by Slanely Cross got a hundred pounds took off him by wee Miss Black, the school teacher.

JOHN (*uncomfortably*). Aye. Heth now, I just call that to mind. And he never got courting at all, I believe.

KATE. It just served him right. He was always a great man for having five or six girls running after him.

JOHN. And she hadn't much of a case against him.

73

KATE. The school children were standing by when he asked her in a joking sort of way would she marry him, and the court took their evidence!

JOHN (*hopelessly*). Aye. Men are always terrible hard on other men where women are concerned.

KATE. And a good job it is, or half the girls would be at the church waiting, and the groom lying at home rueing his bargain. (*She goes out by yard door.*)

MARY (*going up to her father*). Father, has she a good case against you?

JOHN (*after a moment of deep thought*). No. I don't think it.

MARY. Don't worry so much then, father.

JOHN. It's the jury I'm so frightened of. They all come from the mountainy district at this Assizes, and there's not a man of them but wouldn't put a knife in me, the way I get beating them down in price at the fairs.

MARY. I don't think they'd give her fifty pounds when they see her. It's only good looking girls would get big sums like a thousand pounds.

JOHN. It's all very well, Mary, but she could dress herself to look nice enough, the same Sarah, if she liked.

MARY. She could not, indeed.

JOHN. They say, at least Brown was hinting to me, that its yon Scotch fellow, Mackenzie, has put up the McMinns to this business. He and that connection are as thick as thieves.

MARY. He mightn't be so very fond of them. When a man sends post cards to a girl he doesn't know very well he's got a wee bit of a liking for her.

JOHN. What are you talking about? I never sent her any post cards.

MARY. Father, what are you going to do?

JOHN (*despairingly*). I'm d—d if I know.

MARY. Will you defend the case?

JOHN. I don't want to go near the court at all.

MARY. Father! (*Alarmed.*) Father! Sure you wouldn't – you couldn't think of marrying her after all that row that happened? (JOHN *remains silent.*) Wouldn't you rather lose a thousand pounds and keep me, father? (JOHN *breaks a piece of soda bread morosely and eats it.*) Wouldn't you, father?

JOHN. Ah! (*He spits out the bread.*) Heaven save us, what kind of bread's that?

MARY (*taking away the bread and putting it behind her back.*) Father! Ah please, please, don't marry her anyway. Sure you won't?

JOHN (*softening*). There, there, child. I'll think about it.

BROWN (*coming in hastily*). Here's Mr Dan coming up the loaning, sir, that grand looking you'd hardly know him, and a big cigar in his mouth.

JOHN. Daniel back?

MARY. Oh, I must go out and meet him. (*She goes out by yard door quickly.*)

JOHN. Had he his luggage with him?

BROWN. Aye. He has yon big portmanteau of his, and a parcel of something or other.

JOHN. Away out and help him then, can't you? (BROWN *goes out.*) I wonder what kept him in Belfast all this time. I suppose he's spent most of the five pounds I gave him. Like enough. I never mind him coming back yet with a ha'penny on him. (*He sits down at the fireplace and looks again at the letter.*) A thousand pounds! And there never was a breach of promise case known where they didn't bring in a verdict for the woman. Never! (*He becomes absorbed in thought, and as he sits ruminating* MARY *opens the door, carrying a large brown paper parcel, followed by* DANIEL. DANIEL *is dressed fairly well, and seems to be in high spirits.* BROWN *follows him carrying a portmanteau.*)

DANIEL (*brightly*). Home again, John.

JOHN (*morosely*). Aye. It was near time, I think.

DANIEL. Saw quite a number of people this time, John. A great number. They were all very much interested. Fine town, Belfast. Growing very rapidly. Wonderful place.

MARY. Take me with you when you go again, Uncle Dan, won't you? What's in the parcel? (*She looks at it with great curiosity.*)

DANIEL. Ah, that – that's the great secret. Mum's the word. All in good time, Mary.

MARY. It's a secret? (*She looks at it again wonderingly.*)

DANIEL. Yes.

BROWN. Will I leave your bag here, Mr Dan?

DANIEL. Yes. Here's a sixpence for you. (*He hands it to* BROWN, *who salutes and goes out grinning.*)

JOHN. You're brave and free-handed with your money. Giving the like of that bauchle sixpence. The Lord knows but we will be wanting every ha'penny we can scrape together, and soon enough.

MARY. I didn't tell Uncle Dan yet, father.

DANIEL (*seating himself near the workshop door*). Has anything happened?

MARY. Yes. Sarah McMinn has –

75

JOHN. Read that letter, Daniel. (*He goes across and hands* DANIEL *the letter, and goes back to the fireplace to watch him.*)

DANIEL (*taking out his glasses and solemnly perusing the letter*). Um.

JOHN. Well? What do you think of that?

DANIEL (*endeavouring to appear cheerful*). Keep up a stout heart, John. You're safe enough.

JOHN. Oh, heth, I'm not so sure of that. Sure you never heard tell of a jury yet that didn't give damages against the defendant in a breach of promise case. Did you now?

DANIEL. Tuts, man. She has no case.

JOHN. Case or no case it doesn't seem to matter. What sort of case had Jennie Black against John McArdle, of Slaney Cross? None. What sort of case had Maggie McAndless against old William Boyd? None at all. I was at both of them trials, and says I to Pat McAleenan – "the girl has no case at all!" But for all that they brought in a verdict for one hundred pounds against McArdle, and they put two hundred against old Boyd, and nearly broke the two of them.

DANIEL. It's very awkward this.

JOHN. Did you do anything, Daniel, about the bellows?

DANIEL. The bellows? Aye. (*He points at the parcel.*) A good deal, John. It's all there. But it's all not quite settled yet. A day or two more and you'll see. If all goes well I'll have a great surprise for you in a day or two.

JOHN (*disgustedly*). Ach! I suppose you spent every ha'penny of the money, too, that I gave you?

DANIEL. John. Another surprise for you! Those people I met and went to, put me up very cheap for the week. Very cheap. (*He produces some money.*) There's one pound ten and sixpence for you.

JOHN. What?

DANIEL. I'll keep the pound to do me to the end of the month and not to ask you for any more, John, after that. That is if – well – (*He looks at the parcel.*) That thing there is all right.

JOHN (*pocketing the ten and sixpence after counting it carefully*). Daniel. I'm sorry, but there's an account of some thirty shillings I owe the McArdles, and I want to pay it the night. So if you don't mind – (*He holds out his hand.*)

DANIEL (*unwillingly*). Well, I suppose it can't be helped, John. But it leaves me just with nothing. However, there you are. (*He hands the pound over to him.* SAM BROWN *opens the yard door and peeps in cautiously.*)

JOHN (*looking at him angrily*). What ails *you* anyway?

BROWN. If you please, sir, the posty wants the account signed for that letter.

MARY. Oh, I forgot all about it. (*She picks up the receipt for the letter from the table.*) I'll sign it for you, father. (*She goes over to* BROWN, *who whispers something. She nods.*) And I'll give it to him myself. (*She goes out following* BROWN.)

JOHN. It's a serious business, this, about the McMinns.

DANIEL. You're all right, man. Wait a day or two. Take my advice. Do nothing in a hurry. Sit down and think it over the way I do when I'm working out a new idea. Don't rush things. It will all come right in the end. Just you wait and see if it doesn't.

JOHN. Would it not be better to settle before going into the court? You know I couldn't stand being pointed out to of a Sunday morning and one and another talking – "There's the man that Sarah McMinn took the breach of promise case against." No, I couldn't stand that at all. It would be a disgrace to the Murrays for ever. I'm wondering now— (*He pauses lost in thought.*)

DANIEL (*alarmed*). John. Surely you wouldn't – you couldn't think of going back on what you said to me. Would you?

JOHN. I wonder, Daniel, would you mind so much after all if I married her?

DANIEL (*in an agonised voice*). I couldn't stand it. No, John, I couldn't stay. Any other woman but that McMinn.

MARY (*appearing at the door followed by* ALICK MCCREADY). Come on in, Alick.

ALICK. Good morning, Mr Murray. How are you, Mr Dan? So you are back again? We're all glad to have you back.

DANIEL. Thank you, Alick.

MARY. Father. Alick says he heard Andy McMinn talking yesterday to some one at McArdle's shop, and he was telling them all about the whole business, and blaming it all on Uncle Dan.

JOHN. And so the people are talking of me already? Now that I come to think of it, it was your Uncle Dan, and a brave ha'penny it's going to cost me. One thousand pounds!

ALICK. Never mind, Mr Murray. Maybe Uncle Dan will do something yet. What about the bellows? (DAN *makes a horrified movement to stop* ALICK *talking, but too late.*)

JOHN. Aye. Here, Daniel. I'll make a bargain with you. I'll leave you to the settling of the case, and you can find the money yourself to pay for it if you want to. And if you can't find the money, I'll marry her.

MARY. Father, surely—

JOHN. What? That's enough about it. I would as soon do without the marrying if I could. I don't want the woman at all, but I'll marry her before she gets a ha'penny off me. So you can settle it among yourselves. You can take charge of that letter, Dan, and make the best you can of it. (*He goes angrily out by yard door.*)

DANIEL. This is a nice mess you put me in for, Alick. What the divil made you mention the bellows?

ALICK. I'm sorry, Mr Dan. I wasn't thinking.

DANIEL. The sooner you start and think a bit the better. If you don't help to settle the case – (*he looks angrily at* ALICK) – well – I've a good deal of influence with somebody. (*He looks significantly at* MARY, *who is again examining the parcel.*)

ALICK. I'll do my best, Mr Dan, to help you.

MARY. What will we do, Uncle Dan?

DANIEL. I suppose you've no money, Alick?

ALICK. Well, I haven't much ready money, Mr Dan, but I could lend you up to twenty pounds at a pinch.

MARY. Twenty pounds would hardly be enough. Would it, uncle?

ALICK. Better get hold of Andy and ask him.

DANIEL. I don't like going near that woman at all.

MARY. Alick! Could you not slip over and ask Andy to come across? You know what the McMinns are like. He'd come over for a shilling if he thought he'd get one. Ah, yes. You will, Alick. Won't you?

ALICK. I'll go straight across now if you – if you—

MARY. What?

ALICK. If you'd leave us along the road a bit.

MARY. Ach, you're a bother. (DANIEL *goes over to the table, lifts the parcel, and then goes and sits down near the fireplace.*)

ALICK. Leave us a wee bit of the way, anyway. (*He goes towards the door and beckons her. She goes out after him.*)

DANIEL (*feeling the parcel*). I'm afraid, Dan Murray, it's all U.P. this time. I'm afraid it is. (*Then an idea seems to dawn on him, and he looks at the parcel.*) Unless – unless – well – I wonder now if I—
(KATE *and* BROWN *enter through yard door.* BROWN *is carrying a bucket filled with washed potatoes.*)

KATE. There. Put it down there. You didn't know we wanted that much, did you not? You're getting as big an old liar as Mr— (*She stops short on perceiving* DANIEL.)

BROWN (*looking up and then realising what had made her pause.*) Aye. Go on. As who do you say, woman?

78

KATE (*recovering herself*). Just as big an old liar as Andy McMinn.

BROWN. Now, whist. The McMinns were aye decent folk. (*He glances across at* DANIEL, *who apparently is not listening.*) They're near people, and all that sort of thing, but once they say a thing they stick to it.

KATE. They're a lot of mean scrubs, the whole caboosh of them.

BROWN (*nudging* KATE *slyly*). I believe that once Sarah puts a price on a thing like a pig or a sow, or a hen, the divil himself couldn't beat her down in the price of it. She can beat the best dealer in the county from here to the Mourne. (DANIEL, *who has been listening uneasily, gets up and turns round to look at them.*) It's the fine cigar that you were smoking, Mr Daniel, this morning.

DANIEL. Cigar? Yes. Yes.

BROWN. Aye. A fine cigar, sir. There was a grand smell of it. I seen you coming up by the McMinns, sir, this morning on the road from the station.

DANIEL. Yes. On the road from the station.

BROWN. You didn't see them, but I noticed Andy and Sarah coming out to the gate when you had passed them and looking after you a long time.

DANIEL. Is that so?

BROWN. Aye. A long time, sir. I suppose, like myself, they smelled the cigar. Mr Andy, they say, is guy fond of a good cigar, and I understand that he'll be for getting a few boxes of them soon, for the sister, they say, is coming into a lot of money. It's well for the people can afford the like of them things.

KATE. Will you hold your tongue. There! I want no more of you now. You're only a nuisance in the house anyway. Go out and clatter to somebody else. I wonder the master didn't sack you long ago.

BROWN. The master? (*He retreats slowly to the yard door.*) The master knows to keep a good man when he gets one. He doesn't part soft with either good men or money. God bless him. (*He goes out.*)

KATE. Will I make you a drop of tea, Mr Dan? You'll be tired travelling.

DANIEL. It's hard to eat anything, Kate, when I'm worried. (*Despairingly.*) I don't think there's another man living has the same worries as I have. Something awful! Where's the pen and ink, I wonder?

KATE. There's some here on the dresser, Miss Mary was using it to-day. (*She takes it over from the dresser to the table.* DANIEL *rises and goes over and sits down and begins slowly to write.*) Cheer up,

Mr Daniel. Sure you sold the plans of the bellows anyway. Didn't you, sir? They had word up at the McAleenans the other night that you got two thousand for it.

DANIEL (*astonished*). Eh? They said that?

KATE. Aye. To be sure. McAndless told McArdle, and he told Smith the postman, and the postman told the McAleenans, and said he had seen letters about it. And McAleenan was up in McMinns the other night and told them, and I believe you never saw such an astonished crowd of people in all your lives.

DANIEL. He told the McMinns?

KATE. Aye, last night I think it was.

DANIEL. Last night? (*He looks at the letter.*) Yesterday was the 14th, wasn't it? Aye. It was. I wonder did they believe McAleenan?

KATE. I don't think they know right what to make of it. And yon Scotchman was there at the time, and mind you, Mr Dan, they say he looked quite serious when he heard it, and said such things as that happened many's a time.

DANIEL (*incredulously*). Mackenzie said that?

KATE. Aye. You know, I think its maybe because he has a wee notion of Miss Mary, sir.

DANIEL. It's quite possible. Quite possible. A nice wee girl is Mary. Far too good for the half of them about these parts. (*He takes up the parcel, pen, and ink, and paper, and goes across into the workshop.*)

KATE (*looking after him*). Poor creature. I'm feared he's for the road again if he doesn't worry out some way for himself. And God knows he's the one best fitted for it. (MARY *enters.*) Well, did you see him off comfortably?

MARY. Who?

KATE. Alick McCready.

MARY. Kate. I wish you'd mind your own business.

KATE. It's a sore time I have in this house minding my own and every other bodies business.

MARY. Kate. He said I couldn't bake a cake to save my life. I'll just show him that I can, and you're not to help me, mind you. I'm going to do it all myself.

KATE. Very well, Miss. Anything for a bit of peace say I.

MARY. Where's that recipe book? (KATE *hands it to her, and she begins to pore over the pages.*) "Queen pudding."

KATE. Ah, Miss Mary, don't be trying that again. Do you not mind how bad your poor uncle was after it?

MARY. What's this Sarah McMinn was so good at? "Plum cakes." I'll try a plum cake.

KATE (*hopelessly and to herself*). She's clean daft.

MARY (*consulting the book*). I'll want eggs and flour and currants and suet and –

KATE. I think if I was you, I'd try something more easy.

MARY. But plum cakes are easy.

KATE. That's what I used to think till I tried one. I give it up, Miss. It's beyond me altogether.

MARY. I think that you believe I couldn't bake anything. Where's the flour?

KATE. There's none in the house, Miss Mary.

MARY. What?

KATE. You mind it was all used up this morning on account of them cakes you were doing that turned out bad.

MARY. Go down to McArdles, Kate, and get a quarter stone on account.

KATE. Your da told me this morning, Miss Mary, that I wasn't to get any more from McArdles or any other place unless he gives me an order for it. Do you not mind?

MARY (*dejectedly*). So he did. I had forgotten.

KATE. Aye. Quite so, Miss. (*She sits down contentedly.*)

MARY. I wonder is Uncle Dan about?

KATE. Aye. He's in his workshop, Miss.

MARY (*going over and knocking at door of workshop*). Uncle Dan!

DANIEL (*without*). Yes.

MARY. Please, Uncle Dan.

DANIEL (*appearing at door*). Well, Mary?

MARY. Uncle Dan, could you give me sixpence?

DANIEL (*fumbling in his pockets*). Sixpence? Sixpence, Mary? Bless your wee heart. Here. Here's a two shilling bit. But Mary, mum's the word. Don't tell John I gave it to you.

MARY. No. Thank you, uncle. (DANIEL *goes in again.*) There, Kate, quick as you can and don't stop to talk to anybody. Sure you won't? (*She hands* KATE *the money and takes up the recipe book.*)

KATE. I'm not dirty looking – am I, Miss Mary?

MARY (*absorbed in the book*). No. You'll do grand. Flour, – currants, raisins – we have all that – suet – I wonder—

KATE. Ach! You and your currants. Could you not tell a body was her face clean?

MARY. It's lovely. Hurry, Kate. (KATE *shrugs her shoulders disgustedly, and goes out by yard door.*) Flour, currants— (*She goes over to the workshop door and listens*) – raisins – (*A sound as of a blast blowing can be heard.* MARY *becomes intensely interested, and, throwing aside the book, kneels down and puts her head to the keyhole.*) He's actually got something to work. (*She peeps in.*) He has, indeed. (*She laughs, knocks loudly at the door, and then runs to the other side of the kitchen.* DANIEL *opens the door and cautiously peeps out.*) Uncle Danny! Ha! Ha! Uncle Danny! (*Dancing up and down in front of the fireplace.*) Uncle Dan's a wonderful man! Uncle Dan's a wonderful man!

DANIEL (*amazed*). What's all this?

MARY. I'm a cleverer girl than you think, Uncle Dan! I know your great surprise. I've found it out. (*In a disappointed manner.*) And you never told me! (*Pouting.*) I think you might have told me anyway. It wasn't at all nice of you to keep it secret from me.

DANIEL. I just wanted to give you all a surprise, Mary.

MARY. And you've actually got it to work! That's splendid, uncle, isn't it? Father will be awful proud when he hears about it. And you did it all yourself, uncle?

DANIEL. Well, I took those plans, Mary, to a handy chap, an acquaintance of mine, and we talked a long time over it, and he made it out according to my design. I'm not sure – I think it works all right. Is there a screw driver about, I wonder, Mary?

MARY. I don't know. And did you get it sold, uncle?

DANIEL. No, Mary, but I have hopes – great hopes.

MARY. Do you think you'd get more than a thousand pounds for it?

DANIEL. Don't know, Mary, don't know. Very hard to know these things. I must have a look for that screw driver. I think John had it last working at something in the parlour. (*He goes out by door to inner rooms.*)

MARY. I wonder would it really sell for a thousand pounds? (*Knocking at yard door.*) Come in. (DONAL MACKENZIE *opens the door and comes in.*)

MACKENZIE. Fine afternoon, Miss Murray.

MARY (*coldly*). Good day to you.

MACKENZIE. I'm going off to Scotland verra soon, and I thought I would call over to see you before I went off. You're no angry, are you?

MARY. No. (MACKENZIE *seats himself at the table.*)

MACKENZIE. Did you get a post card?

MARY. I got some silly thing this morning that I tore up.

MACKENZIE. I'm sorry. I'm verra fond of you, Mary.

MARY. Miss Murray, please.

MACKENZIE. A girl like you is lost here, you know. Now, if you were a Scotch lassie you would have a great time enjoying yourself. In a place like Greenock we have a theatre, and we have a music hall and a cinematograph show on Saturdays and trains to Glasgow. You could have a grand time in Scotland.

MARY. Do you really like me, Mr Mackenzie?

MACKENZIE. Verra much. Indeed I—

MARY. Well. Look here. I would like you very, very much too, if you—

MACKENZIE. If I what, bonnie Mary?

MARY. I'd even let you call me Mary, and write to me if you wanted to, if you would do me a favour.

MACKENZIE. What's the favour?

MARY. Uncle Dan has brought home his fan bellows, and it works.

MACKENZIE (*laughs*). The fan bellows! I think he'll never make much of a fortune of his fan bellows.

MARY. Do you ever examine new inventions?

MACKENZIE. Aye. I'm a specialist on that, you know. I'm the writer of the inventions column in the Scottish—

MARY. Yes. Yes. That's all right. I know. Are all the inventions you write about good things?

MACKENZIE. Eh? Ninety-nine per cent. rotten, lassie. Ninety-nine per cent perfectly rotten. People don't invent a reciprocating piston that works every day in the week, or a fan bellows either.

MARY. But if you liked the inventor you could do him a good turn all the same?

MACKENZIE. Aye. I did that often.

MARY. Then could you do a good turn for Uncle Dan? For me!

MACKENZIE. Eh?

MARY. Uncle Dan has a fan bellows in that workshop. Go in and look at it, and examine it, and if you like me even a wee bit, you – (DANIEL *re-enters. He stops short on seeing* MACKENZIE, *and seems to become very uncomfortable.*) Uncle Dan! Mr Mackenzie's going to examine your bellows.

DANIEL. I don't allow everybody to go and look at it. No. I refuse. It's my property and no one else's.

MARY. Uncle Dan. (*She looks at him meaningly.*) Mr Mackenzie has promised to give his opinion on it.

DANIEL. It's not protected yet by patent.

MACKENZIE. Andy McMinn is coming over, Mr Murray. He has got orders from his sister to settle the case for her. Are you going to pay the money?

DANIEL. That is a matter of my own deciding. (MARY *goes over to her*

83

uncle and whispers to him.)

MACKENZIE. Verra well. I may go. (*To* MARY.) I would have done you that good turn, Miss Murray; but there's no enmity between us. And – (*lowering his voice*) – I hope you get the best of the McMinns in the bargain. Don't give in, Mr Murray, easy. Take my tip. I'm from the stables, you know. (*He laughs knowingly.*)

MARY. Here's Andy now (*she looks out through the window*), and Alick's with him. (*she opens the door,* ANDY MCMINN *and* MCCREADY *enter.* MCCREADY *glances at* MARY *and* MACKENZIE, *and goes over sulkily to the fireplace.* ANDY *advances awkwardly towards* DANIEL.)

DANIEL (*genially*). Good afternoon, Andy.

ANDY. Good afternoon. (*He looks at* MACKENZIE, *who nods curtly.*) I suppose you know I've power to settle the case.

DANIEL. Well, you wrote the letter, and so, in point of law, I think it is you who should look after all this unfortunate business. Believe me, Andy, I sympathise with you. I do indeed. (MARY *and* MACKENZIE *become absorbed in conversation near the table.* ALICK MCCREADY *stands at the fireplace looking at them and unable to conceal his jealousy, makes sundry odd noises to distract* MARY'S *attention. She pretends not to hear him.*) I have your letters here. (*He searches in his pocket and produces it.*) Yes. One thousand pounds. Do you not think that a trifle high?

ANDY. Well. You know we could have as easily claimed two thousand, but we didn't like to break you altogether; so we just said a thousand would come pretty near it.

MACKENZIE. Mr Daniel, may I look at the bellows?

MARY. Uncle Dan, I'm sure you won't object. (*She makes a gesture as if asking him to assent.*)

DANIEL (*looking hard at her, and then seeming to understand what she is about.*) Yes. Yes. I'll thrash out the matter here with Andy. (MACKENZIE *goes across into the workshop, followed by* MARY. MCCREADY *sits down disconsolately at the fireplace and begins to smoke his pipe moodily.*) A thousand pounds is impossible. Absolutely out of the question.

MCCREADY (*to himself*). Ach. She only torments me.

DANIEL (*looking over wonderingly*). Eh? (MCCREADY *makes no response, but sits with his back to the two of them.*) People behave strangely sometimes, Andy. Very strangely. Now to go on with our business. I don't think, in the first case, that this was an affair of the heart, as the Frenchmen say.

ANDY. Eh?

DANIEL. You don't understand French? Of course not. No. It wasn't a love affair, I mean. I don't think Sarah was in love with John, was she?

ANDY (*hesitatingly*). Well – indeed, now, I don't know that she was.

DANIEL. No. We're all aware of that. He was just what we'd call a likely man. That's all.

ANDY. Aye. He would have been a good match for her.

DANIEL. Yes. Quite so, Andy. (*He makes notes in a pocket book.*) Nothing like notes, Andy. Now, so much for the love part of the business. They never exchanged letters?

ANDY. No. No letters.

DANIEL. Of course in a breach of promise letters are a great help. A great help. I'm very glad, however, just for your sister's sake, that she never wrote any to John. Imagine them reading out the love letters in the open court, and all the servant boys gaping and laughing.

ANDY. It's not nice, right enough. It's one thing I wouldn't like.

DANIEL. Well. No love. No letters. Next thing. He never courted her?

ANDY. Well, he came over and sat in the house a few nights.

DANIEL. Yes. No doubt. But hadn't he always some message on business to transact with you? Loan of a plough or a horse, or something like that?

ANDY (*uneasily*). That's so, of course.

DANIEL. Ah, yes.

ANDY. But I seen him with his arm round her the night of the social at the schoolhouse.

DANIEL. Andy. That's a wee failing of John's. I often warned him about doing that sort of thing indiscriminately. A bit of a ladies' man, John, in his way. I saw him do the same nonsense four or five times that night with other girls. John likes to think himself a bit of a gay dog, you know. It's not right – I don't think myself it's a bit proper to put your arm round a girl's waist on every occasion, but sometimes it's quite allowable. A night like a social, for instance.

ANDY. Aye. Of course a social's different.

DANIEL. Certainly. Well, now. No love, no letters, no courting, no photographs exchanged? (*He looks at* ANDY *inquiringly.*) No photographs exchanged. (*He notes it down.*) No ring? In fact, Andy, no nothing.

ANDY. But he proposed to her right enough.

DANIEL. Who said so?

ANDY (*astonished*). What? Do you mean to deny he didn't?

85

DANIEL. My dear Andy, I don't know. There was no one there but the two, I suppose, when he asked her. There's only her word for it.

ANDY. He wouldn't deny it himself?

DANIEL. Well. That depends on whether he really asked her to marry him of course. And it's not likely that John would be inclined if his memory was at all bad – it is a bad memory he has, you know. He forgets often to return your ploughs and that sort of thing.

ANDY (*blankly*). Aye. He has a bad memory.

DANIEL. Yes. Just so. And the fact that a verdict of one thousand pounds would hang on it would hardly make it any better. Would it? You've a bad case against us, Andy. A rotten case! In fact, looking over the whole thing carefully, do you really believe you'd make even a ten pound note out of us?

ANDY (*despairingly*). I wish Sarah had come and settled the case herself.

DANIEL. Ah, no. You've a better head, Andy, for seeing the sensible side of a thing, far better. (MARY *comes out of the workshop smiling gaily.*) Well?

MARY. Uncle Dan, he's delighted with it.

ANDY. What with? The bellows?

MARY. Yes. Go in, Andy, till you see it.

ANDY. Is it true, Daniel, you were offered two thousand for it?

DANIEL. We'll just go in and have a look at it. (ANDY *and he go into workshop.*)

MARY (*looking across at* ALICK). What's the matter?

ALICK. Nothing. I'm going home. (*He goes across to the yard door.*)

MARY. Alick!

MCCREADY. Goodbye.

MARY. And I was going to go to all the trouble of baking a big plum cake for you, you big ungrateful thing.

MCCREADY (*stopping at the door*). I know what your plum cakes would be like. (*He opens the door and stops again before going out.*)

MARY. Well, get that big, ugly Maggie Murphy to bake them for you then.

MCCREADY (*looking out through door and then coming inside again*). I say, here's Kate and your father coming and a load of flour.

MARY (*in a frightened voice*). Kate and father?

MCCREADY. He seems to be in a bit of a temper.

MARY (*in a frightened voice*). He's caught her with the flour!

MCCREADY (*laughing*). Flour? Aye – she's carrying about three stone of it! Boys, but that would make a powerful pudding!

MARY. It was to have been the nicest one I could have baked.

McCREADY (*coming in and going over to her*). Mary!

MARY. What?

McCREADY. You wouldn't come to my house where there would be no stint of flour or raisins or anything else, and I'd eat all you cooked for me no matter if I was dying after it.

MARY. Go to your house!

ALICK. Aye. Look here, wee girl. I got this— (*He fumbles and produces a ring.*) Let me put that on your wee finger, won't you?

MARY. Oh, Alick, what a lovely wee ring. (*She allows him to put it on her finger, and is slyly kissing him when* JOHN *enters, followed by* KATE, *who is trying vainly to stop a leak in the bag of flour which she is carrying.* KATE *goes to the dresser and places the bag on it.*)

JOHN (*severely to* MARY). Mary. Did you send her for more flour?

MARY (*meekly*). Yes, father.

JOHN. And didn't I leave word there was no more to be got without my orders? (MARY *hangs her head.*) It's lamentable the waste in his house! I was just looking at the pass book last night, and you'd think this house was a bakery to see the amount of flour comes into it.

MARY (*submissively*). I'm sorry, father.

JOHN. When I was out on the road, I seen a trail of flour leading up our loaning, and says I to myself, Jeminy, father, are they getting some more! So I followed up the mark and just caught up on her coming through the gate.

MARY (*a little defiantly*). It's paid for, Kate, anyway. Isn't it?

KATE. It is, Miss. (*She busies herself putting the flour into a box, and then slips out during the next speech.*)

JOHN. Eh? Who give you the money?

MARY (*going over to her father and whispering*). Uncle Dan is in there, father, with Andy McMinn and Mr Mackenzie, the Scotch engineer, looking at his bellows.

JOHN (*amazed*). Eh? Andy McMinn? Is Dan settling the case?

MARY. I believe he'll do it yet.

JOHN (*admiringly*). He has a great head on him, Daniel.

MACKENZIE (*coming out from workshop and going over to* MARY.) Mary, I'm sorry. It's such a rotten thing that— (*He sees* JOHN.) How are you, Mr Murray.

JOHN. Fine day.

MARY (*appealingly*). Mr Mackenzie, what did you say to Andy about it?

MACKENZIE. What did I say? Oh, ma conscience – I said it was a grand thing. (DANIEL *and* ANDY MCMINN *come in from workshop.*)

ANDY (*nervously*). Brave day, John.

JOHN. Aye. It is.

ANDY. Sarah gave me power to settle the case.

JOHN. I'm glad to hear it.

MACKENZIE. I tell you what it is, Mr Daniel Murray. It's a good thing that – a right good thing, and I'll make you an offer for it.

ANDY (*eagerly*). What's it worth?

MACKENZIE (*with a look at* MARY). It's worth – it's worth more than all the damages your sister will get from Mr Murray.

DANIEL (*suddenly*). I tell you what it is, Andy, and believe me when I tell you, I'm sacrificing a great deal. I'll make a deal with you. Instead of a lump sum cash down, I'll hand over all the rights and royalties of that same bellows to you to settle the case.

ANDY (*dubiously*). I – I don't know.

DANIEL. You will have all the expense of the law, the bad name that your sister will be having over the head of being in a breach of promise, and all the expense of solicitors and lawyers. Then, after that, trying to get the money out of us, and, mind you, we will fight you to the last ditch. Won't we, John?

JOHN. Aye.

DANIEL. There now. What do you say, Mr Mackenzie?

MACKENZIE. I tell you what it is, Mr Murray. I'll make you an offer for—

ANDY (*hastily*). I'll take your offer, Daniel.

DANIEL. One second. I drew up a wee agreement for you to sign, and I'll fetch the bellows. (*He goes into the workshop.*)

JOHN. Andy, I think—

MARY. I think Uncle Dan's a fool to throw away the thing that way. I do indeed. (DANIEL *comes out with the parcel and the pen, ink and paper.*)

DANIEL. Just sign your name to that, Andy. It's a sort of agreement to settle the case – you can read it for yourself. (*He hands a sheet of paper to* ANDY *with the pen.*) It's to show that the whole thing is fixed up to the satisfaction of everybody. (ANDY *looks at it and then signs.*) Ah. Good! Now, Alick, and you, Mr Mackenzie, just witness it and the date. (*They both sign.*) And now, Andy, there's your bellows. (ANDY *looks at it, and then takes it under his arm.*) And may you have the best of luck with it. (ANDY *looks wonderingly at the parcel in his arm and moves slowly towards the door.*)

MACKENZIE. Noo, my reward, Miss Murray – Mary rather. (*He goes forward and she stretches out her hand for him to shake, when he notices the ring, and stops short.*)

JOHN. I hope you're satisfied, Andy.

ANDY. I'm just wondering, Mr Mackenzie, do you think—

MACKENZIE. I think nothing for a year. I'll – I'll – I'm for Scotland in the morning. (*He goes out morosely through the door.*)

DANIEL. There, Andy. There's company home for you, and good luck to you. It's a sad heart I'll have this night.

ANDY. I'm wondering what – (*He goes to the door.*) Ach! She couldn't do better herself. No ring nor nothing and a thousand pound bellows. (*He wanders out abstractedly.* DANIEL *closes the door after him and looks sadly but triumphantly across at* JOHN. ALICK *and* MARY *go to the window together and look out after* ANDY.)

DANIEL. Well, John?

JOHN (*with a sigh of intense relief and gratitude*). Dan, I've said it before, and I'll say it again, you've a great head on you, Daniel.

(CURTAIN.)

THE TROTH

CHARACTERS

EBENEZER MCKIE, a farmer
MRS MCKIE, his wife
FRANCIS MOORE, a neighbour
JOHN SMITH, a labourer in McKie's employment

The action takes place in the kitchen of Ebenezer McKie.

TIME – the middle of the nineteenth century.

This play was first produced, by Mr William Mollison's Company, at the Crown Theatre, Peckham, London, on 31 October, 1908, in Dublin on 25 November 1908, at the Gaiety Theatre, with the following cast:

EBENEZER McKIE	W. A. Mackeray
MRS McKIE	Josephine Woodward
FRANCIS MOORE	Whitford Kane
JOHN SMITH	Murray Graham

THE TROTH

The farm kitchen of EBENEZER McKIE. *There is a door at back and a window. To the left is a large, open fireplace, and to the right is a door leading to the bedroom. The kitchen is very scantily furnished and bare. There is a table at the back under the window, and a chair at each side. It is near midnight, and a candle placed on the mantel at the fireplace casts a dim light. An old muzzle-loading gun can be seen hung over the mantel. Outside the house is darkness, and a wind moans loudly as the curtain rises to discover* MRS McKIE *crouched over the fire.* JOHN SMITH *sits a little way off chafing his hands.* MRS McKIE *is a woman of some thirty-five years of age, neatly dressed, but poverty-stricken in appearance.* JOHN SMITH *is some five years her junior, and a stout, brawny type of labourer.*

MRS McKIE (*shivering*). Bless me but that's the cold night. The fire's near out, John. You're a bad hand at keeping up a fire.

SMITH. No wonder, and nothing to keep it going.

MRS McKIE. Get a lump more turf then.

SMITH. I was out just a wheen of minutes ago and there's no more turf about the place, ma'am. I could cut a lot of sticks if you like.

MRS McKIE. Na. We'll need them all for the morning. Deary me, there's not as much heat as would keep a tin of water at the boil. (*She shivers.*) Was it freezing hard?

SMITH. Aye, hard it is, ma'am. You'd hear your neb cracking if you put it round the corner of the door. (*A wind wails mournfully around the house.*)

MRS McKIE. D'ye hear the wee bit of a cold wind singing? It's coming in off the old grey sea, and it would cut you to the bone. (*Wistfully.*) D'ye think the dead be cold, John?

SMITH (*startled*). What? Sure they've neither heat nor cold. It's all one to them. (*Looking at her curiously.*) You're talking strange, ma'am.

MRS McKIE. Aye. And whiles when I be thinking of my wee boy lying his lone in the old graveyard beyont, I be wishing I was near to

93

hap him.

SMITH (*consolingly*). It was a sore loss to you, ma'am. But maybe he's better where he is.

MRS McKIE. He was a bonnie wee boy. My poor wee son.

SMITH. Cheer up, ma'am. There's no way like being right and hearty, and there's nothing to beat arguing to lift you out of yourself. If you like I'll argue politics with you.

MRS McKIE. No. I've no head for them things at all. But 'deed now, John, I hear you're a terrible old Tory.

SMITH. I am, indeed, and right proud I am of it too. And if I had it I'd send every pound I owned to turning all the people Tory.

MRS McKIE (*absently*). I wonder will Ebenezer's sister send us that money?

SMITH. Was it money the master went to fetch the night at Ballyhanlon, ma'am?

MRS McKIE. It was. (*Suspiciously.*) Who told you?

SMITH (*carelessly*). Nobody told me. I was expecting that's what he went for. Is the master's sister a well-doing woman, ma'am? I heard she was.

MRS McKIE. If Ebenezer had treated her a wee bit more decent at the time the old McKie, their father, was buried, he might have had more chance of getting some from her the now. But I'm feared, John. (*Whispering.*) He kept fifty pounds off her that was hers by right.

SMITH. Aye?

MRS McKIE. Whist. Don't be telling anyone about it. He had intended to pay it, but what with the bad harvests this two years and one thing and another I'm feared it's all gone. Ah, John, but this is the terrible time of trouble I suppose you heard they're starting the evicting to-morrow?

SMITH. Aye. D'ye know what I say is at the bottom of all this serving of writs and evicting on the estate, ma'am?

MRS McKIE. Ach, what could it be but the bad harvests this two years, and that hard old niggard of a landlord.

SMITH. Aye. Niggard or no niggard, he wouldn't have done a ha'pworth only for them Moores and Maguires and Maginnesses, and that connection, talking and threatening what they'd do on him if he wouldn't let them off the rent this winter. (*Emphatically.*) Old Colonel Fotheringham's one of the right sort, and don't you be forgetting it, ma'am.

MRS McKIE (*contemptuously*). Ach. You're always backing up the quality. D'ye not know that every tenant on the estate, barring one or two, couldn't pay up, and they're every one of them noticed, there's no odds. And I heard the bailiffs were for Moore's first, poor creature, and be here the next. Och anee, John Smith, we'll be wandering the wide world the morrow. (*She breaks down and cries silently.*)

SMITH (*softening*). Cheer up, ma'am. D'ye think the master's sister would let the old place go and her rolling in money? Man a dear, it'll be lying ready for him the night in Ballyhanlon, don't you be a bit afeared. (*More or less to himself.*) It's the price of Moore and that lot raising all the bad talk against the landlord. Heth the evicting will soon settle them.

MRS McKIE (*hopelessly*). It'll settle more than them, John, I'm thinking.

SMITH. Did you say the bailiffs were for Francey Moore's?

MRS McKIE. Deed they are, John. And him and his poor wee bit of a wife ailing. God preserve us! I heard they hadn't tasted anything but the Indian meal this six weeks, and her dying of the black fever.

SMITH. Aye. It's a pity of Moore in some ways too. But he shouldn't have talked the way he done.

MRS McKIE. A pretty wee girl she was, the same Mary Moore, with her black hair and her bonnie blue eyes. They say there's no chance of her coming round.

SMITH. Aye. I believe he's running about half out of his mind about her. (*He starts.*) I thought I heard somebody in the road outside. (*He goes toward the window and looks out.*) Aye. It's him you were talking about – Francey Moore. (*Knocking at the door.*)

MRS McKIE. Poor soul! Let him in, John. (SMITH *opens the door and* MOORE *enters. He is a nervous-looking man, with unkempt hair, black beard and wild dark eyes.*)

SMITH (*morosely*). How're you?

MOORE. Good evening. (*He seems benumbed with cold, and stands awkwardly near the door.*)

MRS McKIE. Come here, Francey, and warm yourself. You'll be starved with cold that night.

MOORE. It's terrible cold. (*He seats himself to the left of the table apparently unmindful of her invitation.* SMITH *stands near the door to the right eyeing him disapprovingly.*)

SMITH. How's it with you down there?

MOORE (*with an effort to keep back the agony that shows in his voice*). Ah, my God. I couldn't stay in the house. The priest is in, and she's dying. It's only a matter of minutes now. (*After a pause.*) I thought I'd have catched McKie in.

MRS McKIE. He's down at Ballyhanlon the night to see about a bit of money to help to pay the rent. It's the hard and terrible times, Francey.

MOORE. I wouldn't mind it only for the wife, and it's killing her. Aye. *He* killed her.

SMITH. She might have a chance yet, man. I heard that.

MOORE. She – she's dying. I heard the death rattling in her throat, and I couldn't stand it, I couldn't bear it any longer. I came out of the house. I watched my two sons dying, gasping, fighting for air. I canna watch my wife.

SMITH (*listening*). There's the master's step. (MCKIE *opens the door and enters. He is a middle aged man of some forty years and more, of powerful build, but gaunt with privation. He is weary and haggard-looking, and takes but little interest in the people in his kitchen. He throws his overcoat over a chair, and then goes and sits down to the left at the table almost opposite* MOORE, *and lets his head fall listlessly on his hands.*)

MRS McKIE (*watching her husband intently, and speaking with suppressed excitement*). Had you any luck? Was it no there?

McKIE. There was nothing. Not a line nor a scrap. (*Bitterly.*) My God, she might have forgiven me. She might have remembered the old place to no let it go to the strangers – the old home of the McKies. I told her in the letter I sent about remembering when we were children together under the same thatch roof, but she must have hardened her heart agin me. Three times I wrote her and she never—

SMITH. I bid you good night, sir. (*He goes to the door.*) Is there anything you'd be wanting in the morning?

McKIE (*listlessly*). Nothing. Barring you give us a hand to carry out them chairs and things. You're paid up to to-night, aren't you?

SMITH. Aye. You give it to me yesterday, all but ten shillings. But I can thole a bit. (*With a touch of malicious pride.*) I have got a job.

McKIE. Aye?

SMITH. Yes. I'm hiring with the gardener up at the demesne. Good night. (*He goes out and is heard whistling blithely.*)

McKIE (*raising his head, and then suddenly realising that* MOORE *is seated opposite him.*) Is that you, Francey? I didn't notice you before.

MOORE. It is.

McKIE (*turning to his wife*). Not a line nor a scrap did she send. I met Michael Malone, Annie, and he gave me a wee drop – just a wee drop to keep out the cold. (*He brings a small bottle of whiskey out of his pocket. Then, suddenly turning to* Moore.) Who do you

96

think I saw riding in with a policeman ahind him?

MOORE. The landlord.

McKIE. Aye. Colonel Fotheringham himself. I heard he was going to the agent's, so I walked out after him and went there, for I thought to myself that maybe if I could get speaking to him it might turn him. But they ordered me out like a dog when they heard I'd no money with me.

MRS McKIE He's here himself, then?

McKIE. Aye. He's coming back again to the hall the night.

MOORE (*eagerly*). Late? He'll be late coming? He'll no be by yet?

McKIE. No. He'll no be by yet. Maybe you think if you catched him you could soften him to you. (*Bitterly.*) Pah! Could you soften a stone?

MOORE (*intensely*). Maybe –

McKIE (*contemptuously*). Maybe! Do you know what I heard? The old widow Maguire of the whin head give him the black curse on her knees and him riding past. And he snappit his fingers at her and laughed.

MOORE (*half to himself*). Them that gets the black curse dies that same night.

McKIE (*looking in a wondering way at* MOORE, *and then seeing his wife regarding the latter with fear in her eyes*). Here. Get to bed, woman dear. You'll be perished with cold.

MRS McKIE (*rising obediently and going towards the bedroom door*). Deed aye. I'd be the better. Good night to you both and don't be long. I'm feared by myself in the dark.

McKIE. We'll no be long. (MRS McKIE *goes out.*) Here. Take a drop, Francey. (*He pours some of the whiskey into a cup.*) It'll hearten you. Your wife – is she any the better?

MOORE (*broken-heartedly*). May God rest her soul this night.

McKIE. She be dying?

MOORE (*hopelessly*). Aye.

McKIE. I'm sorry for you, Francey. I lost a wee boy of my own. I'm sorry for you.

MOORE. God, but it's hard to loose house and home and wife and wains, and no ways for to beat if off. What are you for doing yourself? Can you pay up?

McKIE. I canna.

MOORE. They're for my place the morrow, and they're for redding you out next.

McKIE. Redding me out?

MOORE. Aye. And then when you're gone the people will be coming and pointing to the place, and the stranger they put in will be coming out, and they'll ask him who it belonged till, and no one to tell them it was once the McKies that owned it. (*With increasing intensity.*) Two years ago you mind there was a bad harvest. We prayed to the landlord to be easy. He told us no. Why? Why? Because, I tell you, Ebenezer McKie, and I know. He had debts of his own – gambling debts – debts of honour as the quality calls them. Next year it was worse. No one got in the crops. They lay rotten in the fields. You and me and the rest went to him again. We might as well have been praying to them big stones up yonder on Slieve Dubh. (*With a sob in his voice.*) Then the sickness come and the wee childre – they slippit away one by one. One that was to be called after you, McKie of Ballyhanlon, and two of my own wee childre – they went away by the dark boreens, and you couldn't call them back to you now. No – not if all the rents of the world was poured into your hand.

McKIE (*tremulously*). Don't, man. Don't.

MOORE (*his voice trembling with intense passion*). A pound or two might have saved them. Aye. Only a pound or two. And now they're lying rotten under the sod, but their wee souls is crying. You can hear them in the wind crying – crying to the God that made them for vengeance. (McKIE *raises his head and looks in a startled way at* MOORE.) Who owed the hand that took and wrenched the very food from their mouths? Who was it swore to the police sergeant – I'll learn them, says he, to obey me. I've a man for every place that knows how to labour the land, not a lot of lazy, drunken swine.

McKIE (*with anger*). He said that?

MOORE. I suppose, says he, for all their talking, they'll just go out with their tails between their legs like the lot of cowardly, snarling curs they are.

McKIE (*passionately*). He called us that, did he?

MOORE. Aye.

McKIE (*wildly*). And by God, Mr Colonel Fotheringham, there was a McKie put the fear of the Lord in your boasting breed in '98, and there's another one will do it again the night. (*He starts up and reaches for the gun, then suddenly suspicious of* MOORE, *he stops and looks round at him.*)

MOORE (*smiling grimly*). You're afeared of me? Wait till you see what I put behind the barrel at the door. (*He opens the door, reaches his hand out and brings in a gun.*)

McKIE (*in an awed voice*). You mean to—

MOORE (*wildly*). Aye. I swore to do it this night, and I swore he would not escape. That's why I come to you. Listen. We can get him as he comes through the Glen. We can each take a side of the road. One side has a hedge with brambly land and the other across from it is most whins with the demesne wall behind. It's the only two places you can get him from. But I warn you. Him that takes the whinny side runs a chance of the rope. Fair do. We'll toss for it. If you win, you can have the pick.

McKIE. Afore I toss will you make me a promise. I want a promise off you, Francey Moore. We two have seen our wee children, as you say, slip by beyont us, and we have seen the brown earth shovelled over them the way you would bury a dog. They were buried the same day – my son and your own. Mine in the old meeting-house green and yours in the chapel graveyard, and you grippit my hand when I met you at the roads end, and you cried like a child. And I lay that same night at the same place we're going to to-night, but the hand of the Lord turned him back, and he came not by me. But I said to myself he should die. And the one thing I ask you to promise is this. If one's catched, he's no to tell tales on the other, and that other will look after his wife for him.

MOORE. I promise you.

McKIE. Swear it, man. Swear it.

MOORE. I swear it by the Lord God in Heaven.

McKIE (*taking a coin from his pocket and tossing it on the table*). Head or harp?

MOORE. Head. (*They both look at the coin.*) I've lost. I'll have to take to the whins.

McKIE. It will be a hard job to escape from your place.

MOORE. I'll chance it.

McKIE. But mind what you swore.

MOORE. You can trust me, and I can do the same with you. I want a cap off you for the gun. That's what I come for the night. (MCKIE *goes across to the mantel, takes down a small box and extracts a few caps from it. He leaves it on the table and hands some to* MOORE.) He'll be here in a couple of minutes. Hurry.

McKIE (*taking down the gun and going across near the door*). I'll lock the door and take the key with me. If John Smith took a notion to come back, I'm feared he'd be for noticing the gun away. (*He follows* MOORE *out through the door and locks it. A pause.*)

MRS McKIE (*without*). Ebenezer! Ebenezer! (*She comes out into the kitchen.*) Ebenezer! He's away. I thought I might have given that poor creature Moore this half pound of tea I found in the drawer.

(*She goes to the door and tries to open it.*) He's locked it! (*She shivers.*) It's cold. (*Uneasily.*) There's something queer about that Francey Moore. His eyes were flaming like that old cat of Mahaffy's looking at you in the darkness of the byre. He's next mad, that man, about his wife. She's not long for this world, I'm thinking. (*Knocking at the door.*) God have mercy. Who's that?

SMITH (*without*). It's me, John Smith. (*He goes round to the window.*)

MRS McKIE. Aye. You can look through the broke pane. What's the matter?

SMITH. I thought I would have got Moore here. His wife died a wee while ago. I'm after hearing it at home from the neighbours.

MRS McKIE. Well-a-well. She was a pretty wee girl in her time.

SMITH. I thought I'd have met the master and Moore coming down, but there was no sight of them.

MRS McKIE. The master – (*She catches sight of the box of caps, lifts them, and then with quick suspicion, her eyes travel over to where the gun used to hang.*) Ah! God bless us!

SMITH (*startled*). What ails you, ma'am?

MRS McKIE (*trembling violently, but recovering herself*). It was a nail catched me. You'd be the better of your bed, I'm thinking. (*A shot rings out in the distance. A short pause. Then another.*)

SMITH. D'ye hear yon? (*With a sudden suspicion in his voice.*) I say, ma'am.

MRS McKIE. Well?

SMITH. Did the master go out with Moore next the Glen?

MRS McKIE. The master? He's no out of the house. He was cold and I was getting him a wee drop to warm him. (*She reaches for the bottle on the table.*)

SMITH. Her head's turned—. (*A sound of shouting in the distance.*) What's yon?

MRS McKIE. What?

SMITH (*listening intently*). Shouting or something down the Glen! (*More shouting.*) Boys, and it's where the shots went off too! (*Renewed noise.*) D'ye no hear it? There's something wrong. I must away to see what it is. (*He rushes away quickly. MRS McKIE listens until assured he is gone and, then, overcome, clutches at the table for support.*)

MRS McKIE. The landlord! He was to come up the Glen to-night. Oh, Lord God, preserve my husband, keep him from evil, save him from the shedding of blood. Save him, ah, God, my Saviour, save him! (*She kneels wildly at the table. A sound of soft footfalls outside makes her catch her breath and listen. McKIE suddenly unlocks the door and appears. He goes lightly across the kitchen, hangs up the gun, and is just going through the bedroom door when his wife calls.*) Ebenezer! What have you been up to? What have you done? (*He remains silent.*) Where is Moore? What has he done? Ah, there was bad in the dark man. I seen it in his eye.

McKIE. Sh. Get to your bed, woman.

MRS McKIE. I'm feared, Ebenezer, for John Smith was round, and he asked had you and Moore gone down by the Glen.

McKIE. Ah, great God! And what did you say, woman? (*He rushes forward and grasps her almost fiercely by the hands.*)

MRS McKIE. I told him a lie. I said you were in your bed. Whist. (*A murmuring of voices can be heard.*) D'ye hear yon? (*The voices come nearer.*)

McKIE. Canny with the light. (*He blows out the candle at the table.*)

MRS McKIE (*going to the window and looking out cautiously.*) Lord have mercy! They're carrying something up the road. (*She turns to her husband.*) Ebenezer! In the mercy of God, speak! Did you do it? (*Hysterically.*) Ah, for God's sake, did you?

McKIE. Whist. (*Sound of footsteps.*) Here's someone. Dinna let them in.

SMITH (*hurriedly coming to the window and speaking in a hushed awed voice.*) God bless us! I never thought he was that mad!

MRS McKIE. What is it?

SMITH. Francey Moore's in the hands of the police yonder. He shot the landlord, old Colonel Fotheringham, dead in the Glen, and they catched him among the whins. He'll swing for it now. I suppose it was the wife dying turned his head. They are bringing him and the body up by the house here to the barracks. (*He goes away back again.*)

MRS McKIE (*in a voice of terror*). Ebenezer! Ebenezer! Was it you or him done it? (*The voices now come very near.*)

McKIE (*standing where the darkness of the kitchen almost hides him.*) Hold your tongue, woman. Are they passed yet?

MRS McKIE (*looking out*). No yet. (*She turns to him with a gesture of horror.*) It was you. I can see it in your eye. You killed him.

McKIE (*breathlessly*). Whist. Are they passed yet?

MRS McKIE (*as the sound of the voices dies away*). They're gone. (*She goes forward, looks into his eyes, and then involuntarily shrinks back.*) It was *you* that killed him.

McKIE. Peace, woman. (*He stretches out his hands towards her appealingly. She makes no movement.*) Moore has no wife.

(CURTAIN.)

101

RED TURF

A PLAY IN ONE ACT

TO

THE RT. HON. W. F. BAILEY,

P.C., C.B.

CHARACTERS

MARTIN BURKE, a farmer
MARY BURKE, his wife
MICHAEL FLANAGAN (the elder), a farmer
MICHAEL FLANAGAN (the younger), his son
JOHN HEFFERNAN, an old man

The action takes place in the bog lands in the West of Ireland.

TIME – the present day (1911)

This play was first produced at the Grand Opera House, Belfast, by the Ulster Literary Theatre, on 5 December 1911, with the following cast:

MARTIN BURKE	Joseph Campbell
MARY BURKE	Josephine Mayne
MICHAEL FLANAGAN (the elder)	Ross Canmer
MICHAEL FLANAGAN (the younger)	C. K. Ayre
JOHN HEFFERNAN	J. M. Harding

RED TURF

A peasant kitchen in the West country, humbly but comfortably furnished. There is a window and a door at the back, the window looking out on low lying lands that fringe a vast expanse of bog. There is another door leading off to an inner room. To the left is a fireplace at which a fire is burning. Some sods of turf piled in a corner near it. The door to the inner room is slightly ajar, and the sound of a woman singing a child to sleep can be heard. It is bright noon-day, and the sun is shining without. There is a rapping at the door, and MARY BURKE *opens the room door and comes softly into the kitchen, She is a well-set woman, with a quick, assertive manner, and somewhat hard of feature. She goes to the door at the back and quickly opens it. An old man,* JOHN HEFFERNAN, *is standing without, with a long bundle of rushes under his arm.*

MARY. Why! Good-morrow, John!

JOHN. The blessing of God be on all here.

MARY. And with you too, John. Come in.

JOHN (*hobbling in slowly*). Its the fine day this, thanks be to God.

MARY. Its the fine weather, surely. (*She gives him a curt look, and places a chair for him at the side of the window.*)

JOHN (*placing the bundle he carries on a small table near the window*). And how is the child, Mrs Burke?

MARY. Sleeping it is now. A fine, strong, little boy, God be thanked.

JOHN (*somewhat shyly*). The bit of a goat I have is run dry, Mary, and I come to ask if you could as much as give me a drop for to tide me over the morrow. It's queer tasting the tea is without the bit of a white drop in it.

MARY. Surely – surely. (*She goes over to a crock near the dresser.*) Did you bring a vessel with you?

JOHN. No, I did not then. For I was thinking to myself if I bring a big vessel she may not like, and if I bring a small vessel she may not like either, so I leave it to yourself, Mrs Burke, and musha, may God be good to you as you may be to me.

MARY (*curtly*). There. There. (*She lifts a can down from the dresser and fills it with milk from the crock.*) I wouldn't grudge the ould and the poor like the pensions officers.

JOHN. No, glory be to God, you would not indeed and deed. (*He takes the can from her.*) Where is himself this day?

MARY. Martin is down by the cross roads at Ballinlea.

JOHN (*curiously*). He'll be waiting someone, so?

MARY. He is waiting the agent and an engineer from Athenry this day.

JOHN. The agent. Are they for settling the dispute between you and the Flanagans this day? Well! Well! I heard Father Nolan say it was the map would settle it surely.

MARY. What needs the map for to be settling it? Isn't it mine, and will be always till time is done.

JOHN (*meekly*). Flanagan told me that when his father bought the holding next you, that he was given a promise of turbary on the bog below you, and was showed it on the map at the rent office.

MARY (*with a flash of temper*). If he had a right itself, isn't it strange that he'd be waiting it till my father was dead and buried. And if Martin isn't for standing up to my rights, it's over my own dead body they will be crossing to draw what was never theirs. It's not on my land with his asses and his carts Mike Flanagan will be coming.

JOHN (*with demure malice*). It's the map will do it surely. Isn't it by the maps all the great lords and ladies be holding of their estates, and be buying and selling of them.

MARY. Martin Burke and myself will be letting no Flanagan be tramping on our lands, John Heffernan.

JOHN (*apparently not heeding her*). It's wonderful the maps is for the truth. The sappers that come here ten years ago were telling me they had come to look an acre of land that was missed from the map of the County of Galway, and it the biggest county of Ireland. And where d'ye think now found it? In John Haverty's purtas! Ah! The maps is the divil surely. (*Curiously.*) And it was this day they were coming, Mary Burke?

MARY. Himself got a letter two days ago from the agent that he was for setting out Flanagan's turbary this day.

JOHN. Isn't it a great thing now to have hard words and fighting put down, and a little scrapeen of a map to be doing it all? (MARY BURKE *does not answer him, but goes over to the fire and puts on some fresh sods of turf.*) And it's great turf entirely that you have, Mrs Burke. Black stone turf. It has the great red colour when the

106

fire is on it so. Turf in dispute aye burns red they say.

MARY. Let you not be naming it disputed turf. There is none but ourselves has the right to it.

JOHN. I will not be raising of you, Mrs Burke. D'ye see this. (*He shows her the bundle of rushes.*)

MARY. I was wondering what manner of thing you had concealed in it.

JOHN. It's many the bite and the sup it gave me surely, this same, when I was a young, supple fellow, and not feared of drowndings and bog holes.

MARY (*coming closer*). Is it the butt of a gun I see sticking in it?

JOHN. And nothing else is it. (*He proceeds to take off the covering of rushes and reveals an old-fashioned fowling piece in good repair.*) I was thinking of leaving it with you, Mrs Burke, for many the bite and sup you gave me.

MARY. I only did what was neighbourly, John.

JOHN. Well, it's getting a done old man I am and near dark, and let alone I with no licence paid this year and the gauger and the sergeant cocking their ears for the sound of it. Keep it for me, Mrs Burke. It's himself will be getting you an odd hare or two and a moorcock or maybe a brattle at a pheasant in the corn.

MARY. I'll tell himself so. Is it loaded?

JOHN. It is. But let you not be feared. Put it by you in the corner. I'm feared of the gauger, Mrs Burke. (*He hobbles over and places the gun against the wall, near the table, then turns and makes for the door.*) Musha and may God bless the kindly heart and the open hand that ye always had for the poor. (*He walks slowly to the door.*)

MARY. God speed you, John. (*He opens the door and passes out, then stops suddenly and peers into the distance.*)

JOHN. Would that be himself yonder with the men?

MARY. Where? (*She comes forward quickly and looks out of the door beside him.*)

JOHN. Down by the haggart they are.

MARY (*after a keen scrutiny*). It's himself, surely. They never come this way.

JOHN. It's by Flanagan's boreen they've come across. Aye, they have the spades with them, and are settling it so. Well, I'll bid you the time of day, Mrs Burke, and please God may you suffer no loss with them down beyond.

MARY (*watching with eager interest the movements of the group in the distance*). If you pass by them, John, tell Martin not to be

107

long coming.

JOHN. I will so. (*He hobbles away.*)

MARY (*after a pause*). Maybe the gentlemen will be coming this way, and they tired and hungry. I will get a drop for them so. (*She goes over to the dresser and busies herself getting some cups. The sound of voices in the distance can be heard. She stops suddenly and listens. The voices come nearer, and it is soon easy to distinguish that one in particular is loud and angry above the rest.*) 'Tis himself so. He was a man aye had this temper handy. (*She goes to the door, opens it, and waits expectantly.*)

MARTIN (*from a little distance without, his voice almost a shout*). I defy you to cut a sod of turf on it. (*There is the sound of a big man's sarcastic laugh in answer.*)

MARY (*working herself into a heat of passion*). It is Martin is wronged surely. (*She calls out.*) What are you laughing at himself for, Mike Flanagan?

MIKE FLANAGAN (*without*). Let you be shutting the door on yourself, Martin Burke, and your wife there, and not be interfering with the law. (MARTIN BURKE *makes no answer, but appears in the doorway. His wife looks at him anxiously and follows him in, closing the door.*)

MARY. Sit down, man. You're all in a fever. What have they been doing on you?

MARTIN (*a small wiry man who shows signs of passion inflamed by drink which he has taken*). Doing on me, is it? (*He flings himself into the chair.*) It's the greatest wrong in the world they have been doing on me. Split my fine stone bank in two and give Flanagan the big half and left me the far end half drownded in water, the ould dirty red turf they left me.

MARY. The far bank to you?

MARTIN. Aye, the far bank, woman. And they give him the one at the end of the land here. The one I was meaning when it was cut for a bit of a bog garden and pasture next the haggart.

MARY (*with a vindictive ring in her voice*). And is it letting that go you be?

MARTIN (*sullenly*). Wasn't it give him this day by the engineer and the agent according to the map. And they had Flanagan with his spade out to come and mark it, for I refused the use of mine to them. And they warned me not to touch a sod of it.

MARY. Oh musha! And you'd be letting go the land that my father and my father's father had from time was – that was part of my fortune to you.

MARTIN. It's not my fault the way it is.

MARY (*sarcastically*). And they'll allow you in the rent so?

MARTIN. Allow in the rent is it? They told me it was never in the rent. That neither I nor you nor your father ever paid a penny piece for it.

MARY. You can take the case to the county court, and the judge will give it back to us so.

MARTIN. Haven't they got it on the map now and it cannot be altered. Didn't they warn me this day not to be going to law like a fool to be throwing my money into the sea.

MARY (*madly*). I would to God you had let me know, and I would have talked to them. You fool soft creature. (*She mocks him.*) With your "I suppose you're right, your honour." and "I suppose the map must be right, your honour," as ye done at the county court when Flanagan won the right of way against ye. Aye, and now he can be coming with the smile on his twisty face, knocking down the stones of the gaps would be in his road, on and past the very door here, down by the haggard and on to the turf, him and his sons and his asses and his carts. Whistling and shouting and laughing they'll be and you within feared to say one word – and them tramping and trespassing—

MARTIN. Who said I was for letting him?

MARY. Och, don't I know ye? Haven't I lived with you long enough now to know the kind of you. Did I ever see you stand up as a man and fight your rights. Never. With your "Father Nolan says this and we oughtn't to go agin his reverence," and "James Haverty wanted that and I would like to oblige him" (*almost crying with anger*) – and now there's my own land slipping from an under us.

MARTIN. Didn't I do and say all that I could?

MARY (*more quietly*). D'ye remember when you come over here to make the match? D'ye remember my father coming down with you and stretching out his hand and saying, "Show me the girl has a fortune of a bank of turf like that, Martin Burke. Stone turf, twice ten spits deep that would keep the hearth lit for a hundred years." D'ye remember that, Martin Burke? And where's my stone turf now and my hundred years' fire? Give away. Give away with your old soft hearted slinking ways. You haven't the guts to stand for your rights and fight for your wife and your children. (*With bitter mockery.*) "God bless your honour," and "Thank your honour for eaving us a bit." Did you think of me and my children, and them that's to come after us? Is it to the Flanagans now

109

they'll be going in time to come begging for a scraw to keep the purtas boiling?

MARTIN (*despondently*). What could I be doing more?

MARY. No. Your like could be doing no more. Oh to God! that I had my father here, that never feared any man. D'ye think the Flanagans dare do the like on him? There never was any talk of these things till you came, and they saw the sort of a man you were.

MARTIN. Didn't the agent tell me himself this day that your father had less claim itself to that bog than the curlews would be flying over it.

MARY. And would you be letting the like of that talk be closing your mouth. Well, if you think so then, let them trample on ye. Let the Flanagans be pushing you in the gutter of a fair day and you with your gentleman's ways stepping aside and thanking of them.

MARTIN (*maddened*). Hold your accursed tongue. (*There is a sullen silence. Then the door swings open and young* MICHAEL FLANAGAN *appears without. He knocks and steps in jauntily.*)

YOUNG MICHAEL. Good day to you both. (*The* BURKES *do not answer.*) My father would be glad of a word with Martin, apart.

MARY. Can't he come himself and be speaking? Is it feared of the house of the Burkes he is?

YOUNG MICHAEL (*with a derisive smile*). It's not feared he is or myself either of any Burke that breathed. But he wanted to have a word with himself there apart.

(MARTIN *starts from his seat as if to go,* MARY BURKE *motions him back.*)

MARY. You'll go none out to speak till him, Martin Burke. Let him come himself and speak if he's wanting.

YOUNG MICHAEL. It was for a civil word I came here, Mrs Burke. And it's because himself there isn't the bad man at heart that my father wanted him by himself and not you to be there raging the heart out of him with your flaming tinker's tongue. (*He steps out quickly and slams the door to after himself.*)

MARY. Aren't you the poor man to be sitting there and let him be speaking that way of your wife?

MARTIN (*quietly*). I was thinking of Father Nolan, and what he was saying about disputes last Sunday from the Altar. And I for the station at Kilglass this night and my sins weighty on me. God help me. (*He seems to mutter a prayer and crosses himself devoutly.* MARY BURKE *looks at him curiously and makes as if to speak, then restrains herself. A silence.*) Let us not be making more bad blood between us this night and more sin.

MARY (*in an intense bitter voice*). It's no more I'll be saying this day. It's an end of talking I've made to your like, surely.

(*The sound of the child waking and crying in the room off.* MARY BURKE *rises and goes in.*)

MARTIN. God knows that if it's a good heart is in you, it's the bitter words is hiding it from me. (*The sound of the child crying.* MARY BURKE'S *voice can be heard soothing it, and then she begins to sing softly.* MARTIN BURKE *rises and goes slowly to the door, opens it and looks out. He apparently sees some one coming and retreats back into the kitchen.* MICHAEL FLANAGAN *the elder, a big powerful man with a masterful strong face, appears in the doorway. He knocks, and then steps in.*)

FLANAGAN. I wanted to be talking to you, and without your wife. Is she out?

MARTIN. She's within there with the child. What is it you're wanting of me?

FLANAGAN. I want to talk straight till ye, Martin Burke. Is it to be the peace between us? Speak out your mind and tell me.

MARTIN. Isn't it all one and the same to your kind now. You have got all ye wanted. What needs ye be seeking more.

FLANAGAN. It's a bit of a spread bank we'd be wanting, and they said we could ask you for it. You can give it or not as you please. Is it to be the civil word and obliging or black looks between us? Say it out to me.

MARTIN. There'll be no civil word between us, Michael Flanagan. Is it coming on my own land that's left you are to spread your blasted turf? Is it not content you are with trampling your right of way across my meadow land making gaps in my fences and cutting turf upon my banks, but you must be coming into my very house—

FLANAGAN. I come none into your house but to ask you a civil question. Is it to be peace or war between us? And if it's to be war between us I'll make you sorrow for it.

MARTIN. Get you without the door.

FLANAGAN (*his temper rising*). Couldn't I break the little snap of a body you have between my two big wrists if ever you tongue me here or anywhere else?

MARTIN (*coming closer*). You can take the word back with you, and tell your wife and your children, and all your connection is a black scourge on the land, that it's war – aye, and bloody war it'll be – between us. So let you be feared of me from this day out.

FLANAGAN. Afeard of you, is it? (*He laughs grimly.*) No, not if all the dykes were full of Burkes on a dark night and them with red murder in their hands would I be feared. So lay to when and where you may, I care not that for ye. (*He snaps his fingers contemptuously.*) I have the right of you and the law of you and what's more, I and my sons are going down to start the facing of our bank this day. So take ease and comfort to your mind with that. (*He turns to go.*) Come out and shout and curse, you and your wife, with her foul mouth on her. (*He slams the door to and goes away.*) (MARTIN BURKE *stands trembling with anger in the kitchen. His eyes light on the gun, and he stares as if fascinated, moves towards it slowly, and then suddenly grips it in his hands.* MARY BURKE *opens the door of the inner room and stands staring aghast at him.*)

MARY. For the love of God, Martin Burke, put down that thing.

MARTIN. Where got ye this?

MARY. John Heffernan left it in. He was feared of the gauger and the police looking the licence. Have a care, man, its loaded.

MARTIN (*with a grim smile*). It's a great weapon, surely. It would kill or scare d'ye think? Eh, woman?

MARY. Put it down, Martin Burke, for the love of God. It's no way to be handling a gun the way you are.

MARTIN. You heard him with me?

MARY. It was Mike Flanagan?

MARTIN. Aye. Wouldn't you know the big voice of him. He would break me is it? Across his two wrists? (*He examines the cap.*)

MARY. For the love of God would you leave it down. Leave it down and go in and look at the child sleeping. It would take the badness from your mind the same as it did with me.

MARTIN (*grimly*). D'ye think it? D'ye think is the badness away from ye? What about the morrow when we'd be raising to see the Flanagans cutting on your great stone bank and trampling your father's meadows. Eh, woman? I know ye. You'll be coming to me with your bitter, biting tongue and your scalding words and what your father would have done. And them without there raising a banter of hell. This night the Flanagans will fear me. This night you'll fear me. You'll fear to sleep the same bed with me and my gallows rope round my neck. (*The sound of horses and carts without and the shouts of the* FLANAGANS.) Aye, they're coming surely, d'ye hear them? Faith and I'll make them have a dread of my land as a fiery flame the like no Flanagan will so much as put his hand across a mearing, fearing it blast and wither him. (*Madly.*) I'll teach him and his breed to keep his bounds this side of damnation for ever. (*He makes towards the door.*)

MARY (*clutching hold of him*). Martin! Martin! Let them be. For the love of God—

MARTIN. Hold off me. (*He throws her roughly aside, pulls the door wide open and shouts.*) Let you all be feared of me now, Mike Flanagan. (*There is a derisive shout in answer.*)

MARY (*struggling with him again*). Ah, for the love of Almighty God, Martin Burke, is it the gallows you'd be making me a widow with. (*He breaks her grasp with brutal strength, and throwing her inside the kitchen slams the door to.*)

MARTIN (*without*). D'ye come off that bank, Mike Flanagan, before I blow your soul to hell.

(*There is a laugh, then the report of a gun. A cry of horror from the younger* FLANAGAN.)

MARY BURKE *falls senseless towards the door. The child in the room off, awakened, begins to cry softly. There is no other sound.*

(CURTAIN.)

PHANTOMS

A COMEDY OR TRAGEDY IN ONE ACT

CHARACTERS

GNU, an old man, maker of weapons
HAG U., his wife
DANON, their bondsman
SEEKI, a tribal chief
THE GOWLAN, an outlaw
SEEVA, his daughter

TIME – the bronze age or thereabouts.

PLACE – the clearing at Gnu's smithy, on a steep mountain-side overlooking rich pasture lands far below.

The smithy hut is on one side; on the other are overhanging rocks; in the background, a stone wall with a gap giving access to an unseen pass and gateway lower down.

This play was first produced at the Gaiety Theatre, Dublin, in December 1923.

116

PHANTOMS

HAG U., *an old woman, is seated on a rough stone at the back near wall, stirring a pot hung over a fire. There are herbs beside her, which from time to time she picks, and throws into the pot.*

From the open door of the hut can be heard the sounds of metal being hammered by GNU, *her husband.*

All kinds of primitive weapons lie carelessly along the stone wall. There are bundles of spear-shafts and lance-shafts near the rocks opposite the smithy. Rough blocks of stones lie scattered in the clearing.

On the stone wall, on a great rock near the gap, DANON, *their bondsman, is perched. He should be putting an edge on the head of a new spear with which he mounts guard. But he has made a lute and is trying to play it softly.*

It is the growing dark of a summer evening.

HAG U. (*sniffing at the pot*). I like this odour. It is strong. (DANON *plays a few soft notes. She stops stirring and looks at him.*) Is it always the birds that answer your fluting?

DANON (*laying down his flute and looking into the valley*). To-night only the thrushes below are singing.

HAG U. You had better finish that spear-head.

DANON. I would rather be a herd with my sheep upon the mountains than a warrior skilled in nothing but the making of spear-heads and the slaughter of men.

HAG U. Gnarr. Fool. (*Looking into the pot.*) This is better. I will try it now. (*She goes over to the wall and searches, catches an insect, and brings it over. She touches it, as it lies on the ground, with the potstick.*) Um! The black beetle is hardy of life, but this . . . this . . . augh . . . the life has gone out of it. That is good. (GNU, *an old gnarled man, black from the smithy, comes wearily out of the doorway. He is lashing a spear-head on a shaft.*)

GNU. That is six spears now we have made to-day. Seeki may barter them from us.

117

DANON. One of the lambs you got from Seeki of the Blue Valley is sick. He will have to give you another.

HAG U. Where is the lamb?

DANON. It is within the smithy, near the hearth.

GNU. I saw it. It may still live. (*Going over to his wife.*) Is the mess good?

HAG U. It kills flies.

GNU. This is not enough. It must kill more than flies. Have you added all the witch-man told you?

HAG U. Aye.

GNU. What more?

HAG U. Listen. (*She whispers in his ear.* DANON *suddenly starts up in alarm.*)

DANON. A cry! I heard a cry. Did you not hear?

GNU. Phtt. I hear nothing. Is there someone coming?

DANON. There is no one in sight.

GNU (*going over to the wall and peering into the valley*). I did not see the Gowlan abroad to-day. That is strange.

DANON. There is no sign of life about his house all day. I do not see any of his cattle to-day by the lake shore.

HAG U. Gnarr! Listen to him. He would like us to believe it was not the Gowlan's pretty daughter he was spying for.

DANON. His sheep are on the mountain, but no herd is with them.

HAG U. The Gowlan may have travelled in the night. He goes long journeys to far places at nightfall.

GNU. There was crying in the night.

HAG U. There was.

DANON (*suddenly*). Listen! Someone cried now. Did you not hear?

GNU. It is the cries of the night you are hearing again.

DANON. The wind was coming from the west last night. It is men in the Blue Valley that were crying.

GNU (*chuckling*). The battle-axes may have been stronger than the spears we sold. (*He looks meditatively at his wife stirring the pot.*) I have been thinking since you began to make this thing to-day. It may not be wise for us to make it.

HAG U. Fool. Is it not things for the killing men you want? Do you not live by the killing of men?

GNU. Aye. But not by the killing of all men.

HAG U. It is as good to kill by poison as by weapons. Did you not sell a score of spear heads to the Gowlan last moon?

GNU. Aye. He gave two milch cows and three lambs for them. It was a good barter.

HAG U. Gnarr. Stupid one. You did not tell his enemy, Seeki. Fool. You do not know how to sell.

GNU. But Seeki bought a score of battle-axes yester evening.

HAG U. Only that I had sent word to him to beware of the Gowlan he would not have so armed himself. Give me that spear.

DANON. There! Did you not hear that cry again?
(*They all listen intently.*)

HAG U. I heard no cry. Give me that spear. (*She dips it in the pot.*) Only for your old wife there would be no trade for your weapons.

GNU. I would sooner see a death by weapons than by this. Men will not drink poison. I am sorry you lost your time making this.

HAG U. (*taking the spear-head out of the pot*). Now, wise one. This spear will make the mouth to drink with.

GNU. That may be true, indeed.

HAG U. (*with a burst of passion*). If I were young and beautiful, I would—

GNU. Stand off. (*He seizes a battle-axe.*)

HAG U. The Gowlan has a wife and many children. Otherwise I think he would be one to my liking. Or Seeki, his enemy. They are both fine men. (*She lunges at him maliciously*).

GNU. Leave down, or I hurl this axe.

HAG U. Peace. I will do you no harm. I am not a fool. I am only an old woman. And you are old. We will not kill old things. it is the young we will slay. Try this spear-thrust on the lamb that is within the smithy.

GNU (*takes the spear and goes within. He appears again at the door*). If it dies, Seeki may not give another.

HAG U. If it dies we will have many more to choose from. (*He goes inside.* DANON *ceases gazing down the valley, and turns uneasily to* HAG U.).

DANON. There is terror on me to-day. And the wind cries in the rocks. I am hearing it all day. It is like the crying of wounded in battle.

HAG U. Let you keep a good watch on the gate.

DANON. Listen. I saw eagles descending from the mountains down into the valley. Look. There goes another. They go to pick the bones of the dead.

GNU (*appearing at the doorway*). It is done. And I only scratched it with the spear-point. Go in and see it. (*The old woman goes within.*) That is a great ointment. A stab with a thorn would be like as strong as a spear. How goes the day, boy?

DANON. The day is almost gone. (*Suddenly rising.*) I see men down

119

below.

GNU (*hurrying to wall*). Those are men surely, and driving cattle. It is not herds that are driving. That is the way a raider drives the cattle of his enemy. (*Loudly.*) Come out, old wife, and see this sight. Look. There is smoke. (HAG U. *appears.*) Come, see this. Look you now. See. There is fire in the valley at the lake.

HAG U. (*grimly chuckling*). Hee. The house of the Gowlan is burning. The fool who bought the spears one moon ago. The battle-axes of Seeki were better buying. It was well for us we took the Gowlan's two milch cattle. That was a great barter. The fool. A warrior he would be, and go aplundering. Hee, hee. He will plunder no more.

GNU. I do not like this. There would have been more profit it he had been left some living. He will be so poor now, he will be able to buy no more weapons.

HAG U. I wish you had driven a harder bargain with him.

GNU. You amy empty this pot. There will be no one to buy arms. We may burn these staves.

DANON. The Gowlan may be alive.

GNU. Phtt! Alive. His house burning. His daughters and his wife, what of them? Did not Seeki tell us he would put them all to the sword? (*Musingly.*) His daughter, Seeva, too. She was lovely to look on. She was beautiful to look at herding her father's sheep upon the downs. I have crawled through the furze to watch her.

HAG U. Shame. Shame, old withered heart.

GNU (*growling*). No shame. Gnarr!

HAG U. (*spitting like a cat*). Phtt!

GNU. An end to this. We are too old to squabble. Come into the smithy, to strip the hide off the dead lamb. Let Danon keep an eye to the gate. (*He goes into the hut.*)

HAG U. If any come to the pass below, remember it is after sunset. If they would speak to us, see they are not armed, and bind them. (*She passes into the hut. A soft, wailing cry comes up from below. DANON grows suddenly rigid in a keen, listening attitude. The cry is repeated.*)

DANON. Who cries below?

VOICE OF A GIRL BELOW. Seeva!

DANON. Seeva! Seeva! The Gowlan's daughter.

VOICE. It is Seeva. Oh, Danon! Open these gates! Open! (DANON *goes swiftly through the gap. The sound of his voice below can be heard. He reappears at the gap supporting* SEEVA, *a beautiful young girl. She is trembling with terror.*)

SEEVA. Hide me, Danon. Swiftly. He is coming.

DANON. Who?

SEEVA. Seeki. Hide me. Oh, I pray you , Danon. I will die if you do not. I will die.

(*Distant shouting.*)

DANON. Here. (*He thrusts her into a crevice between the rocks, behind a bundle of staves.*) You will be safe there until . . .

(GNU *comes out of the hut.*)

GNU. I thought I heard voices—

(*Loud violent knocking below.*)

DANON. Who goes there?

THE VOICE OF SEEKI (*without*). Seeki, Chief Man of the Blue Valley.

DANON. It is after sunset. We cannot open the gate.

SEEKI. Open. Open the gate.

HAG U. (*coming out from smithy*). Who calls at the gate?

GNU. Seeki of the Valley.

HAG U. Bind his hands and noose him. Then he may enter. A man in battle-fury is dangerous. Go. (*Danon goes.*) Dip that spear in the pot. It is well to be ready for treachery.

GNU (*gleefully*). He may want new armoury. I have six new spears ready. And there is death to sell in the pot.

HAG U. We will not sell the secrets of the pot to him – yet. He comes. (SEEKI, *a wild, dishevelled man, enters. His neck is in a noose, held by* DANON, *who follows close behind.* SEEKI'*s hands are bound, but he clutches in one of them a red-coloured girdle.*

GNU (*bowing*). We are honoured, most worthy Seeki.

HAG U. (*grimacing*). We trust you come in peace.

SEEKI. Peace! *You* talk of peace. Foul – filthy – murderous—

GNU. Tighten the noose.

HAG U. Stay. Let him speak, Danon. (*Going over to him.*) Seeki of the Blue Valley seems in a rage. But there is no cause for his rage on us. If it had not been for me, you would not be standing there to spit strong words at humble friends.

SEEKI. You gave the Gowlan arms. Now you would give him shelter. Stand forth and speak, old witch. Where is he hidden?

GNU. Whom seek you?

SEEKI. The Gowlan.

HAG U. We have not seen the Gowlan.

SEEKI. You lie, old hag. He came this way. Only that I stumbled . . . look . . . his girdle . . . it was lying on your passway.

HAG U. That is not a man's girdle.

SEEKI. Ease off your strangling. Ease off, I say. I demand him. He is mine. Send him out, I say. Give me a battle-axe so I may see the red blood tumbling from him.

GNU. Listen, master. The Gowlan is not here. If he were I would sell him to you. He is worth a score of oxen.

HAG U. Seeki would like to kill the Gowlan, would he? What has the Gowlan done?

SEEKI. He came before the dawn last night with half a score of men, and set upon our dun. The gods be thanked that we had taken forethought.

HAG U. Hee, hee. Who gave thee that forethought? Only for the battle-axes of Gnu it would have gone hard with you. And how went the fortunes of the night? It is hard to know these things high up in the mountains.

SEEKI. There is none living now to call the Gowlan master, husband, or father. We shall not rest night or day until we give his body to the carrion birds of the air. Where is he, I say?

GNU. I tell you he came not here.

HAG U. He came not here.

DANON. He is not here.

SEEKI. He may come here.

GNU. He may come here.

SEEKI. He will come here, for he is still alive. He will be seeking arms, for he has none.

GNU. His men? All slain, you say?

SEEKI. All but himself.

HAG U. His wife?

SEEKI. Her body feeds that fire below.

DANON. His children?

SEEKI. They burn with her. We have stamped out all that was once the Gowlan's, so—

GNU. The little one . . . the pretty one . . .

SEEKI. She, too.

HAG U. Oh, the pretty daughter of the Gowlan. Oh, the one that Gnu would watch from the furze bushes. Hee, hee. She, too, is gone, is she? All that was once of her is in the smoke in the air. Hee, hee. It is good to see the young die, when one can be no longer young oneself. Oh, Master of the Valley, that is surely a great thing, indeed, you have done.

SEEKI. Take off this noose.

GNU. Pardon, master, but it is . . .

SEEKI. Take it off, I say. I will not harm you.

HAG U. Gnarr. But he is a fine man, this one. Not as fine as the Gowlan. The Gowlan is a mighty man. He stirs the dried hearts of

122

the old women. Arrh. It is splendid to see big men in their fury. It makes the flesh leap. Oh! It is lovely to see burnings and fires and roastings . . . Gnarr. Roastings and burnings . . .

(SEEVA *moans.*)

SEEKI (*in a white heat of passion*). There . . . is . . . some . . . one . . . hidden . . . in this place.

(*The staves that hide* SEEVA *fall apart, and she steps out dazedly before them.* SEEKI *stands staring at her, speechless.*)

HAG U. Hee, hee. So they were not all slain. There was one left. The pretty one. The young one. The apple of his eye. The delight of his life. *She* was spared, was she? Oh, there will be great clamour on the mountains after this, surely.

SEEKI. Nothing shall save the seed of the Gowlan. She shall die. Release my hand, I say.

GNU. Tighten the noose.

HAG U. No, no. Let him speak. What will you barter for this woman, master?

SEEKI. There shall be no barter.

HAG U. Then we will let her go.

SEEKI. I will follow her. She shall not live.

HAG U. Take her away, Danon. Take her away. You that would let her in. Take her away, and set her free.

(DANON *and* SEEVA *disappear.*)

SEEKI. She will soon be dead. She will burn beside her father. I have taken oath. Give me an axe.

HAG U. It is not good to break an oath. (*She takes up an axe.*) See this one. It is sharp. It is keen. It is worth a great price, for it was tempered ten times in the running water.

DANON (*appearing*). She is gone. Seeki would want to be fleet of foot to follow. He will never find her.

SEEKI. I will find her. Give me the axe.

HAG U. The payment, master?

SEEKI. If the Gowlan fall by my hand to-night, send Danon to my dun at sunrise, and he shall have the pick of the Gowlan's herds.

HAG U. We shall want a token.

SEEKI. Let him bring this girdle. I shall not fail you.

HAG U. Let him go. (GNU *and* SEEKI *pass out.*)

HAG U. So. So it was Danon, the lute player, that had pity on the pretty daughter. It is bad to be pitiful, Danon. A maker of weapons should not be pitiful. He will have no mind then in his work.

DANON. The gods keep her.

HAG U. The gods? They will only laugh. That is all. I, too, shall laugh. In the night I shall think of the Gowlan and his daughter. . . . I shall think of Seeki of the Blue Valley hunting them . . . and I will chuckle. They will hunt one another this night, and the night to come, until they pass into night. They will hide, and they will crawl, and they will creep among the rocks, spying to get the spear-cast first. They will suffer angers and agonies, hungers, thirsts, and weariness, and their minds a hell of hate and burning fires – (*she goes over to the pot.*) to-night and to-morrow night and the night to come.

> (*A sound of distant shouting. They stand silent, listening.* GNU *passes in.*)

HAG U. He is gone?

GNU. Like a hound from the leash. Listen. That is his calling to his men.

HAG U. See that he pays his barter.

GNU. He has sworn by the blood of his enemy. It is enough.

> (*A noise.*)

GNU. There is something at the gateway. I will see to the boltings. (*He goes out.*)

HAG U. Let no more in. Go you, Danon, through the smithy into the ravine behind, and see the flocks are safely houses. (DANON *obeys.*)

HAG U. I can see herds and wealth, and lands and many fine skins and woven cloths within this pot.

> (*Two figures come silently through the gap. It is* GNU *and the* GOWLAN. *The last is a powerfully-built, but worn and haggard man. He staggers through the gap and leans brokenly against the wall.*)

HAG U. (*peering at them*). Who comes?

GNU. The Gowlan.

HAG U. He is not bound.

GNU. There is no need. He has greater bonds than cords upon him.

HAG U. This is not surely he that made terror of the night?

GOWLAN (*feebly*). It is I.

HAG U. Surely that is not his voice? The Gowlan had a voice that called far hills together when he went hunting. Gnarr! I could have turned my body to a hate to go leaping with the joy of fright before him. Was it your voice last night came roaring on the winds of the west?

THE GOWLAN. Last night?

HAG U. Last night, a far-off voice cried going through the rocks.

THE GOWLAN. I was abroad last night.

GNU. There is more smoke drifting on the lake.

THE GOWLAN. It is from my haggards.

HAG U. How does your wife?

THE GOWLAN. There is no wife.

HAG U. Your children?

THE GOWLAN. They, too,

HAG U. Had he no men without?

GNU. He had no men.

GOWLAN. I have no men.

HAG U. The Gowlan speaks but little, and in riddles. Hee. He has no wife. He has no children. He has no house. He has no men. Then there is nothing left?

THE GOWLAN. There is now nothing left.

HAG U. It is true. Gnarr! There is nothing left. Nor even in himself. The Gowlan is not living. He is only a mass of live flesh. His soul is dead. Phtt. He is only meat for the eagles.

THE GOWLAN. I see your face . . . I hear you speak . . . the face is evil . . . and the words . . . I do not care. There is only one thing more to come—

(*Cries far off.*)

GNU. Listen.

HAG U. It is Seeki on the mountains, calling his hounds and men. He is alone. Let you go like a man towards him.

THE GOWLAN. I cannot go . . . to-night.

HAG U. Your enemy was here seeking you. He left this token with me. It is a pretty girdle, is it not?

(*She puts it into his hands.*)

THE GOWLAN. My daughter Seeva's girdle. He left this here. (*He bows his head in anguish.*) My pretty daughter's girdle.

HAG U. Your daughter's girdle. Gnarr! He does not think she lives.

THE GOWLAN (*rising madly*). Lives! You say . . . she . . . lives.

HAG U. Listen. Fool. Stupid one. Dolt. So long as the baying of dogs and the cry of the hunter is on the mountains to-night, know that the hare has life before the hounds.

(*The faint sounds of a hunting party are carried into the clearing.* THE GOWLAN *stands as if transfixed. Then clutching at a spear beside him, vanishes through the gap.*)

HAG U. Now there will be joy in my heart to-night. Now there will be the strong wine of the fury again in him. Oh, that I might see their meeting. There is nothing like the madness of strong men locked in battle to delight the heart.

GNU. I am weary. It is time you had the evening meal.

(*She goes, muttering, into the smithy.* GNU *watches her from beside the pot. When she has disappeared, he looks into it, and a slow, evil thought passes through his eyes. He slowly takes a branch of thorns, breaks off a twig, and shapes a goad.*)

(*The sound of* DANON'S *lute comes from above.*)

GNU. The cunning one. He has the pretty Seeva hidden. He has brought her the secret way into the ravine. (*He laughs maliciously.*) But he is not so cunning as old Gnu, his master. Gnrrh! She is not for you, young man. It is not from the furze I will be watching her to-night. She belongs to me – the master of the weapons.

(*He puts the goad into the pot, withdraws it, and feels the point.*) Come out, Hag U.

Come out. There is something here I would show you. (*She comes out towards him.*)

HAG U. (*shivering*). It is getting cold out here. Cold. And it is getting dark. My hands are numbing. (*She stretches them towards the fire.*)

GNU (*suddenly stabbing her wrists with the goad*). Gurrh. That will warm them for you. (HAG U. *makes no cry, but silently moves towards the wall, and lies motionless beside a spear-head.*)

(GNU *watches her. Curiosity impels him to draw near and examine her face. She suddenly raises herself, and stabs him furiously with the spear. He sinks back, dying, beside her.*)

HAG U. I am glad there is no one to laugh at our going.

(*She sinks back dead beside her husband. The light slowly begins to fade, except for a faint glow that comes up from the valley. The figures of a young man and woman appear in the gap. It is* DANON *and* SEEVA.)

SEEVA. There is no one here, I am afraid.

DANON. Do not be afraid. They will be gone within to sleep.

VOICE BELOW. Ho, there. Ho, there. Awake.

DANON. Who calls?

VOICE. Seeki, the Master of the Valley, bid me give the makers of weapons a message. At sunrise you may call for the fulfilling of his promise. The Gowlan is dead.

DANON. I have heard.

VOICE. There will be great peace now upon the valleys.

DANON. There will be peace. (*A silence.*) The messenger of Seeki is gone. You heard his message?

SEEVA. I have heard his message. (*A silence.*) See the old ones.

DANON. They are asleep.

126

SEEVA. I will not sleep. I will stay here, Danon. Here, in your arms.

DANON. Rest in peace, little one of my heart.

SEEVA. You will not leave me at sunrise to go to the house of my enemies.

DANON. At sunrise we will go together, but not to the dun of Seeki. But every sunrise we shall be a day's journey further from this place. Are you content?

SEEVA. I am content. And you will make no more weapons for the slaying of men.

DANON. I will make no more weapons.

> (*A pause.*)

SEEVA. These old ones . . . are they not very silent in their sleep?

DANON. Let them sleep. They are old.

> (*The twilight gradually fades out.* SEEVA *rests her head on* DANON'*s lap.*)

SEEVA. Play for us that, like them, we fall asleep.

> (DANON *softly plays a simple melody.*)

(CURTAIN.)

PETER

A COMEDY IN THREE ACTS AND
A PROLOGUE AND EPILOGUE

TO

LENNOX ROBINSON

for all the generous aid he gave the author

and

TO F. J. McCORMACK

for his creation of "Sam Partridge of Ballymena"

CHARACTERS
in order of their appearance

BILLY STEPHENS ⎱ students along with PETER
CHARLEY PRENDERGAST ⎰ at an Irish University
ROSIE, the maid at PETER'S lodgings
PETER GRAHAME, an engineering student
SAM PARTRIDGE, proprietor of the Excelsior Hotel, Portahoy
TOM, an old waiter
JOHN MCCLEERY, MRS ANN MCCLEERY, a retired shopkeeper
and his wife, guests at the Excelsior Hotel
COLONEL BLAKE, an old Indian Army Officer
MRS BLAKE, his wife
JOAN BLAKE, their niece
NELSON SCOTT, Inspector for Tourist Agencies
BUTTONS, Page boy at the Excelsior Hotel
MISS VAN DE MEIZER, an American visitor, guest at the Excelsior

Peter was first produced at the Abbey Theatre, Dublin, on the 28th January, 1930, with the following cast:

PETER GRAHAME	Arthur Shields
CHARLEY PRENDERGAST	Denis O'Dea
BILLY STEPHENS	Fred Johnson
ROSIE	Gertrude Quinn
SAM PARTRIDGE	F. J. McCormick
MRS ANN MCCLEERY	Maureen Delaney
MR JOHN MCCLEERY	Eric Gorman
TOM	Barry Fitzgerald
MR S. NELSON SCOTT	P. J. Carolan
COLONEL BLAKE	Michael Scott
MRS BLAKE	Meriel Moore
JOAN BLAKE	Eileen Crowe

GUESTS — Christine Hayden, Frolie Mulhern, U. Wright, J. Linnane

THE BLUE ROOM GIRLS — Sara Patrick, Cepta Cullen, Doreen Cuthbert, Chris Sheelan

BUTTONS — P. Farrell

The play was produced by Lennox Robinson

PETER

PROLOGUE

The sitting room of PETER GRAHAME'S *dingy lodgings on the first floor. A door at back of landing, another to bed-room on the right. A large window to the left overlooking the street. Sideboard, bookshelf, table, piano, chairs; books and glasses, cigarette packets, etc.*
The time is about 1 a.m.

PETER (*shutting door at back*). Goodnight, Stephens. Goodnight, Charley. Goodnight!
   (*A pause. He makes his way wearily over to the armchair, sits down, slowly takes off his collar and tie, then his shoes. He stares moodily at his socks. One of them is badly holed and his toes are showing through it. He pulls it off with an effort and examines it, then throws it carelessly aside, rises and walks slowly towards his bedroom. He suddenly sees his hat lying on the floor in front of him, gives it an exasperated kick, opens his bedroom door and switches off the light*).

(BLACKOUT.)

PETER

ACT I

Same scene as Prologue. The darkness gradually gives way to the bright daylight of a summer morning. No one is in the room. Loud pronounced knocking on door at back.

VOICES. Are you there, Peter? Peter? (*pause.*) Peter!
    (CHARLEY PRENDERGAST *and* BILLY STEPHENS *enter.*)
CHARLEY. H'm – not up yet. Lazy dog! (*Looks at table with bottle and glasses etc.*) Just as it was when we left him last night. Poor devil!
STEPHENS. Is there a tincture in the bottle? (*He examines it.*) There is. Have a nip?
CHARLEY. No. Important appointment with the guv'nor this morning at eleven.
STEPHENS. Further explanation of refusal unnecessary. Well. I'm not going home till Friday. So, here goes. (*He pours out a drink.*) Cheerio!
CHARLEY. Goodluck!
STEPHENS (*looking at bottle*). I suppose Peter could do with some. (*Goes to bedroom door.*) I wonder is the rascal asleep? (*He suddenly sees the hat and picks it up.*) I say, Charley, was he wearing it like this yesterday?
CHARLEY. Don't remember.
STEPHENS. Oh no, you wouldn't. You don't give a damn. You've got through of course, and are off, I suppose, to a nice little job. But poor Peter and I – it doesn't matter what sort of hats we wear – (*at door*) – Poor fellow, does it?
CHARLEY. Is he awake?
STEPHENS (*listening*). Not a mouse stirring. Here, let's give him a bugle call.
BOTH (*singing*). Hey, Peter! Wake up Peter!
              Angles calling
              Houses falling
              Babies bawling
      Hey Peter! Wake up!

If you ain't gonna wake up, we can't wait
One minute longer; the trains am whistling—

STEPHENS (*emits long piercing whistle*). Wake up!
(*Simultaneously the two doors open,* ROSIE *the maid at one, with a breakfast tray on which is also a letter. At the other,* PETER, *in pyjamas. He does a few steps of jazz, suddenly observes* ROSIE *and flies back into his bedroom.*)

ROSIE. Mr Grahame's breakfast and a letter for him. (CHARLEY *makes room for the tray on the table.*) Thank you, sir. Will you tell him – his breakfast, sir—?

CHARLEY. Yes. Looks a very good breakfast too. Very appetising.

STEPHENS. Worth about fourpence I should say! (*To* ROSIE.) Come here Phyllis – Is that your name?

ROSIE. No, sir.

STEPHENS. And what do they call you then?

ROSIE. Rosie sir.

STEPHENS. Ah! Rosie, yes. A rose by any other name. Come here, Rosie.

ROSIE (*retreating*). Will you tell me Mr Grahame? (*She sees the damaged sock and quickly takes it up.*) His breakfast.

STEPHENS. 'Course we'll tell him, my sweet Rose of Tralee. Are you very fond of Mr Grahame?

ROSIE. I am. I only wished he kept better company. Excuse me.
(*Exit.*)

CHARLEY. One for you Stephens.

STEPHENS. Must get him out before the tea's cold. (*Knocks.*)

PETER (*off*). Who's that?

STEPHENS (*falsetto*). It's your own wee Rosie with the breakfast, darling!

PETER. I'll be out in a second.

STEPHENS. Hurry. There's the devil's own breakfast waiting for you out here. Grape fruit, prunes, fillet or plaice, bacon and eggs, marmalade, jam, tea and coffee.

PETER. What? (*He appears at door in shirt and trousers, barefooted, carrying a collar.*) What's that you say?

CHARLEY. Never mind him Peter. Are you shaved yet?

PETER. Just found the razor. I can't find my socks anywhere.

STEPHENS. Letter for you there, Peter.

PETER. Excuse me boys. (*He opens and reads letter. Re-reads it.*)

STEPHENS. The old folks at home – including Uncle Joe – broken-hearted, receive news that the prodigal son has not made good in his final engineering.

PETER. A very good guess, Stephens. It is from Uncle Joe.

STEPHENS. Well. What says our Uncle Joe?

PETER. Ach. (*He throws letter over to* CHARLEY.) Read it out to him, Charley.

CHARLEY (*reading*). "Ballywilder House, Ballywilder, Co. Leitrim."
  "Dear Peter,
      As I expected, your name is missing from the results list. Whatever possessed your unfortunate parents to think you had any vocation for engineering I don't know.
      If you haven't *brains* enough to qualify for an engineer, you might have the brawn, though I doubt it, to be a navvy. You had better though return at once and make arrangements for the future.
                                                        Your Uncle Joe."

STEPHENS. Nice soothing letter-writer, your Uncle Joe!

PETER. Uncle Joe bought Ballywilder after father's death. Didn't give much for it either. (*A pause.*) Yes. I have been. No doubt about it.

STEPHENS. No doubt about what?

PETER. That I've been a bit of an ass. Dancing, singing, play-acting. Fool, idiot. Making goms laugh while I was only wasting their time and my own. (*More cheerfully after a moment's thought.*) Still, I didn't waste too much time at it. Did I, Charley?

CHARLEY (*hesitates*). N. . . . no. Not too much. I suppose.

PETER. It was that old McMenemin stuck me. I know it was. (*He suddenly discovers one sock.*) Ah! here's one sock. Where's the other, I wonder! (*Pauses.*) I know it was McMenamin, I got 50/50 in everything bar geology. I know I got 60 easy in Mat. Physics. 70 in Strains and Stresses, and this time I got near full marks in Docks, Harbour and Canals. But those fossils! Those damned trilobites! What have they got to do with engineering anyway? I hate that old brute. "When you are old, Mr Grahame, you will realise the importance of time even in the formation of geological strata".

CHARLEY. I say. That reminds me, Peter. May I borrow your geology?

PETER. Yes. Take it and welcome. It's somewhere on that bookcase.
    (*Knocking.*)

PETER. Come in.

ROSIE (*entering*). The mistress sent this up with her compliments sir. (*Hands him a letter.*) And she told me to tell you she's waiting below for an answer as she's going out shopping this morning.

STEPHENS. Judging from the breakfast, it won't take long to buy grub for the dinner. Wait a minute, Rosie, till he gets his socks on.

PETER (*after a cursory glance at the note*). Yes, Rosie, my socks. Tell Mrs Murphy I couldn't possibly answer my correspondence till I put on my socks. I've found one but I'm hanged if I can find the other.

ROSIE (*shyly*). I beg your pardon, I'm sorry sir, but – I – I've got the other one. There was a big hole in it, but I'll have it ready for you in a minute or two. I'm putting a stitch in it.

STEPHENS. Bless me, does she stitch your socks! Do you, Rosie?

PETER. She does. Thank you, Rosie. I'll wait for it.

CHARLEY. What's the note about, Rosie? Last month's bill?

ROSIE. Yes sir.

STEPHENS. Got the wherewithal on you to pay it, Peter?

PETER. I had yesterday.

CHARLEY. How much is it?

ROSIE. Six pound ten up to last Saturday night.

STEPHENS. Rosie!

ROSIE. Yes sir.

CHARLEY. Tell Mrs Murphy, he's dressing. That he hasn't taken his breakfast yet, and that in half-an-hour he'll see her and square up.

ROSIE. All right sir. But she said I was to wait.

STEPHENS. Wait? Wait where?

ROSIE. Wait here until he sent it down with me.

STEPHENS. Wait here! Arrah, have some sense about you, Rosie. Fond and all as we are of you Rosie, there's some times ladies are *de trop*. Go down and tell her what Charley said.

CHARLEY. Yes go down and finish off that sock.

ROSIE (*hesitating*). Very well sir. But you – you'll answer it, won't you sir? Soon. If you don't, she'll be up herself.

STEPHENS. God forbid such a calamity should happen! Yes, yes, he will. He certainly will. Won't you, Peter?

PETER. I— might. (*He looks mournfully at* ROSIE).

ROSIE. Your breakfast sir. It's getting cold.

PETER. Yes, yes. Right. I'll have to think this thing out, Rosie.

(*Exit* ROSIE, PETER *seats himself at the table, pours out a cup of tea and rereads the letter.* STEPHENS *sits down opposite* PETER *at the table.*)

STEPHENS. Nice morning's correspondence, Peter.

PETER. Yes. (CHARLEY *extracts a book from the case, and seats himself beside* STEPHENS.)

CHARLEY (*examining book*). Some funny marginal notes here, Peter.

(PETER *makes no reply but looks glumly at the letter.*) Sorry I

135

can't help. I just managed to scrape enough to get home with.

STEPHENS. Misfortunes never come singly. They come in squadrons and platoons. Reminds me of Partridge. Went out with him yesterday before I met you boys, got two punctures one after another. He was talking about you, Peter.

PETER. Who's Partridge?

STEPHENS. Sam Partridge of Ballymena.

PETER. I don't remember any such bird from Ballymena.

STEPHENS (*incredulously*). Do you mean to tell me that you don't remember Sam Partridge, the Dives from Ballymena who dined us all sumptuously last year, the night of the big match?

PETER. No.

CHARLEY. He remembered *you* all right.

STEPHENS. Well, Partridge took me for a spin yesterday on the Bray Road. A huge giant of a car and by jove she could shift. Cabinteely to Bray in four minutes, I thank you. And he talked a lot about you, Peter.

PETER. Did he?

(*The two students eye* PETER *curiously. Pause.*)

PETER. Well? (*He sips his tea.*) Cheerio!

STEPHENS. What's on you now, Peter?

PETER. Ach! Everything. Uncle Joe, exams, engineering, navvying, socks and stitches . . . well, yesterday was yesterday, no use thinking about it, still I can't help. . . .

CHARLEY (*who has resumed examining the book*). I say, Stephens, look!

STEPHENS. I say! Jolly fine. Did *you* draw this girl's face, Peter?

PETER. Where?

CHARLEY. Here. On the margin. Jolly nice girl, Peter.

STEPHENS. Yes. Who is she?

PETER. Oh . . . no one in particular.

CHARLEY. I see something scrawled here underneath her portrait which might be a clue. Listen! (*Reads.*) "Where in the world will you find anything like the beauty of a young girl? Exquisite, like a fragrant rose."

STEPHENS. Hear, hear! Good man Peter.

CHARLEY (*looking critically at drawing*). The chin is a bit – um – too big and her nose is . . . (*with a start*) . . . aha, now I've got you, Peter! She's that girl who passed us yesterday in a big blue Chrysler car and bowed to you, Peter.

STEPHENS. Well, sure we'll probably meet her again, won't we, Peter? Cheer up! Your boat hasn't sunk yet, Peter.

PETER. It sure has now.

STEPHENS. Aren't we all of us little sailing boats tacking this way and that? Trying to dodge into harbour, trying to pass our finals.

CHARLEY. Hopeless for you.

STEPHENS. I agree. Some get in all at once. Here's Charley in for a snug berth, nice fair breeze behind, sunshine, guns saluting, bands playing, flags flying, mammas waving – all that sort of thing. But you and I Peter – well, cheer up old sort, we'll sail into port some day.

PETER. Some day, yes. When we're old men, I suppose.

CHARLEY. Well, I want to be fixed up before I'm old.

PETER (*angrily*). Old! Old! Damn the old! (*He rises and walks about, talking excitedly*). All the examiners, they're old. All the people who give you jobs, who sack you from jobs, who make you swat for jobs, they're all old, old! And they use us, you, me; fetch and carry me this, bring and carry me that; – they sit down and give us orders; kill us or spare us. (*Suddenly.*) Well, there's one thing they can't have, they can't get; they can't take from us. . . .

CHARLEY. Can't take – what, Peter?

STEPHENS. Shut up. His girl, of course. (*Snatching up and waving the book.*) His girl. My girl, your girl, all the girls that we fall in love with. But he's wrong. Some old fellow's bound to nobble them.

PETER (*excitedly*). No, never! They belong to us, not to them. They're ours. We were born with them – they're our own age . . . (*triumphantly.*) Aha! that's where we have those old fellows. The beauty of youth belongs to us, not to them. Bah! They're too old. They don't count. They wouldn't look at them. They despise them.

CHARLEY. Who does what?

STEPHENS. Shut up! Don't interrupt him! Go on, Peter.

PETER. That's the one thing, I say, that they can't rob us of, they can't trick us out of. They'd like to, these old ones. Make it so difficult that we could never win. But they can't and shan't. Never.

CHARLEY (*reading from book*). 'Where in the world can you find anything like the beauty of a young girl? Exquisite – like a fragrant rose."

STEPHENS. Rosie!

PETER (*angrily*). What do either of you know or care about beauty?

STEPHENS. No offence meant. Be a good child now and eat your breakfast, Peter. Here, I'll cut some bread for you. (*He does so. *PETER *sits down again.*)

CHARLEY. Tell us, Peter, about that girl in the big blue Chrysler. Who is she, Peter?

PETER. None of your business.

(CHARLEY *wanders over to bookcase examining its contents.*)

STEPHENS. "The flower that sat in the car, tra-la, has nothing to do with the case."

CHARLEY (*suddenly*). I say, Peter! Do you mind letting me have a loan of your "Stoney"? You won't want it for a couple of months.

PETER. Take it and welcome.

(CHARLEY *is taking the book out of the case when he suddenly drops it, and seizes another one.*)

CHARLEY. Hello! Where did you pick this up?

PETER. What?

CHARLEY. Griffiths "Harbours, Docks and Canals." "New Edition Revised." I say, where'd you scrape together two quid to nobble this? (*He looks inside.*) "To Peter from Joan." Who's Joan?

PETER. She's a girl.

STEPHENS. Is that a fact? And did she give you that?

PETER. She did.

CHARLEY. Jove, I didn't know you had a 'Griffiths.' Lend it, too, Peter?

PETER. No, not that. You can have any of the others.

CHARLEY. Right-o! But I'd have liked to have the Griffiths. Who's Joan?

PETER. Girl I once met.

CHARLEY. Must be a decent sort.

PETER. Why?

CHARLEY. Spending forty bob on a book like this for a fellow she met – (*he pauses and grins*) – once did you say, Peter?

PETER. Well, once or twice maybe. . . .

STEPHENS. Look here, Peter, I'm fed up waiting in this hole; a walk would do you good. We might see a few more beauties of your own generation . . . where's your shoes? (*He begins to search the room.*)

PETER. My shoes? Somewhere about. I suppose, Charley – (*he looks sadly at the note from* MRS MURPHY) – it's not much use – asking you to help with this?

CHARLEY. Six-ten? No Peter. (*Looking at the books.*) Sorry, but I'd give you a quid for the "Griffiths" if you'd part.

PETER. No.

STEPHENS (*finding a shoe and flinging it over*). Here's one shoe, anyway. And here's the other. But you can't go about with only one sock on. Has she never got it it stitched yet? Cheer up, Peter!

138

We might see that blue Chrysler girl again.

CHARLEY. Who was that blue Chrysler one, Peter?

PETER. That's Joan.

CHARLEY. What!

STEPHENS. Where did you meet her?

PETER. One day this winter I was swotting up Geology, looking for specimens up in the hills, and a girl drove past.

STEPHENS. Fast?

PETER. She was driving slowly. I was on the road looking at a lump of quartz and she nearly ran me down. She stopped, or the car stopped; she laughed and I laughed, and then I helped her to start it again; then she gave me a lift down . . . and . . . that's all.

STEPHENS. I see! (*Intones in a high pitched clerical voice.*) And he thereupon told her *all* about himself and all about Docks, Harbours and Canals.

CHARLEY (*like some sauve "uncle" in a Children's Hour broadcast*). "Yes, and then, dear children, he met her in secret, and without the knowledge or consent of her parents or guardians, and told her the story of poor engineering Peter."

STEPHENS (*suddenly clutching* CHARLEY *in a frenzied embrace*). "And Joan, – Oh Joan darling – honestly I'm afraid I'm going to fail in my final. Joan darling I really know nothing about the one great subject I'm specialising in – Docks, Harbours and Canals." (*In his ordinary voice.*) And so he got the book. (*Mischievously.*) Sounds rather like the truth, Peter.

PETER. It is. Told by a pair of cynics.

CHARLEY. I see. That's how you got 90% in Docks and Harbours. Good man, Peter!

PETER (*angrily*). You two can go to hell. Get out! A fool I was to tell you.

STEPHENS (*who has crossed to the window*). I say boys, here he is!

CHARLEY. Who?

STEPHENS. That fellow. He's at the door now, below. Gee, what a car the man has! Brass and silver and blue and gold! (*Knocking below.*) Yes, that's just the way he would knock.

PETER. Who is he?

STEPHENS. The chap I met yesterday. The football dinner man. The big pot, Partridge. I told him we'd be here, this morning.

PETER. What's he wanting with me anyway?

(*Loud knocking at the sitting room door.*)

PETER. Come in. (*Enter* SAM PARTRIDGE. *He is middle aged, but quick and alert in manner, speaks with a rather boisterous self-*

assurance in a pronounced Ulster accent and is very smartly dressed.)

PART. Excuse me. *Pardonnez-moi.* Aye. You're here allright, Billy – what's this your name is? And this, I suppose, is Mr Grahame?

STEPHENS. No, that's Prendergast. This is Grahame here.

PART. Och aye, aye. How're ye, Mr Grahame? I suppose you remember me.

STEPHENS. Mr Partridge, Peter. (PETER *bows*.)

PART. (*shakes hands, brusquely*). Aye, I'm Sam Partridge of Ballymena. D'ye remember me? Och, go on with you! D'ye not remember the night of the football *conversazione*? Peter Grahame! Isn't that you?

PETER. Yes, I'm Peter Grahame.

PART. Of course you remember. And your pal here. Wasn't he there that night?

STEPHENS. Yes. Charley Prendergast – Mr Partridge.

PART. Prendergast, aye. He came over in Strongbow's time! Ha, ha! Looking for Eva. Did you find her yet, Charley? Ha ha! How're you, Charley?

CHARLEY. Quite well, thank you.

PART. Aye. Indeed you look it. And how've you been doing since, Peter? Any coorting? Well, 'pon my soul, Peter, you were the great value that night. Great! Cripes, Peter, but you were the hell of a man at the Irish Jig, and dancing the Billy John Ashcroft breakdown . . . let alone the Jazz and the Rooshian dancing. It's a year ago now, but I never forget you. So when I seen the Billy artist here yesterday, the first thing I says to him, "Where's that Grahame fellow?" (*A pause.*) I hear you got stuck in the exam, Peter?

PETER. Yes.

PART. (*interrupting*). Aye. Ah well, you can't do everything, can you? (*Looking at* CHARLEY.) I remember Charley now. Wasn't it Charley played the accompaniment for you?

STEPHENS (*grinning*). Yes.

PART. Aye, oh aye. Charley, he done his part well, but man, Peter, you were the star turn of the night! I'll never forget you. Says I to McLoughlin, the Chairman of the County Council – he was there that night – says I, that fellow would make his fortune, a regular fortune, man, on the stage. (*Looking delightedly at* PETER.) You couldn't help but laugh at that fellow even if he done nothing but look at you. Ha ha! (PETER *looks reproachfully at him*). That's it! That's it! The doleful Jester in the Yeoman of the Guard. Jack

140

Point! The dead spit of him! But for the Lord's sake, Peter, buck
up. You're not dead yet.

PETER (*maddened*). I'm damn near it.

PART. (*delighted*). Ha ha ha! Well, soul, you do make me laugh.
You're an artist. (*Looking at the tray.*) Are you just after your
breakfast? (*Examines it.*) Holy God, what a breakfast! Well, that's
the last breakfast of the kind you're going to eat, my son.
(*Suddenly.*) D'ye know Portahoy?

PETER. Portahoy?

PART. Aye – on the sea-coat.

PETER. Yes. I was there once, I think, about ten years ago with my
Uncle Joe and mother.

PART. (*contemptuously*). Ach! Your mother and uncle Joe! Spade and
bucket, down for the day, eating cockles. I wish to God your uncle
Joe seen it now! It's booming, man, booming. None of your
ordinary charabanc trippers' business, but real class like. Great!
Kind of an Ulster Lido like, if you could imagine the thing. Last
year – great! This year – better! And who done it? One man and
one man only. And who's that? Me! Sam Partridge of Ballymena.
And how? Art and beauty. Nature supplied the beauty – it's a
beautiful place, there's not the like of it in the United Kingdom –
Blackpool and them places, bah! nothing naturally beautiful
about them. Portahoy and Killarney – Heaven's reflex – Portahoy!
But it wanted art, and Sam Partridge, he supplied the art.

STEPHENS. Up the Partridges!

PART. I practically own the place, you know. I bought up all the
leaseholders and have the biggest share in the big new hotel –
Hotel Excelsior – just got it done up in the latest style; sofas and
cushions and armchairs; late dinner at night – and choked off all
them old commercials by charging them 20/- a night; bed and
breakfast – none of your seven bob touches for me. And now I
have a real nice place for the idle rich and them classes. Don't let
me be stopping you eating your breakfast, Peter, but by the holy,
you should see the breakfast I put up for them people. Six
courses, man! grapefruit and prunes and porridge, fish, bacon,
ham and eggs, scrambled eggs and poached, and bacon and
fish . . .

PETER. Any jam?

PART. Aye, and jam, and marmalade – and I've got the best *maitre
d'hotel* special over from Deauville, and the best *chef* out of the
Savoy, and you could go on eating all day in the dining room and
never want to leave it. Simply gorgeous!

141

PETER. Look here, Mr Partridge, what's the good of coming here and telling me about these things at your wonderful hotel? Is it a way you have of asking me to breakfast or dine there, or what is it?

PART. It is. (*Looks at* PETER *and laughs knowingly.*) It is. Ha, ha, ha! It certainly is!

PETER. Thanks very much. To-day or to-morrow?

PART. For a fortnight – longer, maybe. I want you and Charley here – what d'you call him – Prendergast. (*Looking at* STEPHEN.) This Billy fellow, he's no good for me, but I want the two of you boys to eat, dine and drink and sleep like that for a solid fourteen days, and longer . . .

CHARLEY. Sorry I can't possibly . . .

PART. Right. But I want Peter. I must have Peter. You'll come.

PETER. I don't quite get you, Mr Partridge.

PART. I told you about the breakfast; would you like to know what you'd have for lunch?

PETER. Woa! Wait a bit. All this eating business doesn't quite appeal to me. I don't want all that grub, I want something else. I don't suppose I'll ever see it.

PART. Ha, ha, ha! Good! Lord, when you look like that you do put me into fits. Well, look here; you know the sort of danger a hotel like that gets into. Too many old fellows and women sitting in the drawing room and the lounge doing nothing but playing patience and dozing and smoking and knitting and taking a turn round the esplanade and the cliff head and that sort of thing. Well, that's no use to me. I don't want the place turned into a sort of high-class Turkish Baths for old crocks. I want a bit of life and jizz about it, you know. I want young ones as well. They're the ones that matter. Use them – always use the young ones for the benefit of the old ones. And if you like the place, they'll make the Pa's and Ma's and the Uncles and Aunts stick it. But you got to amuse them. Use them and amuse them. Now Peter, you're just the sort of young fellow I want.

STEPHENS. What he's trying to get you to see, Peter, is that he's offering you a job – the run of your teeth and a free bed.

PETER. Yes, that's plain enough. For a fortnight?

PART. Aye, and longer if it suits.

PETER. Yes, well, you do that. What do I do?

PART. Well, look here. Take the morning. You get breakfast – grapefruit and . . .

PETER. Yes, yes, I know. Consider we've had breakfast, What then?

PART. Well, after breakfast, some old fellow wants a game of golf.

142

PETER. Golf?

PART. Yes, 3 holes or 9 or 19. He tells us in the office and I give you the tip and you goes off to him and fixes up a match. Or maybe an old lady wants a game of croquet.

STEPHENS. Croquet?

PART. Yes, croquet. Right! Peter gets the tip and offers to play. D'ye understand Peter? Then in the evenings you drop into the drawing room and do a turn or two at the piano, not professional like but nicely and artistically as if it were the usual thing to do Paderewski or Chopin at the piano, and I buzz round the place and say that's a clever lad at the piano and nobody should miss hearing him, and they all come in like, then I gets Peter here to give them a bit of a song. And then my little orchestra plays, and there's dancing, and then comes along my young dancing quartette – kind of a cabaret business – but nice don't you know – all the latest foxtrots—

STEPHENS. What! Your young dancing quartette?

PART. Aye, or sextette or whatever you call it.

STEPHENS. Young, are they?

PART. Of course . . . I wouldn't have anything else. Now, Peter. Don't you see?

(*The latter gets up and walks moodily towards the bedroom door.*)

PETER. Just a moment. (*Enters room and closes door.*)

STEPHENS. Partridge! (*He hands him over* MRS MURPHY'S *note.*) Square this for him.

PART. (*looking at it*). *Six-ten* . . . Right! Look here, you two boys go down and square the old lady. (*He gives* STEPHENS *some notes.*) And wait for me in the car. I want to speak to Peter a minute or two alone. (*Exit* STEPHENS *and* CHARLEY. PARTRIDGE *whistles.*) Peter!

PETER (*Off*). Yes. Just a moment. (*Enter.*) Sorry I'd forgotten to brush my hair.

PART. You hard up, Peter?

PETER. Yes, broke.

PART. Ach! Don't you worry. Leave that to me. Free quarters, Peter, best of grub and a fiver a week. And have a nom-de-plume or whatever you call it. Call yourself say, Peter Gordon. (*He crosses and closes entrance door carefully.*) I don't want those two fellows to hear this, Peter. (*Bashfully.*) The thing is, Peter, there's a very special girl coming to the Excelsior.

PETER (*more interested*). Yes?

143

PART. And its time Sammy Partridge was hooking on; you know?

PETER. Well?

PART. Well, from all the talk of Stephens and that lot, you seem to have a way with the weemin', Peter . . .

PETER. No I haven't. But I like them.

PART. Aye. Sure that's what has been reciprocating! Well, this special girl, Peter – she's a nice-class girl, you know – came last two summers and any amount of dough, not that I want that very much – I've plenty of that all right – but Peter, I'm terrible gone on this particular one. I never done much in the coorting line when I was – well – a bit younger like you, and I feel terrible awkward now with nice class young girls, talking and laughing and gagging and doing the gay like, don't you know Peter, and if you and me and she and the cousin . . .

PETER. Cousin? What cousin?

PART. Her cousin or her aunt, or whatever other woman company she has, like if we all went for a stroll in the evening, and you did most of the talking . . .

PETER. That's impossible.

PART. Well, you done most of the arty sort of talk like, and amused them; you could then nose off with the cousin and give me a bit of scope like, with the . . .

    (*Knocking at the door.*)

PETER. Come in.

ROSIE (*with note on salver*). Mistress said to give you this, Mr Grahame, and I'm sorry to have kept you waiting so long for this. (*Hands him a sock.*)

PETER. Thank you, Rosie. (*Exit* ROSIE.)

PART. Well, Peter?

PETER. Wait a moment. (*Putting on sock.*) I can't answer till I've put on my sock and read my correspondence. (*Reads.*) Great Scott! "Paid with thanks!" (*Looking at* PARTRIDGE.) You did this?

PART. Aye, och yes. It's nothing, you know, Peter. Sure you'll do just as much for me and more. Pack up your troubles in your old kit bag! Will you come?

PETER. Six pounds ten down and the rest in weekly instalments! (*Suddenly with delight.*) When do I begin work?

PART. Day after to-morrow. I'll call for you and bring you down. Come with me now and I'll give you a spin in the car, and lunch with me at Jammets.

PETER. Go ahead. I'll follow you down.

PART. (*pulls papers from his pocket*). There's a couple of prospectuses and views of the hotel and the new grounds.

PETER (*reading*). The Excelsior Hotel . . . Portahoy. Very fine it looks. What's that beyond the hotel. Out to sea in the distance, below the mountains?

PART. Oh that! That's a big new harbour they're working at. Tremendous thing – worth seeing. Don't be long Peter. (*He goes out.*)

(QUICK CURTAIN.)

ACT II

A few days later.
One of the lounges of the Excelsior Hotel, Portahoy. It commands a view of the hotel grounds, sea and mountains beyond. In the foreground can be seen a new harbour in course of construction. The lounge is empty. PARTRIDGE *can be heard talking, then suddenly appears in immaculate morning dress. He is followed by* TOM *the waiter assisting a large stout gentleman who is rather unsteady on his feet.*

PART. All clear. In here, Tom. This way Mr Scott!

SCOTT (*insistant on stopping to look out to sea*). Woa! Yes. That's an extraordinary fine view. Have you no telescope . . . for guests? Why haven't you . . . a telescope? What's that thing out there to sea in the distance? Just below the mountains?

PART. Oh that? That's a new big harbour they're working at. Tremendous thing. Worth seeing.

SCOTT. Yes. If you had . . . telescope. Should have telescope. Essential for first-class seacoast hotel. Take a note of that, please, waiter. I insist on . . . on telescope. Most essential.

PART. Right. Take a note of that Tom.

TOM. Yes sir. We'll have one for you to-morrow.

SCOTT (*slightly mollified.*) Hm. S'nice view . . . all ri'.

PART. Great. (*proudly.*) To the right . . . (*he points*) . . . South Foreland Rockery. Choicest of Alpine flowers and shrubs . . . to the left . . . the Rhodendrums . . . left centre . . . the Lovers' Walk.

SCOTT. Yes . . . (*chuckles delightedly.*) I . . . I like that . . . "The Lovers' Walk" . . . first class hotels . . . should always have . . . "Lovers' Walk" . . . v' good . . . that is. Romance . . . Romance, most important. You go one up on that.

PART. That's great. Right. Turn to starboard, Tom (*They steer* SCOTT *towards a seat.*) Now. (*He is deposited carefully in it.*) Now isn't this a nice cosy kind of place to pass the afternoons. The snooze parlour I calls it.

SCOTT (*annoyed*). No . . . no . . . no . . . no. Tut . . . tut . . . tut. Not

146

snooze. Snooze . . . vulgar . . . common word. Use word like . . . eh . . . siesta. Yes, that's it. Siesta room . . . lounge.

PART. Right. Make a note of that, Tom. Put that cushion round a bit more. This way, Tom. (*He looks critically at* SCOTT.) Now. How d'ye like that for a snoo . . . for a . . . for siesting?

SCOTT. Excellent. Thanks v' much. (*he settles down.*) And a most excellent lunch. V' good indeed. Hm. v' comf'ble here. Very.

PART. Good. (*The sound of a loud-talking merry party coming along the passage outside.*) Tom. Stop that crush coming in here. Can't have any disturbance of Mr Scott's siesting. Quick. (TOM *hurries off and can be heard shepherding the party elsewhere.*)

SCOTT. V' comf'ble here. Nice. M'yes. Good place for snooze . . . siesta . . . snooze . . . siesta . . . snoo. (*He falls asleep.*)

(PARTRIDGE *satisfied that all is well, goes off. An elderly couple drift slowly into the lounge and seat themselves. They are* MR *and* MRS MCCLEERY. *The latter carries a capacious work basket from which she extracts a large ball of wool. Her husband has a note book in which he writes at odd moments.*)

MRS MCC. (*after a long pause*). Have you done much, John dear? (*She commences to knit.*)

MR MCC. No. (*irritably.*) It's terrible hard work, this. My brain isn't as quick or alert as it used to be.

MRS MCC. Well dear, sure your heart is in the work anyway. These few days down here and nothing to worry about, and them dinners and lunches, its doing you good, dear. Could I help you, dear?

MR MCC. (*testily*). One moment, Annie. (*To himself.*) Bog . . . fog . . . bog . . .

MRS MCC. I'm sure I could help you, dear. Whats the word, darling?

MR MCC. Bog.

MRS MCC. Bog. Bog. Were your thoughts on the bog, darling? (*The ball of wool slips away.*)

(TOM *re-enters. He is rather taken aback to find the* MCCLEERYS *instaled in the lounge, but says nothing.*)

MR MCC. Yes. Bog . . . fog . . .

TOM. Yes sir. Excuse me, sir. (*He retrieves the wool and hands it to* MRS MCCLEERY.)

MRS MCC. Oh, thank you, Tom.

MR MCC. (*meditatively*). Bog . . . bog . . .

TOM (*puzzled but interested*). Excuse me, sir. You want some – what sir?

MRS MCC. Oh, it's alright Tom. Mr McCleery only wants a little word to rhyme with bog. That's all.

TOM. Is that so, sir. (*He tries to peer into* MCCLEERY'S *notebook.*) Excuse me, sir. Bog, did you say sir? Well now, there's . . . bog and there's fog . . . and there's log . . . and there's . . . ach! sure there's thousands of words that end in og. I never was much good at them sort of things, but wee Joe, the night boots, has a great head for that sort of thing. (*He produces a small notebook and a stumpy pencil.*) That's it! That's it! I heard Joe at one a few nights ago. "There was once a young man in a fog – (SCOTT *stirs and grunts.*) Excuse me ma'am. Have to . . . you know. Very important gentleman over there ma'am. (*He crosses to* SCOTT *and stands waiting the latter's awakening.*) "There was once a young man in a fog."—

PART. (*entering briskly.*) Tom! Tom!

TOM. Yes sir.

PART. Have you seen Mr Peter?

TOM. Mr Peter? Mr Gordon, sir? Yes sir. He was up very early this morning, sir, down at the new harbour, and he's been out golfing with Colonel Blake since breakfast.

PART. (*looking over at the* MCCLEERY'S). Who are the old couple?

TOM. No. 18, McCleery, sir. (*Reassuringly.*) It's all right, sir. Very quiet, sir. Wouldn't disturb a fly, sir.

PART. Right. Well, under no account have Mr Scott disturbed either. (*He crosses to the* MCCLEERY'S.) Nice afternoon, Mrs McCleery.

MRS MCC. (*gratified by the attention*). Very nice indeed. (*She hastily nudges her husband.*) John! This is Mr Partridge. (*Sotto voce.*) The owner, darling, of the hotel. (MCCLEERY *looks up and bows.*)

PART. How d'ye do! I hope you're being well looked after. Would you not now prefer the main lounge to sit in? Its brighter and gayer than this place.

MRS MCC. Oh thank you so much, Mr Partridge but my husband likes rest and seclusion for his literary work, and I – well, what my husband likes I like too. So we just sit here in this nice quiet corner every afternoon.

MR MCC. I find I can write here better than anywhere else at this time of day.

PART. Right. (*Crosses to* TOM.) If Mr Scott wakes up and wants . . . well, you know . . . a little nourishment . . . the best in the house . . . see he gets it, Tom.

TOM. Yes sir.

PART. I don't mind that old couple, but anybody else that comes along – young chatty people or any noisy ones – shunt them along to the main lounge.

TOM. I will sir, certainly sir.

PART. I told you before what he is, Tom, and what he means to this hotel. So don't forget. (*Pauses.*) Aye. You said Mr Peter was out golfing with the Colonel?

TOM. Yes sir.

PART. Aye. Well, here. (*Produces card.*) I want you to give him a note of these extra arrangements, and tell him that I want to see him. Urgent business. And he's to pay particular attention to Miss Van de Meizer. Lady up in No. 45.

TOM (*taking card*). I know the lady, sir. No. 45. Yes sir.

PART. And in case I miss seeing him, tell him privately that he wasn't just up to the whack last night at the singing. He'll have to put a bit more jizz in it than he done last night.

TOM (*marking card*). More jizz. Yes sir.

PART. Make Mr Scott a bit more comfortable with that cushion. (TOM *does so. Exit* PARTRIDGE.)

TOM (*going carefully over card, making notes on it*). Do him well, the best in the house, Mr Scott, No. 45, Miss Van de Meizer, extra attention. Singing, more jizz, Mr Peter. Right. (*He moves over to* MCCLEERY.) What's this we were at when we were interrupted? Poetry! Aye. "There was once a young man in a fog"—

SCOTT (*drowsily*). Um. Um. Um. (*Blinks at* TOM.) Oh! Waiter.

TOM (*at attention*). Yes, sir.

SCOTT. Another . . . um . . . um . . . another whiskey and soda.

TOM. Yes, sir. Certainly sir. Large or small, sir?

SCOTT. Um. Um. Large. (*Suspiciously alert on seeing* MCCLEERY.) No . . . Small. (*Nods to* MCCLEERY.) How do! Um. Small.

TOM. Yes sir. (*exit.*)

SCOTT. Um. Yes. Very good. Nice here. Um. Comf'ble. (*Settles down again.*) Um.

MRS MCC. (*after a scrutiny of* SCOTT.) Do you know the gentleman, darling?

MR MCC. (*looking over his glasses at* SCOTT). Don't think so. (*Suddenly.*) Oh! I've got it! I've got it! Dog!

MRS MCC. Of course, so it is. Isn't that splendid, love! I just knew you'd do it. How many lines have you got now, darling? And would you let me hear them, love? There's no one listening.

MR MCC. (*reassured on this point after a glance around*).
"Away where the curlews cry on the bog,
There sounds the faint wild bark of a dog,
And Oh! to be there

149

When the . . ."

TOM (*entering, up L., with glasses*). Excuse me, sir. Your drink, sir.

SCOTT. Um. Very good. Um. Yes. Put in all in the soda. Um. V' nice here. Comf'ble. (*As* TOM *pours out a drink, there is a long prolonged sound of a syren as from a great distance away.*) What's that?

TOM. Syren sir. The new harbour works, sir. They generally give two blasts sir.

SCOTT. What they blow twice for? Um?

TOM. First one is warning – tide has turned enough to get up steam – get ready for work sir. Second one means commence work sir. It won't go for a long time yet, the second one sir.

SCOTT. Um. Second one what?

TOM. Second one means – commence work, sir. If you were inclined to bathe sir, them syrens is very useful.

SCOTT. Um. Bathe? No. No, not just now. Later. Um. V' comf'ble here. Bathe? (*Decisively.*) No!

TOM. No sir.

(SCOTT *sips his drink, then closes his eyes.* TOM *looks at him admiringly. Once more the ball of wool slips from* MRS MCCLEERY'S *lap.* TOM *retrieves it.*)

MRS MCC. Oh, thank you so much.

TOM (*to* MR MCCLEERY). Excuse me, sir, but we were talking about . . . aye . . . bog, sir. Bog . . . fog . . .

SCOTT (*sleepily*). Um. V'nice here. Comf'ble. (*Stares in a stupified way at the whiskey and soda then closes his eyes in slumber again.*)

MRS MCC. (*after a critical survey of* SCOTT). Who's the gentleman?

TOM. Mum's the word, ma'am. (*Impressively.*) I wish I was him. What a job! (*Confidentially.*) He's the Astronomer Royal ma'am.

MRS MCC. (*to her husband*). Darling! Toms says the gentleman over there is the Royal Astronomer.

MR MCC. (*after a sharp look at* SCOTT). Nonsense!

TOM. 'Tis a fact ma'am. He marks places like this with stars, d'ye understand. He's the Chief Inspector for the United Tourist Agencies Recommended Hotels. One star – fair. Two stars – good. Three stars – very good. Four stars . . . ! ! ! My job is to get this place marked four stars. "Do him well now, Tom," says Mr Partridge. And I'm doing him (*Crosses to* SCOTT.). Excuse me sir. Little more soda, sir?

SCOTT. Um. Yes. Um. Small lil' drop. (TOM *pours it out.*) Thanks. Nice here. Comf'ble.

TOM. Yes sir. Shall I put this cushion round a little, sir?

150

SCOTT. Um. No, no. Quite all ri'. Comf'ble.

TOM. Yes, sir. Hope you liked your lunch, sir?

SCOTT. Um. Lunch! Um. Very nice. Comf'ble. Nice.

TOM. Thank you, sir.

(*A little buttons enters with programme cards which he proceeds to distribute. He attempts to give one to* SCOTT.)

TOM (*interposing*). Keep away from the gentleman. (*Seizes card.*) What's this?

BUTTONS. New programme. To-night. Special, with Mr Partridge's compliments. (*He hands one to* MCCLEERY *who, irritated at this interruption, glances at it and throws it away. The* BUTTONS *gives one to* MRS MCCLEERY.) "BLUE ROOM GIRLS – first appearance tonight. Special." With Mr Partridge's compliments. (*exit.*)

MRS MCC. (*reading the programme*). Oh! Dear! This is nice. John – John dear! The new programme, dear.

MR MCC. The what?

MRS MCC. Last night, Mr Partridge announced he had got something very special arranged for this evening.

MR MCC. (*annoyed*). Sh! Sh! Just getting it.

MRS MCC. Are you darling? I'm so glad.

(*She puts the programme aside after a glance at it, and resumes her knitting.* SCOTT *relapses into sleep.* TOM *seeing no need for further attention to* SCOTT, *puts programme on table in front of Scott, and comes over to* MRS MCCLEERY.)

TOM (*sotto voice and motioning towards* SCOTT). Nice gentleman that, ma'am.

MRS MCC. Yes, he seems very contented.

TOM. Yes ma'am. Mr Partridge's orders – "Keep him full and contented. The best in the house." (*coming closer.*) The best room in the house – No. 3. A grand room ma'am. Canopy bed, tapestry curtains, cost two hundred guineas. (*Pause.*) When he wakes first thing in the morning, double gin and ginger and dash of lemon. Half an hour later, China tea and crisp toast. Quarter of an hour after, grapefruit and slice of melon. Breakfast – prunes, porridge, Finnan haddock – he must have the stomach of an ostrich. But he has brains too. He's got more brains for guzzling, eating and drinking than the old Roman Emperors down in the catacombs.

(*The noise of guests arriving outside suddenly puts him on the alert. He goes towards the entrance. There is a loud burst of laughter.* TOM *hurriedly goes out.*)

VOICE (*off*). Let's go in here for tea.

TOM (*off*). Excuse me, gentlemen. Excuse me, ladies. The other lounge, sir. Round the corner. (*Another party of guests suddenly appear at opposite entrance.*) No sir, not here. Round the corner. Thank you sir. Thank you ladies. (*He re-appears looking at* MRS MCCLEERY *for sympathy.*) Awful life, this, ma'am.

MRS MCC. (*who has again taken up the programme*). John. John, dear.

MR MCC. Sh! Don't interrupt.

MRS MCC. But this is interesting. Did you see this?

MR MCC. What?

MRS MCC. They're actually going to have a cabaret show here this evening. (*She reads.*) No. 1 Rumba "Halfway to Cuba."

MR MCC. (*irritated*). Don't . . . don't interrupt please, Annie.

MRS MCC. (*unheeding*). No. 2 Slow Valse. "Missouri". No. 3 Special . . . Peter. (*Repeats*) Peter.

SCOTT (*drowsily*). He's . . . a funny fellow . . . is Peter. Um . . . yes. Um . . . Very . . . Um . . . funny.

MRS MCC. Tom!

TOM. Yes, ma'am.

MRS MCC. Who's Peter?

TOM. Peter, ma'am? D'ye not know Mr Peter, ma'am?

MRS MCC. No. Where is he?

TOM. Mr Peter's out playing golf with Colonel Blake, ma'am.

MRS MCC. Oh, Peter plays golf too, does he.

TOM. Oh yes. Plus four man, ma'am.

MRS MCC. Dear me. (*She continues to read.*) "Last item. The Blue Room Girls, who have now arrived, will appear in a special Cabaret scene with Peter this evening."

TOM. Yes, ma'am. Ballet cabaret and tap dancing, croquet, tennis, golf, badminton, all one to Mr Peter.

MRS MCC. John! John dear!

MR MCC. (*testily*). Yes. (*He goes on writing.*)

MRS MCC. John darling!

MR MCC. (*exasperated*). Yes. Yes. What is it?

MRS MCC. Do you know anything about this young man they call Peter?

MR MCC. I don't know anything about him and I don't want to.

MRS MCC. I saw him last night. He's terribly like your sister-in-law's first cousin.

MR MCC. (*irritably*). What's that?

MRS MCC. They always were a bit inclined, your sister-in-law's family, for dancing and capers. It's in the blood.

MR MCC. What is?

MRS MCC. Ach, nothing darling. I'm sorry to interrupt you. Are you getting on all right?

PETER (*without*). Tom. Tom. (*He enters hurriedly with a golf bag and almost stumbles over* SCOTT'S *outstretched feet.*) Damn. Oh. I beg your pardon. I'm so sorry. Oh Tom. Tom. Lend me a couple, quick. Pay you back when I've seen Partridge.

TOM. Easy sir. (*He indicates* SCOTT *with a warning gesture.*) Be quiet. Boss's orders. No account to be disturbed. (*Fumbling in his pocket and producing notes.*) There's two. Wait. One second sir. Note of your engagements—

MRS MCC. (*excitedly to her husband*). John. John dear. John. It's him.

MR MCC. (*angrily*). Who? What's the matter?

MRS MCC. Nothing darling. Nothing.

TOM (*handing* PETER *the note of engagements given by* PARTRIDGE). From Mr Partridge. Your engagements for today. And he said to pay particular attention to No. 45, sir.

PETER (*studying the note*). No. 45? No. 3 and all following dances with Miss Van de Meiser. (*Anxiously.*) What's she like, Tom?

TOM. Number eleven. Outsize. American. And rehearsal again tonight at 6.30 in the annexe.

SCOTT (*drowsily*). Yessm. Partridge 'll keep um busy.

PETER. What's this in pencil opposite No. 3. Is it "M.J."?

TOM. Yes sir. Excuse me sir. Little note of mine. (*Whispers.*) Boss seemed a little upset today, sir.

PETER. At what?

TOM. Wants more jizz, sir.

PETER. More what?

TOM. More jizz, sir. "Tell Mr Peter, says he, that he wasn't up to the mark last night at the singing. Tell him to put more—

PETER. I quite understand. "M.J." means more jizz.

TOM. Yes sir. (*The sound of an angry altercation outside.* COLONEL BLAKE *appears.*)

COLONEL. Gordon? Where the devil are you?

PETER. (*Simultaneously*). Come on in here, Colonel.

TOM. Ah, Mr Peter, keep that old gentleman out.

COLONEL. So here you are. (*Sees* SCOTT.) Who's this?

TOM (*despairingly*). Oh, James's Gate. Here's Typhoon now. No more siesting for you, Mr Scott. (*To* PETER.) Afternoon teas in the other lounge sir.

COLONEL. No. None of your wishy washy teas for me. Whiskey soda. For two. And here. We stop here. Must sit down.

TOM. Over here, sir. (*He guides them to a table as far away from* SCOTT *as possible.*)

COLONEL (*looking at* SCOTT). Sleepy sot. Hate that sort of life.

Guzzling food all day and no excercise. Snoozing in armchairs all day. (*Suddenly addressing* SCOTT.) Fresh air. That's the tonic you want. Wake up, sir.

TOM (*To* PETER). Careful sir. Don't disturb him sir. You're having tea, gentlemen?

PETER. Yes.

TOM. The other lounge, please, gentlemen.

COL. No. No tea. And I stay *here*. Bring two whiskeys and sodas, here. (*Exit* TOM.)

PETER, I say, that reminds me. Sorry Colonel (*He hands over notes.*) I owe you two over the last game.

COL. Oh. Right! Yes. Two. (*Counting.*) Right.

SCOTT. Hm. How do, Colonel. Um? Nice game golf. Um.

TOM (*hurriedly entering with the drinks*). Pardon me, Colonel. Excuse me, gentlemen. (*He places drinks on a table still more distant from* SCOTT.) More comfortable over here, gentlemen. (*To* PETER.) Pardon, sir. Star man you know Mr Peter. Inspector . . . Hotel Vet, sir. Keep off the grass. Excuse me. Keep the man of war off the rocks, Mr Peter.

COL. Look here, what about another 18 holes tomorrow first thing? Nine o'clock?

PETER. Right.

COL. And the usual guinea? Right (SCOTT *snores.*) Damn that fellow. Stop that, sir! I hate snoozers. Drum them out of the service. (*A piano sounds faintly.*) What's that?

TOM. It's Mrs Blake and your niece, sir. The young lady's in the drawing room playing the piano.

COL. My wife down from her room, then?

TOM. Yes sir. Came down after lunch, sir.

COL. Good. Your very good health young man. Glad to have met you. (*Drinks.*) Saw you dancing last night. You sing also.

PETER. I try to, sometimes.

COL. Sing? Why?

PETER. Well . . . Partridge thinks I can sing.

COL. Oh! Well pardon me. I don't. And I hate singing. Never could sing. Don't like it. Like sport, horses, fresh air. None of your singing business for me. Wouldn't object so much but I served 25 years in the 5th Mahrattas, Bungapore. We sang "Old Lang Syne" once a year. Christmas. Rotten tune. Rotten head next morning. Take my advice, stop singing. Leads nowhere.

PETER. I have to. Sometimes. And to-night I must. With more jizz.

COL. Must! Bosh! My wife said to me . . . "We'll try the Excelsior again this year. I believe it's really fine now." So I said, "Right. One condition. No more singing doleful things in the evening. Can't stand songs like "Mona" or "In the Gloaming." Too much like cattle lowing. (*He looks hard at* PETER.) You remind me very much of somebody, Gordon.

PETER. That so?

COL. Yes. Funny. Ever meet you before anywhere else, did I?

PETER. Not to my knowledge.

COL. No? Must be wrong then. Damned funny though. Was sure I had.

PETER. Why?

COL. Ah! (*After another sharp scrutiny.*) Now I know who you remind me of! Jordan! That's it.

PETER. Jordan?

COL. Yes. Bungapore. Devil called Jordan from the sappers came out there to fix up a waterworks or something. Never did it. Too much this. (*He motions to the whiskey.*) What about a walk after dinner, before our bridge? Go and see the new Harbour Works, what?

PETER. Sorry. I couldn't possibly. Do you take an interest in Harbours?

COL. Well, I'm Chairman of Company building that new harbour out there. Didn't want the d-d post – refused it last time. Funny thing, my niece Joan takes an interest in it. Most extraordinary girl! Actually found her once reading some book about Docks, Harbours and Canals or something. (PETER *smiles.*) I said to my wife, "Joan's gone potty." What the devil does a woman want knowing anything about Docks or Harbours? Bosh! Ridiculous! Waste of time. All right for someone like you or Jordan. (*Suddenly.*) What do you do?

PETER. I . . . you mean what's my profession?

COL. Yes. What the devil do you do for a living?

PETER. Oh, at present – nothing. Just on a loose end at present. Sorry. I suppose . . . I'm somewhat vague.

COL. Hm. Vague. Vagueness. Vacuity. Hm. Don't like that in young people. (*Suddenly.*) Stop being vague. Do what Joan *shouldn't* be doing. Read up Harbours and Docks and go and dig something – Suez Canal or something.

(PARTRIDGE *enters.*)

PART. Tom! Tom!

TOM. Yes sir.

PART. (*suddenly seeing* SCOTT). It's all right. Still here I see. You did him all right, did you?

TOM. Yes sir. (SCOTT *looks up.*) You're all right, aren't you?

SCOTT. Um. How do, Partridge? Um. Very nice here. Most comfortable.

PART. Good. Right. Maybe he'd have a couple of coronas.

TOM. Yes sir. I'll get them sir. (*exit.*)

PART. Brave day, Colonel. How's the golf?

COL. Fair, fair. Do better tomorrow. Getting the stiffness off. (*Looking at* PETER.) Made another couple of guineas off this rascal today.

PART. Good. (*He takes out a newspaper.*) And my heartiest congratulations. There's todays "Times". You might want to see it, Colonel. There's reference to your election as Chairman of the New Harbour and Port Co., here.

COL. Yes; didn't want it. Refused election last time.

PART. (*handing over paper*). I marked it for you – page 3. One moment, Peter. Excuse me, Colonel. (*He beckons.*) Come here, Peter.

PETER (*rising*). Yes? (PARTRIDGE *draws him aside.*)

PART. So he won off you again at golf did he?

PETER. Yes. One up on the last green.

PART. Aye. I seen the last of the match from the office. You missed that last putt on the 18th nicely. Did you pay him yet?

PETER. Well . . . yes I did. But you told me on Monday that . . . (*he hesitates.*)

PART. I told you what?

PETER. That you'd stand the racket and not to worry . . .

PART. I know. Aye. Well, that's alright, I'll leave it for you in the office. But Peter, here . . . I'll be wanting a little more return for all this cash invested you know. Six quid in three days . . . a bit thick you know, Peter. I don't just hand out money for nothing. It's due to me to get some credit for it too, you know.

PETER. But I can't very well tell him it's your money, can I?

PART. No (*A pause.*) But you needn't just pay him for staying on here by missing putts. (*He looks meaningly at* PETER.) The aunt . . . she's come down.

PETER. Who?

PART. The aunt. (PETER *looks at him somewhat puzzled.*) You've been paying a little too much attention to a particular young lady, Peter.

PETER. Have I?

PART. Yes. Do you not remember I told you of a particular young lady?

156

PETER. Yes.

PART. Aye. Well, I haven't mentioned it to you yet, but . . . well, that's her now. Playing the piano. She's the old warrior's niece. So mind what I told you and nose off. Look after him and the aunt.

(*Piano ceases.*)

PETER (*aghast*). So then Miss Blake . . .

PART. Aye. Miss Blake . . .

PETER. She's the . . . she's the . . .

PART. Aye. She's the one.

PETER. She's the nice girl that . . .

PART. Aye. The nice class girl that Sammy Partridge told you about. That's her. D'ye understand? (PETER *makes no reply.*) And the aunt has come down now. Do you see?

PETER. Her aunt . . .

PART. You seem to be a long time taking it in Peter. You were just paying a little too much attention to the niece. D'ye follow, Peter? Well, just you transfer that attention to the auntie. And give me that bit of scope that we arranged. D'ye see, Peter? The gooseberry season now commences. D'ye follow.

PETER. You never told me this before.

PART. No. But it struck me after last night when I saw you dancing with her, the sooner I told you the better. The auntie's been laid up since they came, but she's up to-day, I understand. So keep her and the Colonel in good humour. I don't mind investing a couple of quid a day in this old warrior, but I'm the preference shareholder in this business, Peter. You follow?

PETER (*grimly*). I do.

PART. Right. Now just a word more. You weren't quite up to the mark last night in the singing. Course I understand you being a bit . . . well . . . I know the crowd was a bit stiff, but . . . put a bit more jizz into it. Have a ball or two of malt. Just enough like. Sure you needn't mind if you do make a bit of an idiot of yourself. No one will mind you.

(MRS BLAKE *enters.*)

MRS B. Why, here you are, Tiger. And you never came to inquire how I was. But you needn't bother now. I'm quite fit again, thank you.

COL. Oh, sorry. Bit tired. Just done 36 holes. No lunch.

MRS B. No lunch! Gracious! Have you had your tea?

COL. Wait for dinner now. Far better. Um. Most introduce my partner. Um. This is . . . what's this they call you, young man?

PETER. Grahame. I mean Gordon.

COL. Oh yes yes. Gordon – something – Grahame. Gordon Grahame of Claverhouse. My wife, Mrs Blake, Claverhouse. Wife's been laid up since she came here. Just down first time to-day.

PETER. I'm sorry to hear that.

MRS B. Oh, I'm quite recovered now. And I'm very grateful to you. It's been such a rest having Tiger off my hands for the last couple of days.

COL. Now, now, Eh? (JOAN BLAKE *enters. She is a handsome young girl in the early twenties.*) This is my niece Joan. Joan–Claverhouse.

JOAN (*smiling*). We met before.

COL. (*sharply*). When? Oh yes, yes, of course. I saw you dancing with him last night. Hm.

PART. I hope you like your room, Miss Blake.

JOAN (*delighted*). I think my room's a charm, Mr Partridge. There's a most exquisite view from the western window. And there's another – (*she laughs*) – do you know, it looks right down on this lounge, Uncle! (*She takes* PETER *up the lounge.*) That's it up there. On the first floor!

MRS B. Sorry I can't say there's a view from mine. What on earth made you choose that awful room, Tiger?

COL. Air. I want air. Give me big windows. Don't give a hang for scenery. Windows. That's what I want.

MRS B. Well, you certainly got them all right! It seems all windows. No view, though. I just got so tired of the wallpaper, I got up and came down after lunch. (*Crossing to* PARTRIDGE.) Oh, I say, Mr Partridge, I do want to see your new grounds. I've been hearing so much about them.

PART. Certainly. And with the greatest of pleasure, Mrs Blake. Right now if you like.

MRS B. I hear you have a wonderful new rockery garden.

PART. (*proudly*). Spent six hundred on it last year. Great. A mass of blooms at present. You could almost smell them from here. I'll be delighted to show you round.

MRS B. Come and see it with us, Tiger.

COL. Excuse me, Mary, but I'm too stiff at the moment. You go along with them, Claverhouse.

JOAN. Come along then, Peter. (*Exit with* PETER.)

MRS B. What did she call him?

PART. Everybody here calls him Peter. If we go down to the right and follow them, Mrs Blake, you'll see the new walk I made last year. Full of rhododendrums. The scent of them on a balmy night in June . . . ach . . . I couldn't describe it to you. You'd never forget it as long as you lived. (TOM *enters with cigar box.*) Don't forget the

158

Colonel, Tom, with them Coronas. Have a couple, I can guarantee them, Colonel.

COL. Not now. After dinner I will. Prefer pipe at present. (MRS BLAKE *and* PARTRIDGE *go out.*)

TOM (*bringing box to* SCOTT). Cigar, sir, and Mr Partridge's compliments.

SCOTT. Um. No. Not now. After dinner. (*He examines them, however.*) "Corona de Corona"! Um. Nice. Um. (*He extracts a handful of cigars and puts them in his pocket.*)

COL. Here, waiter!

TOM. Yes, sir.

COL. I'll have one if that clown leaves any . . .

TOM (*hurriedly*). Yes yes. Certainly sir. (*Bringing the box.*) They're the real thing sir. We only keep the best here, sir.

COL. Remains to be seen. (*Takes and lights one, then looks hard at* SCOTT.) Is that fellow awake yet?

TOM. Oh yes. Yes sir. (*Suggestively.*) Little walk would do you good, sir. What do you think? (COLONEL *shakes his head.*) Excuse me sir. (*Sotto voce.*) Would you mind, sir, if I asked you a request, sir – just a little favour sir. (*Motioning to* SCOTT.) The gentleman's an invalid, sir.

COL. Devil of an appetite for an invalid.

TOM. Yes sir. He's got what you call it, the eating diabetes, sir.

COL. Um. More like sleepy sickness. (*He scrutinises* SCOTT *disapprovingly.*) Lazy devil.

TOM (*soothingly*). Perhaps you'd like the other gentleman, sir. (*Nodding to* MCCLEERY.) Very nice gentleman and his wife over there, sir. No. 18.

COL. What?

TOM. No. 18, sir. Poetry.

COL. What?

TOM. Poetry, sir. Ulster poet, sir.

COL. Ulster what?

TOM. Ulster poet, sir.

COL. Bosh! Never heard of such a thing, did you?

TOM. No sir.

COL. Not at all. (*He rises and walks up and down, occasionally stopping to eye* SCOTT *disgustedly. The ball of wool slips from* MRS MCCLEERY'*s lap and attracts his attention. He picks it up.*) What's this?

MRS McC. Oh, I beg your pardon. It's mine. I'm so sorry. I'm afraid. . . .

COL. (*amiably*). Don't apologise. Don't apologise. Useful work,

knitting. (*He hands her the ball.*) When it's well done. If it's not –
awful. (*He looks at* MCCLEERY.)

MRS McC. (*nudging her husband*). This is my husband, Colonel. . . .

COL. How do, No. 18? Must have a name of some sort, eh?

MR McC. Oh, I'm just plain John McCleery.

COL. Um. Good old Ulster name. Mine's Blake. 5th Mahrattas.
Bungapore. Twenty-five years out there. (*Testily.*) Hell.

MRS McC. Indeed life in India must be a very trying thing indeed. I
believe the heat . . . .

COL. Quite. Heat. Mosquitoes. (*Looks at* SCOTT.) No snoozing in
India. 130 degrees in the shade, Bungapore. Hottest station in
India. (*He looks hard at* MCCLEERY.) Ulster Poet?

MR McC. Well, I'm not exactly a Poet. I'm just in my old age indulging
in a little versifying.

COL. Um. Ever publish anything?

MR McC. Well, "The Whig" took one or two little things I made out
last winter.

MR McC. Oh indeed he's just a little too modest, Colonel Blake. They
took one in "The Bell" the other day.

COL. Um. Did they?

MRS McC. And now he's thinking of getting out a little book of verse.

COL. Um. Read me one of them. Short one.

MRS McC. Go ahead, John. It's no harm to see what a man like the
Colonel would think.

MR McC. (*diffidently*). Well, I was just working out a wee one here. It's
a wee bit like what you know Mr Yeats would be trying. I think
it's something is his style like:

"Away where the curlews cry on the bog,
    There sounds the faint wild bark of the dog,
And oh! to be there
    When the canavan fair
Billows and sways in the evening air."

COL. (*delightedly*). Right! I say, jolly good! Bog – dog. Damn fine!
Love bogs and dogs. On you go. Another verse.

MR McC. I'm just working at the next one. I – well – I – I haven't quite
got the idea for the next one.

COL. (*enthusiastically*). Well. Extraordinary. Yes. Jolly good idea. Now
let me see. We're out in the bog. Yes. I have it! Next verse. Grouse.
Drive. Butts. Grouse coming over you with a following wind. 90
miles an hour. Grand! Next verse. Get into the butts. Describe the
grouse coming over with the wind. H'up! Over they go! Bang!
Bang! Right and left barrel. Got 'em! Good dog! Fetch 'em!

MRS McC. (*hastily*). Of course, it's very difficult work you'll understand Colonel.

COL. Oh quite, quite. (*The ball of wool slips again, he retrieves it.*) Your ball, madam.

MRS McC. Oh, thank you. I'm afraid this ball of wool of mine is a bit of a nuisance.

COL. Yes yes, quite. Husband here should invent something. Pocket or something to keep it in. Cartridge bag or pocket.

MRS McC. That's a nice young man you had out golfing.

COL. Oh, yes yes. Quite.

MRS McC. I suppose you know him very well, Colonel?

COL. Don't know the rascal from Adam. Got here on Monday. Told Partridge I wanted a game. He put up this Claverhouse chap. Ha, ha! Took a couple of guineas off him so far. Must have another rattle at him to-morrow. (*Suddenly – going towards entrance.*) Must have a little stroll before dinner. Must see what's become of my womenfolk. (*Looks at* SCOTT.) Lazy devil! Get up, sir.

TOM (*hurriedly*). Excuse me sir! I think I see your party out there, sir. (*The* COLONEL *looks, nods and goes out.*) Thanks be to God! He puts me in a tremble every time he looks at you, Mr Scott.

SCOTT (*sleepily*). Um.

TOM. Yes sir. Drat them flies. (*He flicks serviette.*) It's all right, he's gone out sir. (SCOTT *opens an eye and nods sleepily.*) Never mind him, Mr Scott. A dasint ould gentleman, but he can't stand still for two seconds. Not like you, Mr Scott.

SCOTT (*drowsily*). Um. Yes. Um.

TOM. Yes sir. Them Indian soldiers has all their livers gone wrong. Eating nothing but curried chicken and Bombay duck. Not like you, sir. (*He busies himself attending to the screen and cushions, and talks soothingly to* SCOTT.) Not like you, sir. You know what's what. None of them made-up dishes for us connoisseurs, Mr Scott. You and me, we knows better than that. No shepherds pie for us, Mister. Not likely. (SCOTT *grunts.*) Another little snooze sir. Right. (TOM *retires to watch him from a distance, then catches* MRS MCCLEERY's *eye.*) The boss getting on well, ma'am?

MRS McC. (*warningly*). Shush! Yes, Tom, very well.

TOM. That's good. (*He looks hard at* MCCLEERY *who has all the appearance of distraction.*) D'ye know, ma'am, he should get Mr Peter to help him.

MRS McC. Peter?

TOM. Sure, isn't that what Mr Peter is here for? Helping people.

MRS McC. I wonder who he is!

161

TOM. He just landed out of the sky like, one day with Mr Partridge. And I suppose he'll go off again the same way.

MRS McC. I wonder where he comes from.

TOM. THE divil a one of us knows, ma'am. But Mary, the housemaid up on No. 5 floor, tells me he has some old label on his bag with an address on it. Something like . . . Bally . . . Bally . . . something, Co. Letirim.

MRS McC. I wonder by any chance could it be Ballywilder?

TOM. That's it. That's it. Ballywilder!

VOICE (*off*). Waiter.

TOM. Yes, sir. (*He goes out.*)

MRS McC. (*excitedly*). There, there. I just knew it was him! John! John! darling!

MR McC. (*angrily*). What?

MRS McC. Wasn't it at Ballywilder in Leitrim that John Grahame, the wild young man lived, who made the run-away match with your sister-in-law's first cousin?

MR McC. Yes, yes. Why? These people are all dead long ago, thank goodness.

MRS McC. Indeed, nothing of the kind. There was a young boy and girl left, anyway. And your sister-in-law's first cousin died and then he died, and the place was sold afterwards to Joseph Halliday, their uncle. And they were all living there two years ago.

MR McC. Don't interrupt me any more. (*Heatedly.*) The old Colonel has the whole thing destroyed on me.

MRS McC. Ah, don't say that, darling.

MR McC. He has, he's got my imagination into them butts and I can't get out of them. (*Maddened.*) Damn him with his right and left and bang! – bang! That sort of thing is alright for epic poets but I'm a lyric poet . . . .

MRS McC. (*soothingly*). Indeed, you're a lyric, darling.

MR McC. And the last thing you want in a lyric is guns and shots and bangs!

MRS McC. Yes, yes, I know that, darling. But it's interesting, isn't it, to get the outlook of that class of people on your work? After all, it's him and his class that really reads anything worth while. Isn't it, love?

MR McC. I wonder!

MRS McC. (*musingly and to herself*). The same name too. I just did right, I know I did, to write Joe Halliday that letter yesterday.

MR McC. Write? What were you writing to Joe Halliday yesterday? If there's one man I detest it's that Joe Halliday. What did you write to him about?

MRS McC. It's all right, darling. Don't worry. (*A pause.*) Do you not think we should go and dress for dinner, darling? You didn't do it last night, but to-night's a bit special. And a wee rest would do you good. You've been a long time now composing.

MR McC. Ach! Damn that man and his right and left and bang! . . . bang!

MRS McC. There, there, darling. Let's go upstairs for a change. Come along.

(MCCLEERY, *grumbling, obeys, and they both go out. There is no one left in the lounge but* SCOTT, *who snores contentedly. A gong sounds, booming through the lounge.* SCOTT *wakes suddenly, yawns and stretches himself.*)

SCOTT. Um. Where's everybody? Um. Company seems to have gone. Um. Must dress . . . Better have a little walk before dinner. Um. (*He picks up the programme, feels for his glasses and puts them on.*) Um. Not menu. (*He throws it down.* COLONEL'*s voice, off.*) Um. Must have a little stroll. Um. (SCOTT *exits hurriedly.*)

PART. (*off*). Off for a little walk, Mr Scott! Good. (*Enters with the* COLONEL *and* MRS BLAKE.)

MRS B. I must say, Mr Partridge, the view from the little walk was certainly exquisite.

PART. Aye. Your niece seems to be taking a long interest in it.

MRS B. Well, certainly no one could keep from admiring it. I couldn't blame her. (*A pause.*) Didn't we hear a gong going?

PART. Aye. We sound one three quarters of an hour before dinner as a warning to dress, like.

COL. I see – Snoozer's wakened up and gone out. Only thing wakes him up!

MRS B. Joan had better hurry. You'll tell her, Mr Partridge? We'd better dress now, Tiger.

COL. Poet's gone too, I see. Bog. Dog. Hm. Funny.

(*The* COLONEL *and* MRS BLAKE *go out.*)

PART. (*looking out L.*). What's keeping that young pup! After me warning him, too.

(*He watches moodily.* JOAN *and* PETER *suddenly enter.*)

JOAN. We stayed to see the sunset. It was really wonderful. Do you know, Mr Partridge, I've seen very few views to compare with that from the old Cromlech. The picture you get there of the little village in the sandhills at the foot of Slieve Aughlish across the bay is most remarkable.

PART. (*somewhat mollified*). Maybe you'd do a little picture of it

163

sometime. (*He picks up a Hotel Guide.*) There's a photograph of it here, of course, on this, but I would prefer something a bit more arty, like.

JOAN. You certainly chose a beauty spot for your hotel.

PART. Sammy Partridge o' Ballymena isn't backward when it comes to recognising the beautiful. (*Looking at her.*) Beauty always appealed to Sammy Partridge.

JOAN (*laughing*). I believe you.

PART. (*emboldened*). In old days, popes and noblemen and the like encouraged the Arts. They're not able to afford the like now. So it's up to us, to them that has it, to take their places, like. (*Looking at his watch.*) It's getting close on dinner time, and you Peter, you have a rehearsal –

JOAN. What?

PART. It's all right, Miss Blake. I just want a word with Peter.

JOAN. Oh. I really must thank you Mr Partridge for that lovely room. Last night it was wonderful to see the new harbour away in the darkness, all lit up with flares . . . I must be off. See you later, shall I, Peter?

PETER. Yes. (*Exit* JOAN.)

PART. Aye. Sit down here, Peter. (*The latter does so.*) You seem to be forgetting something.

PETER. What?

PART. Aye. I suppose . . . (*Suddenly.*) She's a nice girl, isn't she, Peter?

PETER. Yes.

PART. Aye. (*A pause.*) You managed that very nicely.

PETER. Managed what?

PART. Oh aye. Oh, you're very simple, oh yes. You done it very well. (*Sarcastically.*) Peter the Great! Peter Simple, the Midshipman! But don't try it on again, Peter.

PETER. I don't understand what you're driving at.

PART. Didn't you agree to do something for me?

PETER. Yes I did. I'm doing all you asked me.

PART. Aye. And a bit more. Didn't I tell you that was the girl?

PETER. Yes.

PART. Aye. Well, that girl's for Sammy Partridge, not for broken Peter Grahame, the botch student. I'm one that likes a bargain to be a bargain. Your job is gooseberrying. None of your love-making. You can do that with them Blue Room Girls if you want to. (*Suddenly and furiously.*) What d'ye give me the slip for?

PETER. I didn't, I never thought of you, not for one second. She wanted to see the view from the Cromlech so I took her there.

164

Why shouldn't I?

PART. Aye. View from the Cromlech! You leave me, young man, to show her the views of the place. D'ye understand? Them views is mine. I've paid for them. And I've paid for you to mind your business. (*Angrily.*) D'ye hear me? Keep that old fellow going with his golf. I'll pay the damages. And if the old lady wants a bit of a walk, go and show *her* the views if you wish. But stand aside when it comes to the young one. That's your contract – keep it.

PETER. I want to tell you something, Partridge. When I entered into this contract, I . . . I had no idea that it was . . . well, that it was Miss Blake . . . was the particular girl you mentioned to me.

PART. (*sarcastically*). Did you not, Peter.

PETER. No.

PART. And what are you going to do, then? (*A pause.*) You going to fight me for her? All right. Go on then. But if you do – clear out of the Hotel. And hand me back what you owe me before you go. There's a tidy little sum owing me as you know. Can you square it up?

PETER. You know well I can't.

PART. Right. What are you going to do then?

PETER. I . . . I . . .

PART. Aye. What can you do? Don't be a fool. What hope is there for you, man? Honest? Is there any? I suppose you think because you're young that you'll win her some day! Twenty years hence? Don't be a fool, Peter. Leave her alone. Leave her alone to them that has a right to claim her. Have you any? Have you any money? Have you any brains?

PETER (*With a movement of anger*). I . . . I have a right to . . .

PART. Have you anything at all that gives you a right to even ask for her? Have you? (PETER *does not answer.*) You haven't! Then keep your word to me. Stand clear of the course. That's all.

PETER (*despairingly*). Very well.

PART. (*delightedly*). That's the way. Besides it's not fair to her, you know, Peter. You're a kind of half-baked student with nothing but cabarets and capers to live on. Leave her for them that suits her. (*Suddenly.*) Here, we'll have a nip in my room before the rehearsal. Where's Tom? Tom! Are you there, Tom?

TOM (*entering*). Yes, sir.

PART. Tom! Send a couple of cocktails to my room, quick.

TOM. Yes sir. (*He looks round excitedly.*) Where is he?

PART. Who?

TOM. The "Star" man, sir. Mr Scott. He's given me the slip.

165

PART. He's all right, Tom. I saw him out there, having a breath of air, I suppose.

(TOM *goes to one entrance.* PETER *is leaving by the other when he catches sight of someone at a window above. Forgetful of* PARTRIDGE, *who is watching, he smiles and waves as if in answer to a signal.*)

PART. Humph!

(PETER, *suddenly conscious of* PARTRIDGE, *exits hurriedly.*)

PART. Tom! Here Tom!

TOM. Yes, sir.

PART. D'ye see that window up there.

TOM. Yes, sir.

PART. Isn't that in No. 6?

TOM. Yes sir.

PART. Miss Blake's?

TOM. Yes sir. (*He looks at* PARTRIDGE *enquiringly. Then it dawns on his consciousness that there is something afoot which he cannot quite grasp.*) Yes, sir. Anything I can do for you sir?

PART. No.

(TOM *looks at him, then up at the window, and goes out silently.* PARTRIDGE *remains as if awaiting further developments. Moves towards the entrance as if to look up at the window, then changes his mind. He sits down.*)

PART. Right. Aye. Right, Mr Peter, right. We'll see.

(CURTAIN.)

ACT III

Some hours later in the evening of the same day.
Another lounge of the Excelsior Hotel. There is a large archway at the back closed off by curtains. A similar archway at the side, with looped curtains, gives access to the ballroom which is visible from the lounge. A dance band is playing and an occasional glimpse of the dancers can be seen through the archway. The only occupant of the lounge is MRS BLAKE *who is seated at a table sipping some coffee and listening to the music. It suddenly ceases; there is the usual applause and the guests who have been dancing come into the lounge. With them is* PETER *accompanied by* MISS VAN DE MEIZER, *a large imposing figure of a woman. They sit down at a corner of the lounge. Following them after a short interval, enter* COLONEL BLAKE *and* JOAN *who go over and sit beside* MRS BLAKE.

(PARTRIDGE *suddenly appears through the curtains from the back.*)

PART. Pardon, ladies and gentlemen. Just before you go off for some refreshment, I want to say that there'll be a longer interval than usual before the last item. I think some of you already know what it is, so I needn't say very much beyond hoping that you'll all appreciate it. I think it only right to mention that most unexpectedly, Viscount and Lady Merton and their party have just arrived and are honouring us with their presence this evening. It is a great pleasure to welcome them, both as regards the management and, I am sure, all the guests who are here to-night, and all I can say is that I hope they and all the other guests assembled here to-night will enjoy their stay in the Excelsior Hotel. Supper now ready. (*Exit*).

(*Faint applause. All dancers disperse except* PETER *and his partner,* COLONEL BLAKE, JOAN *and* MRS BLAKE *who remain behind.* BUTTONS *enters from Ballroom.*)

BUTTONS. No. 18 wanted. No. 18 wanted. 'Phone telegram, No. 18. No. 18 wanted.

167

COL. What's that?

BUTTONS. No. 18 'Phone telegram.

COL. What name, boy?

BUTTONS. McCleery. No. 18.

COL. Oh yes. Hm. The poet. Go on!

(TOM *the waiter enters from back. He pounces on the* BUTTONS.)

TOM. Here. Didn't I tell you to watch Mr Scott? What d'ye mean going off like this, shouting?

BUTTONS. The head boots told me to.

TOM. The head boots has no business to do anything of the kind. Go back at once and look after Mr Scott, and don't let him attempt to go up to his room without letting me know. Off with you at once.

(*Exit* BUTTONS. TOM *goes slowly round the room examining the seats.*)

MRS B. "Poet" did you say, Tiger? (*Laughing.*) Are you actually getting interested in poetry?

COL. This fellow's quite good. Good sport. Something like that Australian bushranger chap who wrote about horses. Forget the name. Entree reminded me of him.

JOAN. The what?

COL. Entree. Snipe we had at dinner. Bog. Hm. Just took a note before dinner in case I saw him again, all the game you find on a bog. Grouse, hare, duck, teal, widgeon – forgot snipe.

VAN. Gee, I say kid, you suits me just cruel.

PETER. Beg pardon, Miss Van de Meizer?

VAN. I say I guess you just suit me A. 1. You didn't tramp on my Paris footwear or anything. Say, do I book you again in the office or do you carry a slate?

PETER. Why?

VAN. 'Cause I'm just going to have a cinch on you, kid, for a few lessons. Do you know what I want most particular before I goes back to Sunflower Country and Chico City? Can't you teach jigs and reels?

PETER. It all depends on the pupils.

VAN. Gee, aint you modest. (*Laughs.*) Well, I gotta book you for to-morrow and next evening, so just put me on your slate right away.

PETER. Very well.

COL. What about supper?

MRS B. (*rising*). No, I'm going to the drawing-room to finish that Edgar Wallace.

COL. Joan?

168

JOAN. No. No supper for me, thanks, Uncle. I'll stay on here. Shall I keep your seats?

COL. Not for me. Can't stand this dancing business. What about a game of bridge?

MRS B. Couldn't you rest yourself, Tiger! You had a very strenuous day. Give your brains a rest.

COL. Oh – game of bridge wouldn't hurt anybody's brains. My mind – quite active now – must do something. Compose poetry or bid 5 no trump or something (*He sees* TOM.) Waiter!

TOM. Yes, sir.

COL. Any party looking for a fourth for a game of bridge? Gentlemen preferably.

TOM. Sixpence, shilling, halfcrown or pound a point, gentlemen, sir?

COL. Oh, halfcrown.

MRS B. Shilling's quite enough, Tiger. Be careful.

COL. Halfcrown. Not going to spend my brains on shillings. Halfcrown, waiter.

TOM. Yes, sir, I'll see. You won't be occupying this seat, then, sir?

COL. No.

TOM. Thank you. Excuse me, sir. (*He slips a card on to back of chair behind* COLONEL.) For another gentleman, sir. Whenever you leave, sir; no hurry. (*Exit.*)

MRS B. What on earth has he put behind you, Tiger?

JOAN (*reaching over for the card*). "Reserved." Oh, I suppose the Viscount wants this particular seat.

MRS B. Well, keep mine for me, darling, if you're not coming. Don't be too long at the bridge, Tiger. (*Exit.*)

VAN. When I see Mr Sam Partridge again I'll sure give you some boost, kid. How many dollars a week you getting here?

PETER. Oh, I'm all right that way. Please don't worry.

VAN (*persistently*). What you getting? Fifty dollars?

PETER. Thereabouts.

VAN (*reflectively*). Um. Fifty? 'Taint much. Yep. Guess I can be of some help here all right. Say, did you ever hear of the Helpers' League, over here in Ireland?

PETER. Can't say I did.

VAN. Well, Fire Chief Mulligan of Chico City, he started it. Help someone, somewhere, every day. That's our motto. And I was just wondering who I'd help here, and I guess it's you, kid.

PETER. Thanks very much, but really . . . I don't need help.

VAN. Now, don't say so. Everybody needs help. You sure need some more dollars and a boost up. I'll speak to your friend Sam, and you bet Sam'll listen to Van de Meizer. You know why?

PETER. I don't.

VAN. There's a party, 25 of us firm Chico City, doing Europe, and they always send me on in front for enquiry. They're all waiting up in Eustonville Hotel, waiting on Van to send 'em word – cut out or come along.

PETER. I see. Twenty-five.

VAN. Yep. You guess I let our friend Sam know size of our party pretty quick when I came along here. That's how I got room 45 and you for dancing partner. (*Suddenly.*) Guess I'll phone them to-night and confirm all O.K., when you and me we've seen Partridge.

PETER. I don't want to see Partridge.

VAN. Well, I gotta see him (*Rises.*) Say kid, I want to tell you, and you believe it. There ain't no Hotel where Van de Meizer of the Helpers League has stayed at in this whole country, where there ain't someone special on the hotel staff – bellhop or chef or waiter, that ain't got a rise in wages 'cause of me and my Helpers League. Ain't that what you call helping people?

PETER. It certainly is. (*They go off.*)

COL. (*rising*). Any money, Joan?

JOAN. I'll stand in with you for a five. (*She gives it to him.*) Is that enough?

COL. Oh, quite, quite. Sight's getting very bad. Wasn't that Claverhouse?

JOAN. Yes, it was.

COL. Oh. What the devil does he dance with all the old dowagers for, all night?

JOAN. Why does he play golf with cross old Tigers all day?

COL. Oh that's different. Totally different. Can't compare golf with dancing. Bosh!

TOM (*entering*). I've got three gentlemen for you, Colonel. On the main landing. Five shilling gentlemen, sir.

COL. Right. Mum's the word, Joan. (*Exit.*)

TOM (*arranging chairs*). Excuse me miss. For Mr. Scott.

JOAN. Who?

TOM. Mr Scott, Miss. A very quiet gentleman, miss. But how long he'll stay that way this evening, I don't know. Terrible commotion this evening, miss. (*Confidentially.*) Had to change him out of No. 3. We're putting the Viscount into it. "Keep Mr Scott well dosed, Tom," says the boss, "and he won't be a bit the wiser. And keep him downstairs at all costs out of the way." But I tell you, Mr

Scott isn't just as stupid as he looks. You don't hold a job like that without brains stowed away somewhere. (*Suddenly stopping and looking at* JOAN.) Are you fond of dancing, miss?

JOAN. Yes.

TOM. Aye. Why wouldn't you be? Excuse me, miss, but do you know what I think is the loveliest thing in the world? A young girl dancing! Rosebuds in the springtime. Be me soul, but it is too short a time that they are that way too. Aye. The Lord be with them. Here he is! (SCOTT *escorted by* BUTTONS *appears chewing an unlit cigar*). Here's Mr Scott now. Excuse me miss. Now sir. Your seat. (SCOTT *nods vaguely but pays little attention. He insists on examining the texture of the curtains.*)

TOM (*to* BUTTONS). Were you with him all the time since?

BUTTONS. Yes.

TOM. You're sure he didn't go upstairs?

BUTTONS. No.

TOM (*with sigh of relief*). That's all right. Did they get all the Viscount's stuff into No. 3 yet.

BUTTONS. Not yet. I never seen as much baggage to get in. And – (*pointing to* SCOTT) his was just as bad to get out.

TOM. Tell them to hurry. I can't keep the gentleman downstairs all-night. (*Exit* BUTTONS.) Now, Mr Scott. Your seat, sir. How does it suit you?

SCOTT (*settling down*). Excellent. V' good. (*He sees* JOAN.) Excuse me. Hope you don't object to cigar, um?

TOM. Ach, the young lady won't mind. Sure you don't, miss? Smoke away sir. (*He lights a match.*) Now sir. A good long strong pull and all together. That's it. Going strong now, sir?

SCOTT. Um. Thank you. V' good cigar. Um. Nice room. Um. Programme please.

TOM. Programme? Here you are sir. (*Hands him one.*) All over now but the last item, sir. The ballet, sir.

SCOTT. Um. Yes. Ballet. Um. Waiter! If you see that boy Peter, tell him I want him. Um. Most important.

TOM. Certainly sir. I'll get him for you. Like a little curaçao and brandy sir? Go very well with the cigar, sir.

SCOTT. Um. Quite so. Um. (*Looking at* JOAN.) Young lady like something too?

JOAN. Oh no thank you. I have some coffee here.

SCOTT (*to* TOM). Um. V' good. And about so much brandy – Courvoisier.

TOM. Yes sir.

SCOTT. Can't read this programme without glasses. Must go up to No. 3 and get them. (*He attempts to get up but is restrained by* TOM.)

TOM. Don't attempt to be running up and down them stairs, sir. Bad for you. Where are the spectacles, sir?

SCOTT. Room No. 3. Um. On the dressing table.

TOM. Yes sir. And don't stir sir, whatever you do, till I come back. Curaçao, glasses, Courvoisier. Right. (*Exit.*)

SCOTT. V'obliging fellow that waiter. Um. Splendid hotel this. Um. My room No. 3 couldn't be beaten for comfort in the Hotel Cecil. (*Looks at programme.*) Orchestra keep very good tempo. Um. Don't you think?

JOAN. Yes.

SCOTT. Partridge very clever. Does it well, you know. Um. (*Laughs knowingly.*) Um. Oh, clever! Picks up talent all r'. Good sense. Um. Good staff. Um. Chefs and waiters. Um. But . . . Peter! I like that boy! Um.

JOAN (*beginning to take new interest in his talk.*) Do you? Really?

SCOTT. Yes (*confidentially.*) V'funny last night. Partridge gave lil' party in his room. Peter there. V'funny. Clown. Um. Partridge sort of ringmaster. Um. Made me laugh. Um. But Peter . . . extrar . . . extraor . . . extrtaor . . . Life very ex . . . ex . . . extra . . . must get away from that word. Life very . . . much up and down . . . round and round . . . v' difficult . . . constant movement . . . river flowing along . . . um . . . carry you along . . . um (PETER *enters.*) Hm! V'man I wanta see. 'Scuse me. Goo' boy. goo' boy. (*Fumbling in vest pocket.*) Pardon me, my card. (*Producing it.*) S. Nelson Scott. S. for Seosamh. Irish part. In Eire – Seosamh N. Scott. In Northern Ireland – S. Nelson Scott. (*He stares hard at* PETER.) I want most particularly speak to you, Peter. (*Turns suddenly to* JOAN.) This young lady . . . interested in you in any way? Um? (JOAN *looks at* PETER *and smiles.*) No? V'well. You and me, Peter, we talk. You stand there. Just a moment. Now. (*He pauses.*) What's the most important thing in life? Um? Peter?

PETER (*smiling at* JOAN). Hard to say.

SCOTT. Well, I don't consider it hard to say; it's being absolutely thorough. (*Emphatically.*) Whatever you do . . . do it . . . thoroughly. (*He sips his drink.*) Yes, thoroughly. For instance, I thoroughly vet and examine this hotel. Don't I? Yes, I do. Thoroughly. And I have to see what it's like to sleep in, and eat in, and drink in. And I do it – thoroughly. And that's why I'm Chief Inspector of the . . . um . . . the doesn't matter. Understand?

PETER. I do. Thoroughly.

SCOTT. Right. (*He turns to* JOAN.) Colonel thinks I snooze all day on sofas. Quite entitled to his opinion. But I do more'n snooze all the time. Quite wide awake is S. Nelson Scott. Quite. Quite. If you want to be . . . engineer . . . be an engineer. If you want to be cabaret artist . . . be one . . . but be thorough. Very well, now. I help you. I go . . . other hotels. Much finer . . . bigger than Excelsior. And I'm interested in you Peter. Sufficiently to write to big hotel man at Llandadero . . . inth . . . and I got letter back. Letter I want most particularly show you. (*Fumbling in pocket.*) Must have left it in my lounge suit. (*Suddenly.*) Wait. Wait. Just you stay here. Most important. Secret. Um. Get it from my room. No. 3. Important letter. Um. Keep my seat. (*He rises.*)

JOAN (*laughing*). Oh please, Mr Scott . . .

SCOTT. Won't laugh when Peter sees letter. Must get it. Um. (*Exit.*)

JOAN. Forgive me, Peter, for laughing. I can't help it. Tom was asked to keep him back while they were changing his room. (*She grows serious. A pause.*) Peter!

PETER. Yes.

JOAN. You seem afraid of something.

PETER (*breezily*). No. I'm not. I don't care. (*Sitting by her.*) There. He can do what he likes.

JOAN. Who?

PETER. I'm near you again, so it doesn't matter. That's all I care about.

JOAN. What are you doing in this place, Peter?

PETER. I thought you might have guessed by this time.

JOAN. Partridge has bought you?

PETER. Yes.

JOAN. For how long?

PETER. As long as he likes to keep me, I suppose.

JOAN. Peter, last night when I looked out and saw away across the bay the big flare lights and shadows of men, and gantries, and the great blocks of stone moving into place . . . I . . .

PETER. Yes?

JOAN. I was sure you'd be out there among them, somewhere, and instead . . . Oh Peter! It's hard to say what I think, down here . . . in this place.

There was once upon a time a Peter who told me he couldn't build harbours or docks or canals until he got a certain book . . . (*she pauses.*) But when he got it . . .

PETER. Joan!

JOAN. . . . he forgot all about it and went off to play. You won't need

173

that book any more now Peter, so would you please give it back to me?

PETER. Give back . . . your book?

JOAN. Yes. It won't be any use now . . . any more to you, Peter. But I would like to keep it . . . just as as memory of a boy who once – passed by.

PETER (*desperately*). No, I won't. You don't understand . . . it's no use trying to explain to you, I suppose, but I'm not going to give up that book . . . that's something of you I'll never give up. Never.

(TOM *comes in with tray and glasses, put it on table beside* PETER, *then looks up with a gasp of dismay*.)

TOM. Oh! James's Gate! Where is he?

PETER. Who?

TOM. Mr Scott.

PETER. Gone to his room to get a letter.

TOM. Heavenly Father! I'm ruined. (*Hastens out, muttering*.) Them four stars will remain in the heavens, now and forever, amen! All the Holy Apostles Peter and Paul . . . (*Exit*.)

PETER. Joan. I . . . I want to tell you something. You believed in me once . . . I know you did . . . That's true. Isn't it?

JOAN. Yes.

PETER. I didn't tell you before Joan, that I . . . I failed. Went down in the final. That seemed to end everything. Then Partridge came and offered this – this chance of an escape. I took it . . . that's why I'm here. And I tried down here to forget all that happened until I suddenly met you last night. When you spoke to me, I knew that you hadn't guessed the truth. (*Despairingly*.) That big wonder work out there . . . that great new harbour that you saw . . . it has been calling out at night to me with its syrens and its gantries . . . "tell her the truth, Peter Grahame, so that she might forgive – and say goodbye."

PART. (*without – loudly*). Peter!

PETER. That thing shouting . . . it owns me!

JOAN. No no . . . I . . .

PART (*loudly*). Peter! (*Enters*.) Ah, this is where you are! Time you was changing for the ballet. Go and put on your clown's clothes, man. You're late.

PETER. Good-bye then, Joan.

JOAN. Until I see you again, Peter, good-bye.

(*Exit* PETER.)

PART. I'd like to see you after the show is over, Miss Blake. There's something I'd like to talk to you about. It . . .

(McCLEERY *enters. He peers anxiously round room.*)

PART. Looking for something, Mr McCleery?

MR McC. Yes, my wife and I have been looking for Mr Gordon or Grahame, or Peter, I think you call him. We have important news for him. (*Sits down wearily.*) Oh, dear; Oh, dear! It's very hard to get anything done in this life. He's not here?

PART. He won't be available until the ballet's over.

MR McC. How soon would that be?

PART. Very soon now. A word with you afterward, Miss Blake. (*Exit.*)

MR McC. A most extraordinary thing. This young Peter man turns out to be a relative of mine that's been missing from home for some time.

MRS McC. (*entering hurriedly*). Did you find him yet, John darling?

MR McC. No, he's dressing for the ballet.

MRS McC. And here's his Uncle Joe coming to-night – expected any time now – and if he finds him in the middle of all this goings-on sure we'll only have made things worse than ever.

MR McC. Worse! I should say so. And what about me? Oh dear! It's been the same for forty years as far as I'm concerned. Just when you get the inspiration coming and just when you're on the tick of getting exactly what you want and believe is right – there's a knock at the door, or the dinner gong goes, or that military gentleman butts in or some child borrows your pencil or your pen, or you . . . you with your putting your nose into things you've no business to put them into . . . sending off messages to Ballywilder and bringing that fellow Joe Halliday down here. A man I have the utmost abhorrence for. An old Jansenist heretic that never saw beauty in anything but the Bank of Ireland on a pound note. You bring the horror of my life down here on me, and for what? What's this young fellow to you or to me? Or what matter does he make to either of us one way or the other? (*Excitedly.*) If he want to go to hell his own way, let him!

MRS McC. (*soothingly*). Well, sure I did it for the best darling. And there now, there, now that there's quiet here, perhaps you could just try that wee last line again? Wouldn't you darling? Do!

MR McC. (*grumbling, taking out pencil and notebook*). Some of these days I'll just go ahead and finish what I'm at, and everybody else can go to Beelzebub.

(*A gong sounds the warning for the ballet.* SCOTT *appears accompanied by the* BUTTONS *and* TOM, *carrying a glass.*)

TOM (*luring* SCOTT *with the glass*). Here you are, Mr Scott. (*Mops his brow.*) And here's your whiskey and soda, sir. (*Arranges chair and*

175

speaks excitedly to JOAN.) Thanks be to God, miss, he seen the Colonel on the landing and that delayed him till I caught up on him. (SCOTT *puts on his glasses, and wanders slowly over to* MCCLEERY.) It took three of the best green chartreuse in the house, and the head waiter himself, to keep him downstairs while I went up and found the letter he wanted, and the spectacles he wanted, and stuck them in his pocket. Bad luck to him! (*Suddenly finding* SCOTT *has wandered off.*) Come on, Mr Scott, here's your seat. Over here, sir. (*To* BUTTONS.) If he attempts to leave that seat, or this room, and you don't tell me, I'll have you drummed out of the service. Don't dare leave him. (*Exit.*)

SCOTT (*sitting down*). Oh. Um. (*Bowing to* JOAN.) How do? Oh. Yes. Um. We were interrupted that time. Um. I . . . most interesting man – head waiter – I've met for a long time . . . mos' interesting. Um. Now. (*Fumbles in pocket.*) Letter here from Llandanderorinth – head waiter knew – hotel there well . . .

> (*A second gong sounds, and the orchestra is heard playing a lively air.* PARTRIDGE *enters from back followed by* PETER *dressed as a Pierrot and both cross to ballroom off-stage. The lights in the lounge grow dim, but the ballroom lights throw as beam on* PETER *as he moves towards it.*)

SCOTT Goo' boy Peter . . . I . . . (*There are cries of "Hush" and he is silent. Exit* PETER *and* PARTRIDGE. *The lights dim slowly then blackout, to indicate the passing of a few minutes, as the music swells. Suddenly they grow bright again, the music ceases, and there is a loud burst of applause from the Ballroom.* PETER *enters exhausted, and makes for exit at back.*)

SCOTT (*endeavouring to catch* PETER, *but restrained by* BUTTONS). Peter! Just take this letter and read it. Offering you engagement – winter season – Llandanderointh. Ten a week . . . don't stay – hic – here, Partridge – hic – no good, not big . . . go to Llandanderointh. (BUTTONS *brings the letter to* PETER.) Read letter and come up and see me later in my room. No. 3. Talk it over. Going there now to wait for you. Ta ta! (PETER *takes the letter hurriedly, motions at* JOAN *to stay, and goes out followed by* SCOTT *and the* BUTTONS.)

MRS BLAKE (*entering*). Time you were going to bed dear.

JOAN. Yes Auntie. I . . . I'd like to stay just for one minute or so. I'd like to speak to Peter.

MRS B. Peter? Oh. The boy who was dancing?

JOAN. Yes. I want to say something to him.

MRS B. Say it to-morrow, darling. Come long with me. Come. (*She *and* JOAN go out.)

MRS MCC. We'll wait and see Peter, John. We must see him. We must save him if we can. I don't know if you agree, but it's a kind of squandering of youth, this sort of life. I'd like to get him back to earth – to realities, I mean. (PETER *enters centre.*) Oh Peter, Peter! (*Rushing to him.*) Peter, do you not know me?

PETER. No.

MRS MCC. And your cousin John, John McCleery?

PETER (*dazed*). McCleery? Yes, I do now, faintly. You were at Ballywilder once . . . long ago.

MRS MCC. Ah, he remembers! How well he remembered! The poor, poor boy. Peter dear. Peter. Joe . . . your Uncle Joe, he's coming to-night to take you home.

PETER. I haven't any home.

MRS MCC. Yes yes, you have. You poor wandering boy. Your Uncle Joe – he'll take you back again. He wired us to-day. (*Producing telegram.*) "Am certain it is he. Tell him be ready return with me to-night. Have situation ready for him here."

PETER. I . . . I thank you, Mrs McCleery, for all your kind thought but – (*bracing himself.*) – I'm never going back to Uncle Joe – Never, never!

MRS MCC. When he comes and you see him, you poor wandering boy, you'll think better of it. Indeed you will. Won't you now?

PETER. Never! I'll say goodnight – and thank you. (MCCLEERY *looks at him and then shakes his head.*)

MRS MCC. Maybe tomorrow! You'll . . .

PETER. Never. Goodnight.

> (*The* MCCLEERYS *go out sadly. There is a pause. The lights dim.* PETER *sits down dejectedly.* JOAN *appears suddenly. She tiptoes over and puts her hands over his eyes.*)

JOAN. Guess!

PETER. It's you, Joan.

JOAN (*laughing*). Yes. I couldn't go to bed until I came to see you, first. And then – to kiss you goodnight. (PETER *rises, they embrace.* PARTRIDGE *enters and stands looking at them.*)

PART. Peter! (*They fall apart.*) Come on. I have a wee party. The Viscount and Lady Merton and some friends in their private drawing-room.

PETER. Again? To-night?

PART. Yes.

PETER. I just wanted to tell you . . .

PART. Now go on and none of your fool talk. Go and get changed and smarten yourself up. And do what you're paid for and what you promised to do. You're a man – you're supposed to be one anyway. You made a man's promise. If Sam Partridge said to a man "I'll do it" – Sam Partridge does it.

PETER. I've tried to.

PART. Tried, have you? Do you want to know the truth about him, Miss Blake?

PETER. She knows the truth.

PART. Oh, does she. Does she know you got ploughed in the exam? Does she know you got thrown overboard by your people? That you daren't go back to face them? An idle, useless, floating straw; no money, no means, not even enough to pay his lodgings. Does she know all that? Did you tell her how I found you down and out? Yes, I found him like that Miss Blake. And what does I do? Pays his debts for him, feeds him, keeps him, gives him a fiver a week. Tell Miss Blake the truth! Aren't you just a botched student without one farthing – that's only fit for the job he's at? (JOAN *moves*.) I'm sorry Miss Blake – I lost my temper. And I'm sorry, Peter. I . . . I want to show these big people what you are – an artist, man. Show them if you can't build harbours, you can do a few fancy leps.

PETER (*grimly*). I didn't tell Miss Blake quite all that you have said to her, but Joan . . . he has told you the truth. (*He goes off through the curtains at the back.*)

PART. Right. (*A pause.*) He's gone. (*To* JOAN, *suddenly.*) Forgive me, Miss Blake. I . . . I hope you'll excuse me. I only want to tell you that at the back of me . . . inside of me . . . I'm not really so rough, uncouth. (*Overcome with genuine passion.*) Pardon my keeping you, but . . . I've seen you coming here, off and on . . . and would you remember – perhaps you'd hardly – all the little things you've said to me, the little hints you dropped about making some difference here and there in this place. (JOAN *moves.*) I beg of you – don't go. Listen. Last year you said you thought a rockery garden would look wonderful down at the south Foreland. It's there now. It is wonderful, isn't it? But it's only for you it was made, only for you. Your room up there – that blue room – you said once you liked a soft blue shaded room. I got it done! Special from France it come, that wallpapering – 20/- a yard! If it had cost 50/- a yard, do you think I'd grudge it if I knew you cared for it? And there's hundreds, aye, thousands of little things I'd do for you. Say the word and all I have is yours – yours for all time if Sam Partridge can make it so. (*The lights in the room begin to wane still further. He continues madly.*) Let that little dancing Pierrot go; he's not a man. I'm one, I tell you. Fighting Sam Partridge o' Ballymena! I'm yours, do you hear? I'm your's ever always . . . Now the truth is out . . . and I don't care no more. (*The figure of* PETER, *still dressed in the Pierrot costume, reappears through the curtains at the back, dimly seen in the fading light.*) What is he? Cut him out. Only fit for the job he's at. A dancing jig-penny. A lounge lizard. Something to cod the hours away with . . . not to use them!

    (*The light fades still more.*)

VOICE OF PETER. Listen to him, Joan, for he speaks the truth.

PART. All he's got is youth! That's all – youth! Bah! But oh, believe me . . . I couldn't keep it back no longer . . . even though I'm not fit to kiss the hem of your garment – I'm not, I know I'm not – but I've money, money; and if money can make you happy, all that Sam Partridge has, ever will have, ever can hope to have, all that is yours, yours to throw, spin, gamble, buy, bind, lose, bury, toss to the sky – every penny, every sovereign, all of it, all of it – d'ye hear me? Hear me?

VOICE OF PETER. Do you hear him, Joan?

JOAN. I have heard him. (*The room is now almost in darkness.*)

VOICE OF PETER. And what is your answer?

JOAN. That you are my own love, Peter, ever and always.

    (*Sudden blackout, and roll of crash of thunder. The syren of the Harbour works begins to sound as curtain fall.*

    The syren continues to sound until curtain rises again on the Epilogue.)

EPILOGUE

(*The syren blows softly. The darkness gives way to a dim glow of light. As it grows clearer,* PETER *is discovered lying asleep in bed in his shabby lodgings. It gradually becomes full daylight. On either side of the bed are* STEPHENS *and* CHARLEY PRENDERGAST. STEPHENS *is blowing into* PETER'S *ear with a small syren whistle.*)

PETER (*mumbling in his sleep*). Do you hear him Joan?

STEPHENS (*stopping his blowing*). What was the name, Charley?

CHARLEY. Sounded like "Joan". Here, wake up! (*He shakes* PETER *vigorously.*) Wake up, Peter!

(*They both shake him.* PETER *wakens, stares at them dazedly. They laugh.*)

STEPHENS. Joan heard you, darling.

PETER. (*bewildered, rubbing his eyes, hoists himself up in the bed.*) Yes, yes. (*A pause.*) This is the queerest . . . Where is she?

CHARLEY. Who?

PETER. I . . . I don't quite understand what's happened. (*He laughs joyously, then begins to grasp the fact that he is in bed in his dingy lodgings. He gives a gasp of dismay, and buries his face in his hands.*)

CHARLEY. What's the matter Peter? (PETER *makes no reply.*)

STEPHENS. Poor devil, he's had a nightmare! Usual thing after exams. Hi there Peter! Cheer up, man! What you crying for on a morning like this? The bright and glorious morning of your deliverance man!

PETER. The morning . . . of my deliverance.

STEPHENS. Sure is. Poor old Peter! Were you dreaming, son? (*Thumping him on the back.*) You're through, man, through!

CHARLEY. Can't you take it in, Peter? Look here. (*He pulls a newspaper out of his pocket.*) There you are, you old stupid – I marked it for you. Final Engineering Examinations. B.E. Peter Grahame. No. 3 on the list! Distinguished answering in Docks, Harbours and Canals!

180

PETER. Docks, Harbours and Canals! Her book – and she wanted it back again!

STEPHENS. Who did?

CHARLEY. Wanted what?

PETER. Nothing. It was . . . only a dream I had. And you tell me I'm through . . . honest?

CHARLEY. Read the paper, idiot. (PETER *reads, puts it down in silence.*)

STEPHENS. Do you believe us now?

PETER. Yes.

CHARLEY. We met your Uncle Joe this morning.

PETER. Uncle Joe?

CHARLEY. Yes.

STEPHENS. Just in from Ballywilder.

PETER. Ballywilder.

CHARLEY. Yes, he'll be round to see you in an hour or so, after the cattle market's over.

STEPHENS. Peter! He's in great form, Peter. Heard it yesterday, he says.

CHARLEY. And he has that job for you.

PETER. Job? What Job?

CHARLEY. Clerk of Works on a new Reservoir near Ballygilder.

PETER. Reservoir near Ballygilder.

CHARLEY. Yes, said you'd get it easy now and certain, with the degree in your favour. That's all he was waiting on. Said he had the crowd all squared up in the County Leitrim . . .

PETER. County Leitrim . . .

CHARLEY. Yes, County Leitrim. Two guineas a week and you can get digs there. Five bob a day and all found.

PETER. Five . . . five bob a day and all found.

CHARLEY. Yes. You'll be able to save a bit on it. He says so.

PETER. Yes. Two guineas a week and five bob a day. Seven shillings a week. How long was it, Charley, before the Israelites reached the Promised Land?

CHARLEY. Forty years, I believe.

PETER. Forty and twenty are sixty. So then all the young Israelites who started off for it were over sixty when they got there. They had all grey heads and grey beards. Forty years . . . in County Leitrim – the land of mud and rushes. What a life! (*A pause.*)

STEPHENS. Here. Your socks, Peter. (*He throws over a pair.*) Rosie found them in the sitting room. One of them had a hole in it and she put a stitch in it. Darned it, I mean.

CHARLEY. And by Jove! I nearly forgot. Sorry Peter. Letter I picked up for you in the hall below. (*Handing the letter to* PETER.) Hurry up and get dressed. We'll wait for you outside. (*Exit with* STEPHENS.)

PETER (*glancing at envelope, then opening it excitedly*). It's from Joan! (*He is dismayed on finding only an Illustrated Circular.*) "The Excelsior Hotel, Portahoy. . . . Dining Room . . . Drawing Room . . . the South Foreland Rockery . . . the Lover's Walk . . . " (*A pause.*) This is surely the queerest – the funniest thing . . . Ah! Here's something she has written. "Old Tiger consented when he saw your name on the lists. Says you're to come here and start work at once on the new big harbour they're making here at Portahoy. We are staying at this hotel. It's owned by a man called Sam Partridge of Ballymena. I wish you heard him talking about it last night – and the wonderful new wallpaper he put specially in my room. He also talked about some young student he is bringing down to entertain the guests, who it appears is an absolute genius at "singing dancing and capers." (PETER *pauses for a moment, then resumes reading.*) "Some boy called Jordan. He showed me Jordan's photo. I couldn't help laughing and then crying because he is so like you, and because you often told me you were better at that sort of thing than at Docks, Harbours and Canals. Are you, I wonder? What matter if you are. You are my own love, ever and always." (PETER *folds the letter.*) And she said that to me in the dream. (*He repeats joyously.*) She said that to me in the dream. . . .

(CURTAIN.)

BRIDGE HEAD

A PLAY IN THREE ACTS

AUTHOR'S NOTE

In the West of Ireland are those areas of overcrowded little tenant farms known as the Congested Districts. They are the rural slums of Ireland.

The tragic history of the Plantations is explicit from the character and situation of the land on which these small-holders earn their livelihood. These congested areas are to be found fringing the western seaboard, the bog and moorland plains of Mayo and Galway, and the lower slopes of the mountains of Connemara, Kerry and Donegal.

Sometimes adjoining, but more often at a distance are the larger holdings . . . an odd still-existing demesne of one of the former landed gentry, or the wide pasture fields of the grazier tenant.

Successive efforts of legislation since 1891 have been directed towards obtaining this external land for allotment to the people of the congested areas either as enlargements of their little holdings or as new holdings for migrants, whose surrendered lands are used to ameliorate the lot of their neighbours remaining at home.

But the clan feeling of territory still exists, often in a narrow parochial form, and the advent of the congested migrant into a new holding in a strange district is rarely welcome to the local people.

To deal justly with those who have to give up their land so necessary for relief of the congests, to allot this land equitably to the numberless applicants and to instal the migrants in the teeth of what is often determined and strenuous opposition, is not an easy task.

The brunt of this work falls upon the local officers of the Irish Land Commission. On the manner in which they deal with all these varying elements of the local population depends the success or failure of land settlement in these remote districts.

It is in memory of those officers who, like Stephen Moore, have given their life and vision to this work, that "Bridge Head" has been written.

Rutherford Mayne

CHARACTERS

Bridge Head was first performed in the Abbey Theatre, Dublin, on June 18th, 1934, with the following cast:

STEPHEN MOORE	F. J. McCormick
MARTIN	Arthur Shields
HUGH O'NEILL	Denis O'Dea
MRS MARCUS MORRISEY	Maureen Delany
INARI GOSUKI	Michael J. Dolan
DERMOT BARRINGTON	Tom Purefoy
CECILY BARRINGTON	Eileen Crowe
JOHN KEARNEY	Eric Gorman
DAN DOLAN	Barry Fitzgerald
MAURICE MOCKLER	P. J. Carolan
MICHAEL MORRISEY	W. O'Gorman
PHILIP WATERSLEY	Joseph Linnane

The play was directed and produced by Lennox Robinson

It was subsequently produced under the direction of Michael MacOwan at the Westminster Theatre, London, for the London Mask Theatre on May 9th, 1939, with the following cast:

STEPHEN MOORE	Wilfrid Lawson
MARTIN	John C. Bland
HUGH O'NEILL	Stephen Murray
MRS MARCUS MORRISEY	Christine Hayden
INARI GOSUKI	J. Hwfa Pryse
DERMOT BARRINGTON	Edward Lexy
CECILY BARRINGTON	Ruth Lodge
JOHN KEARNEY	Adrian Byrne
DAN DOLAN	Charles Victor
MAURICE MOCKLER	Tony Quinn
MICHAEL MORRISEY	Jackson Gillis
PHILIP WATERSLEY	John Brooking

BRIDGE HEAD

ACT I

The sitting-room of STEPHEN MOORE *in Mooney's Hotel in Western Ireland. One door opens on to a landing outside. Another door leads into* MOORE'S *bedroom. An old-fashioned fireplace and mantel at the back. A large window on the right looks out on the Market Square. The room is furnished with side-table, chest of drawers, a large table, four or five chairs and a couple of old armchairs. There is a litter of maps, ordnance sheets, files, etc., in all sorts of nooks and corners of the room.*

It is late afternoon of a day in Autumn, and MOORE, *who is seated at the table, has just finished writing. His correspondence has been thrown over into one of the armchairs, which serves as a receptacle for his outgoing mail.*

MOORE'S *appearance is that of a hardy, grizzled, weather-beaten official of middle age, with a brusque, alert manner, used to command of men and to working amongst them.*

The chimes of the village clock strike the hour. MOORE *rises, stretches himself, and then quickly goes over and rings. There is no response. He rings again impatiently and then resumes his seat, takes up a sheet of paper and starts in an abstracted way to write on it. The door suddenly opens, and* MARTIN, *the boots, enters.*

MARTIN *is elderly, clean-shaven except for a large drooping white moustache, and his connection with the hotel is indicated by an old braided cap which he seldom or ever discards.*

MARTIN. Did you ring, sir?
MOORE. Yes. I tried to. Bring those letters there to the post. Are the
    bells out of order again?
MARTIN. Gone to hell, sir. I'm sick telling the boss about them.
MOORE. Where is he?
MARTIN. Ballyhaunis Races. The only bell he gives a damn about is
    the starting bell on a racecourse.
    (*He goes over to the letters.*)
MOORE. Hm! (*he goes over to the chest of drawers, extracts a map and*

sits down to study it.) Is Mr O'Neill back yet?

MARTIN. No, sir. That reminds me, I was given this picture card to give him. (*He produces a photo-card and reads the writing on it.*) "The Rose Garden, Mount Nevin." If I knew as much as I did, he'd have been back in Kilrea a couple of hours sooner.

    (*He replaces the card in his pocket and starts collecting* MOORE'S *correspondence.*)

MOORE (*with a sharp glance at him*). Why?

MARTIN. Ach! He's not like you, sir. Sure, you're a kind of a monk. But Mr O'Neill is young yet, and so is she.

MOORE. Oh! So *she* is young, is she?

MARTIN (*confidentially*). She is. They always begin with sending picture post-cards, young ones do. (*He sorts over the letters, reading the addresses.*) "The Secretary" . . . "The Secretary" . . . "The Secretary" . . . Aye. . . . That's the gentleman never answers the letters, but never forgets the rent. (*He suddenly peers closely at one of them.*) "Dermot Barrington, Esq., Mount Nevin House." (*A pause, then with a look at* MOORE.) That's the father.

MOORE. The what?

MARTIN. The father of the lady. Mr Barrington, he's just come into town and sent word he was calling to see you. I needn't post this, sir.

MOORE. All right. Put it upon the mantlepiece.

    (MARTIN *obeys.*)

MARTIN. I hear yous are going to give out land up in that country.

MOORE. Who told you?

MARTIN. Sure Mr O'Neill and Mr Kearney went off that way with that little man from Addergoole that was down waiting in the yard this morning.

MOORE. You've a great intelligence, Martin.

MARTIN. Be the same token, Mr Moore, you'd be wise to be putting no migrant up into that country. Begor, the rising that was in "sixteen" will be nothing to what's coming on yous, if you plant strangers up in that bedlam.

MOORE. I daresay.

MARTIN. It's not blathers I'm talking. Maybe that fellow might refuse to go.

MOORE. He might, if he's fool enough.

MARTIN. If he does, maybe you'd remember Mickey Hennessy . . . my first cousin . . . that I spoke to you about a Wednesday, that's living up at Sheskin above Gort on the Clare side. Hennessy would take land at the North Pole, if yous would give it to him.

And what's more, would pay any rent yous asked him for it.

MOORE. Here, I'll go out for a breath of air to the Post Office. Give me the letters and I'll post them. Clear up this litter and get those windows opened and a breath of fresh air into the room.

(*He folds up the map he has been studying and throws it on the side-table.*)

MARTIN. Right, sir. (MOORE *goes out.* MARTIN *starts to clear up and tidy the room. Goes to the window, opens it and calls out.*) Hi, Jimmy!

VOICE (*without*). What?

MARTIN. Any sign of the boss?

VOICE. No.

MARTIN. Right! (*He goes over to the table where* MOORE *has been writing, tidies up the papers, and then picks up the scrap on which* MOORE *has been scribbling.*) Bal – Balnasheeda. . . . The name of God, what's he writing about back o' beyont about! Something scratched out. O . . . O'Neill . . . He's been writing O'Neill and scratched it out again. Kearney, and scratched it out again. (*The door opens and* O'NEILL, *a young man dressed in rough old tweeds, enters. He is flushed and excited looking.*) Oh! Begors, are you back, Mr O'Neill?

O'NEILL. Yes. Where's Mr Moore?

MARTIN. He was expecting yous and Mr Kearney long ago. What kept yous?

O'NEILL. Business. I got a good stroke of business done.

MARTIN. You're a great man, Mr O'Neill. And there's more than yourself thinks it. Now. Here's a picture post-card for you.

(*He hands it to* O'NEILL.)

O'NEILL. Oh! (*Reads.*) "The Rose Garden, Mount Nevin." Yes. She said she'd send me this. Beautiful, isn't it? (*He puts it on the mantelpiece.*) Where's Mr Moore?

MARTIN. Gone to post the letters. (*Pointing to the mantelpiece.*) Bar that one.

O'NEILL (*lifting the letter and looking at it*). Oh!

MARTIN. I told him Mr Barrington was in the town.

O'NEILL. Oh, is he?

MARTIN. Yes. And has the young lady with him!

O'NEILL. Oh! (*Suddenly.*) I say, Martin!

MARTIN. Yes?

O'NEILL. You wouldn't notice anything, would you?

MARTIN. About you, sir?

O'NEILL. Yes.

189

MARTIN (*after a contemplative examination*). No, sir.

O'NEILL. Well, Kearney told me not to be going near Mr Moore for a couple of hours.

MARTIN (*sitting down*). Well now, if I was Mr Moore and was your Commanding Officer, do you know what I'd tell you?

O'NEILL. No.

MARTIN. Go and get Miss Mooney to give you a big double of brandy, and go and brush your hair, and then come and tell me all the great business you've done. And I'd have a great character of you then to give Mr Barrington. (*Maliciously.*) Tell me, Mr O'Neill, did you ever hear of a place called Balnasheeda?

(*Knock at the door. It opens and a large buxom woman peeps in. It is* MRS MARCUS MORRISEY.)

MRS MORRISEY. Is Mr Moore at home?

MARTIN. No, ma'am, but he'll be in presently.

O'NEILL. Martin! I'll be back in a minute or two. Tell Mr Moore.

MARTIN. Yes, sir.

(O'NEILL *bows to* MRS MORRISEY *and goes out.*)

MRS MORRISEY. Who's that young man?

MARTIN. Mr O'Neill of the Commission.

MRS MORRISEY. Oh! I think I seen him now, somewhere before.

MARTIN. Aye. With somebody, maybe?

MRS MORRISEY. Aye. Just so. Aye. Just so. And a couple of times or more, maybe. (*Suddenly spying the card on the mantelpiece.*) What's that up there?

(MOORE *enters suddenly.*)

MARTIN. Mrs Marcus Morrisey, sir.

MRS MORRISEY. And how is yourself, Mr Moore? And I'm glad to see you. And thank you, Martin— you may go. It's just a few words in private I'd like to be saying to Mr Moore before the rest of the beagles get at him.

MARTIN (*sententiously*). The land for the people!

MRS MORRISEY. Thank you, Martin, I'd be obliged if you'd attend to them people that's down below waiting this last half hour for news of what Mr Mooney is to bring home from the races. (MARTIN *withdraws.*) And I'd be obliged if you'd shut the door after you. (MARTIN *does so with a bang.*) Now!

(*She sits down and smiles genially at* MOORE.)

MOORE. You're Mrs Marcus Morrisey?

MRS MORRISEY. Ah, indeed, and well you know it. And often I've heard of you, Mr Moore, and your kindness to the people. (*A pause.*) Them were terrible nice young men you sent down to our

190

country to work amongst us, Mr Moore. Terrible nice young men, indeed. Ah, but they hadn't the wisdom of Mr Moore. That's what I said to Marcus. They hadn't it. It wasn't there. Ah, nothing like the real gentlemen for wisdom. Give me Mr Moore every time, Marcus, says I, for he's the gentleman for me!

MOORE. Hm! (*He gives her a hard, sharp look, takes out a notebook and begins writing.*) The land as usual I suppose!

MRS MORRISEY. Well . . . we'll come to that presently. . . . I managed to get a lift with Mr Barrington – the gentleman in the big house – Mount Nevin – that you took the land from at Ballyglass. I see a photo of his garden up there. (*She nods towards the mantelpiece.*) Ah! Isn't it nice? A very nice man is Mr Barrington. Ah, there's nothing like the real old gentry, Mr Moore. Nothing like them! The manners of them! Ah, the manners of them! I've often said to Marcus, it's a pity to be taking the land off them, the creatures, but sure it must be done. And Mr Moore will do it, I'm sure, in as nice a way as anyone in the Government will do it. Ah, leave that to you, Mr Moore, you'll always do it nicely.

MOORE. Very hard to do everything nicely, Mrs Morrisey.

MRS MORRISEY. Indeed it is. (*A pause.*) Ah, but you – you'll always do it nicely, but them young men of yours – they mean well, Mr Moore, but they don't understand.

(*She gives a meaning glance at the card on the mantelpiece.*)

MOORE. Understand what, Mrs Morrisey?

MRS MORRISEY. Well . . . Just the right way to do things . . . and then . . . there's . . . the . . . the country people. They just think the land's there to be given to them. And they don't understand all the examination and the selection of them that's selected. It's hard on them, the creatures. They come in and talk in my place in the evening and indeed they have it all planned out. Who is to get and who isn't. But you and I, we know better than that. (*She laughs.*) Heah! Aye! Aha! We— (*She laughs immoderately.*) We know better than that – indeed we do, Mr Moore. The poor creatures! (*Knocking.*) Come in.

MARTIN (*opening the door and looking in*). Beg pardon. Mr and Miss Barrington's below and wants to see Mr Moore. (*He looks knowingly at* MOORE.) They said they had an appointment and are waiting.

MOORE. Hm! All right – I'll see them presently.

(MARTIN *disappears.*)

MRS MORRISEY. I'm glad now Mr Barrington's calling. Pay particular attention to him, Mr Moore. He'll speak the right way of it, and so would Mr Mockler if you happened to know him, the County Councillor. He's a splendid man, is Mr Mockler. And I'm so glad you gave that fine holding to Pat Morrisey, the herd. Ah, that was justice . . . the poor creature! Many's the hour and day that poor creature used to come and tell me his hopes and fears. Ah, but you were the kind gentleman to him. Indeed, I could just kiss you, Mr Moore, for the way you treated that unfortunate man. He's my first cousin by Marcus's side.

MOORE (*drily*). I see.

MRS MORRISEY. But Pa's brother Jack— Ah now, Mr Moore, you must do something for poor Jack. The nicest, decentest poor creature that ever walked. Wait till you hear the Barrington's about him.

MOORE (*hopelessly*). I'm sure.

MRS MORRISEY. Well now, we heard to-day, and I could hardly believe it, that Mr Kearney had brought some strange outsider of a man from Addergoole down to show him the land. Indeed, I pity Mr Kearney. He doesn't understand, you know, Mr Moore. (*With a sudden change, and vehemently.*) They'll never tolerate anyone outside the parish getting land at Ballyglass. Oh, indeed, Mr Kearney may make up his mind to that. (*She rises, goes over to the door, opens it, listens and then determinedly closes it and puts her back to it.*) Is there any chance now, Mr Moore, that I'd get a portion? You see, the licensed business doesn't pay anything like it used to, and there's my two sons, Michael and James, and I fret about their future. You won't forget about them now, Mr Moore? It would be a great thing now that you have that new house and out-office vacant that you put one of my boys into it.

MOORE. No. I'm sorry, but that's impossible.

MRS MORRISEY. Oho! (*Bridling with fury.*) And is it to that little scampeen and cattle-jobber and outsider and stranger from Addergoole that the best land in Ballyglass is going to be given?

MOORE. Yes. It's to be given to Dolan, if he'll take it.

MRS MORRISEY. Oh, indeed! If – if he'll take it! And my two sons that always were foremost in the fight and poor John Morrisey that was the same, they're to be given the go-bye, are they, for the stranger, and the outsider? Oh, we'll see more about this, Mr Moore. We'll see more about this Mr Moore!

(*Knocking at door.*)

MOORE. Come in.

MARTIN (*opening the door and speaking to someone behind him*). Come along, sir. (*In a hurried whisper to* MOORE.) Japanese

192

gentleman to see you, sir.

(*He ushers in a little dapper Japanese. It is* INARI GOSUKI.)

GOSUKI (*bowing low, and taking in his breath*). Eh. Go men ma sai. Misterre Moore, I presume. . . .

MOORE. Yes, I'm Moore.

MARTIN. The little Japanese gentleman has just landed by car from Dublin, sir.

GOSUKI. Yes. Dublin! (*He produces card case and hands card to* MOORE.) Card. (*Produces a letter.*) Note of introduce— (*He hands both to* MOORE.) Not . . . English . . . good . . . speak . . . but . . . (*tapping his ear*) understanding . . . (*he smiles*) . . . good!

MRS MORRISEY. There's a deal in this country very hard to understand. I shall come again, Mr Moore, and I know you'll not say no. Ah! it's not all over yet, please God. It's not all over yet between us. Good day, gentlemen, good day.

(*She and* MARTIN *go out.*)

MOORE (*reading the card*). "Mr Inari Gosuki. House of Representatives. Diet of Japan."

GOSUKI. So.

MOORE. I see by your letter, you are studying the land problem in Europe.

GOSUKI. Eh . . . especial Ireland. Irish peoples land problem . . . much interest.

MOORE. I see. By the way can I offer you anything? Tea?

GOSUKI. Arignato. No. I thank. No.

MOORE. They didn't send any word from Dublin you were coming.

GOSUKI. No. Excuse. I . . . to Dublin's people say "Surprise visit . . . allow . . . please."

MOORE. I see. So you want to know what we're doing here. What our work is.

GOSUKI. Yes. So. Is not all Irish farmer owner of his lands?

MOORE. Yes.

GOSUKI. Den excuse me. Why more want? Do farmer want land and . . . ze sky also?

MOORE. Mr Gosuki, did you ever look at the sky . . . at the stars on a clear night?

GOSUKI. Oh. So. Yes.

MOORE. Some parts of the sky, there are thousands of little stars, all close together. Then there's other parts of the sky . . . almost bare . . . with very few . . . but very big stars.

GOSUKI. Eh so.

MOORE. Well, all the places where the little stars cluster together would be like the congested districts of Ireland where the little farmers are huddled together, same as they are around here (*he makes a gesture*) at Kilrea. Thousands of them. If you don't move them out, make the big stars give them room – space – their lights grow dim and are quenched.

(*A low, cheery voice is heard outside, then a loud knock at the door. Without further ceremony it is opened, and* BARRINGTON *enters, with his daughter* CECILY. BARRINGTON *is elderly and shabby, but unmistakably one of the "quality." His daughter* CECILY *is a young, handsome girl in the twenties.*)

BARRINGTON. Aha! We've got the villain in! How are you, Moore? I don't think you've met the daughter before. Cecily, this is Mr Moore. (*With a look at* GOSUKI.) How d'ye do?

MOORE. Oh! May I introduce Mr Inari Gosuki?

(*The introduction is duly made.*)

BARRINGTON. Japanese or Chinese, sir?

GOSUKI. Please . . . not . . . Chinese. No. Japans belong.

BARRINGTON. You're a long way from home, sir!

GOSUKI. Eh! Yes. (*Rising.*) Perhaps this meeting of family . . . and . . . not . . . official.

BARRINGTON. Stay where you are. We don't care a hoot, if it's all one to Moore. I only want to see him about the land.

GOSUKI (*delighted*). Ah! So!

(*He extracts a notebook and waits eagerly, pencil in hand, to take notes of the conversation.*)

BARRINGTON. You sent down two of your staff to our place to-day, Moore, with some rascal from the Addergoole country.

MOORE. Yes.

BARRINGTON. And do you mean to tell me that you're in earnest, planting a stranger like that up there? Bad enough stripping the land off me, but to go and put tinkers from Addergoole on it under my very nose. . . . Well, you're asking for trouble!

MOORE. From whom?

BARRINGTON. From the locals.

CECILY. It is quite true, Mr Moore. There will be trouble. I've already told Mr O'Neill.

BARRINGTON. Who's O'Neill?

CECILY. He's one of Mr Moore's Inspectors.

BARRINGTON. With all respect to you, Moore, that's no recommendation in his favour. (*To* CECILY.) Bless me if I know the half of these people you run about with. Was it that long thin fellow I saw, when we were shooting at Muckanagh Bog?

CECILY. Yes. He's in charge of all that new drainage and roads you admired so much.

(*She smiles mischievously at* MOORE.)

BARRINGTON. Admired, did you say! The best duck shoot in Ireland ruined. Absolutely ruined.

GOSUKI. Excuse. Zis gentlemans . . . is . . . landlord class?

MOORE. He is.

GOSUKI. And . . . enemy of . . . peoples?

BARRINGTON. No, sir. I never was . . . nor any Barrington that lived! That blackguard there (*he points to* MOORE) . . . at least, that blackguard department he belongs to, they're the real enemies of the people. Taking land off people that knew how to use and work it, and giving it away to a lot of useless tinkers and tailors that let it or sell it the minute they get hold of it. Confiscation. That's what I call it.

GOSUKI. You . . . in Japans . . . same as . . . daimio. In Japans also confiscations of daimio.

BARRINGTON. The whole damned world's gone upside down.

GOSUKI. Eh! So. Not nice for daimio. For young ladies . . . (*he looks and bows to* CECILY) troubles also?

BARRINGTON. Yes. She probably won't have a fluke.

GOSUKI. Please what mean fluke?

BARRINGTON. Pounds . . . pennies . . . money.

GOSUKI (*writing solemnly in his notebook*). Irish daimio angry . . . lands confiscations . . . childrens not money much.

BARRINGTON (*impatiently*). Moore. What about our own tenants up there. Are they going to get any of that land left over.

MOORE. Any of your tenants who were entitled to land got it.

BARRINGTON. Oh yes. I know all that old official rigamarole. I know that you gave land to Paddy Moran and Johnny Smith, and Mary and Kitty Walsh, and some dozens of other small holders, and that Pat Morrisey, the herd, got a holding. But they didn't get as much as they should have, and you've kept back forty acres of the best of the land. And now the latest is that you're giving it to some outsider from Addergoole. There'll be hell to pay if you do, Moore. Listen. There's a string of hungry greedy devils, sons of the larger tenants and others that you left out, and they'll raise Cain. And what about John Morrisey, the herd's brother? You've done nothing for John.

MOORE. No.

BARRINGTON. Something must be done for John Morrisey.

CECILY. What has Mr Moore got to do for him?

195

BARRINGTON. Provide the rascal with land. When the land is there, why shouldn't he get it? He's the head bottle-washer of all that crowd up there, and if he doesn't get it now from Moore, they'll turn round on to me, and that means good night to Mount Nevin for me. Something must be done for John Morrisey. He's entitled to that land, and a deuced sight better than any outsider.

CECILY. Is he, Mr Moore?

MOORE. No. Our orders were to put in a migrant and we're doing so.

GOSUKI. Please! What migrant?

MOORE. A migrant, Mr Gosuki, is a person who surrenders land for the benefit of others, and migrates to a new holding.

BARRINGTON. Yes. Well, put your migrant somewhere else than Mount Nevin.

CECILY. There always seems to be a lot of bother over land down here. Will it ever come to an end?

BARRINGTON. There'll be a miaow over the land till Kingdom Come.

GOSUKI. Excuse, please. What miaow?

BARRINGTON. Cat calls. Pussy calls. (*Mewing.*) Miaow!

GOSUKI. Arignato. (*Smiles.*) Understand. Cry of cat . . . nako . . . milk want. Irish peoples land wants no miaow.

BARRINGTON. Exactly.

GOSUKI. Arignato.

BARRINGTON. Look here, Moore, if you don't give something to those local rascals, life won't be worth living at Mount Nevin. I might as well pack up and get out. So be a sport and a friend of mine and get it done, or else—

(*He makes a gesture of despair.*)

(*Knocking at door.*)

MOORE. Come in.

(KEARNEY, *a middle-aged, nervous individual, dressed in old tweeds, wearing glasses, enters.*)

KEARNEY. Oh, I'm sorry, Moore. I didn't know you had company.

BARRINGTON (*looking hard at him*). Oh, it's you, Kearney! Come in. You're mixed up in this business, too.

KEARNEY. In what?

BARRINGTON. Putting some tinker into land up at my place. You and that long thin fellow. And I'm doing my best to tell Moore I object, and in the strongest way I can put it.

KEARNEY. Oh! (*He looks at* MOORE.) The tinker, as you call him, wouldn't take it. How d'ye do, Miss Barrington? (*He nods to* GOSUKI, *who bows.*) You're the Japanese gentleman that's arrived? How d'ye do? (*To* MOORE.) Yes, Dolan's refused. And

196

sorry to be so late, but O'Neill had to come home by O'Flaherty's at Killasolan.

BARRINGTON. I know the chap. He has a pub there, hasn't he?

KEARNEY. Yes.

BARRINGTON. Well, I'm very glad to hear you didn't succeed with your business. And don't try any more of that game up there if you value your skins.

O'NEILL (*entering, after knocking*). Oh, sorry!
(*He makes to retire.*)

MOORE. Don't go, O'Neill. Come in. (O'NEILL *comes in.*) This is O'Neill, Barrington.

BARRINGTON. How d'ye do? You know my daughter, I believe.

O'NEILL. Yes. (*He smiles at* CECILY.)

BARRINGTON. Well, young man, if you want to continue on friendly terms with her father, don't be out on any more jobs bringing small fry from Addergoole up there.

MOORE. By the way, I was almost forgetting, Barrington, there's an official note for you on the mantelpiece.
(O'NEILL *hands it over to* BARRINGTON.)

BARRINGTON. Excuse me. (*He opens it and reads it, then turns and looks hard at* MOORE.) Moore! What's the meaning of this?

CECILY. What is it, Daddy?

BARRINGTON. It's a notice of inspection of our old home. (*With an effort to hide his feelings.*) On Monday 8th inst. at 11 a.m. (*He bows his head.*) So it's come to this at last, has it? (*With a sudden bravado.*) Here, Moore, you can kill two birds with one stone. Come up and see the old place as my guest on Sunday. Come up, the whole crowd of you, and have a few sets of tennis and a bite of lunch.

MOORE. I'm sorry, I can't.

BARRINGTON. Oh, come on, Moore, and share pot luck, and bring Mr What's-his-name – we might raise a couple of racquets somewhere.

MOORE. I'm sorry. It's impossible.

BARRINGTON (*turning to* O'NEILL). You'll come, then? The day after that I'll meet Moore . . . officially. Goodbye, everybody. Coming, Cecily.

CECILY. Yes. (*With a quick smile, to* O'NEILL.) Be sure to come.
(BARRINGTON *and* CECILY *go out. There is a pause.* KEARNEY *looks at* O'NEILL *and laughs sarcastically.*)

MOORE. So Dolan refused! That's bad news! I want that man put in. (*Moodily.*) Refused! (*Sharply to* KEARNEY.) Why?

KEARNEY. Said it was the worst bit of land he's ever seen.

MOORE. Did you tell him the annuity on it?

KEARNEY. No.

MOORE. Where is he?

KEARNEY. Below waiting to see you, in the hope of getting land somewhere else, I suppose.

MOORE. We haven't any other holding. He refused me twice before. It's my last chance to get him sanctioned for exchange.

O'NEILL. It's hard on the Barringtons if he accepts.

MOORE. Why?

O'NEILL. If that forty acres were left to Morrisey and the other people up there, they'd leave Mount Nevin alone.

KEARNEY. Aye. For another three or four years.

O'NEILL. Cecily hoped—

(*He stops suddenly, a little abashed.*)

KEARNEY. Who?

O'NEILL. Miss Barrington told me her father hoped that in another four or five years, he would be able to stock and work it again, himself.

(MOORE *rises and goes over to the chest of drawers, unlocks it, and extracts a map. It is evident from the way he handles it that it is of importance. He looks over at his two juniors as if slightly hesitant. Meanwhile they continue talking.*)

KEARNEY. Same old yarn her father told Moore and myself ten years ago. The cruel fact is, O'Neill, that the flood of life around this Kilrea countryside can't afford to let people like the Barringtons stay on the land. So some day (*he nods his head to indicate* MOORE) he'll have to do the butcher.

O'NEILL. I hope he never will.

KEARNEY (*with a slight remorse for the youngster*). I say, Moore. Could you possibly drop that idea of using that forty acres at Ballyglass for a migrant . . . for Dolan? Make some sort of special plea that it would be in the interests of peace and law and order . . . all that stuff . . . to use discretion and give it to the locals. What?

MOORE. I can't. (*He brings over the map and spreads it on the table.*) And here's my reason. There's Addergoole. Where Dolan lives. Sixty to seventy wretched holdings all in miserable patches of rundale. Look at them. Like a mosaic pavement. But that's not all. (*Impressively.*) Look where Dolan's holding runs from the main road down to the River Shivna.

KEARNEY (*somewhat indifferently*). Yes. I've seen it often enough.

198

O'NEILL (*who has certainly taken a keen interest in the map*). I see what Moore's driving at. Fitzgormanstown Ranch and its three thousand acres of prairie over the River Shivna!

KEARNEY (*derisively*). Fitzgormanstown over the River! Good Lord, Moore! talk of the River Jordan? A bridge would cost thousands. And we'll never get Fitzgormanstown. You can't. Not under the present Acts.

MOORE. No. But it will come in some day. Nothing can stop it.

O'NEILL (*excitedly*). I say . . . Kearney . . . look at this! Why, it's actually a scheme map of Fitzgormanstown with new roads, new holdings, plantations and fences and sites for new houses all planned. Hundreds of new holdings! (*He looks at* MOORE *with wonder.*) Hundreds of new holdings! (*Sadly.*) But on a place we may never get.

MOORE. Yes. Hundreds of new holdings on a place we may never get. To struggle to get forty acres to-day, for just one migrant, and then to look across the Shivna and see that three thousand acres of magnificent kindly land stretching out to the sun. No shivering little gossoons on that side of the Shivna on a winter day, herding the cow on a rundale patch! We must . . . we must get Dolan's land and drive a road right through it right up to the River there.

KEARNEY. And then?

MOORE. And then wait.

O'NEILL. Reserve a bridge head?

MOORE. Yes. Dolan's holding is the one point, the only point on the Shivna where we can fling a bridge across. No ashplant on a cattle drive ever struck a beast on the three thousand acres of Fitzgormanstown. Why? Because the Shivna saved it. But some day we'll capture it and get the money for that bridge. S. Dolan must come out. (*He replaces the map in the drawer.*) Where's his agreement?

KEARNEY. O'Neill has it. (*There is a pause. They both turn to look at* O'NEILL, *who sits lost in thought.* KEARNEY, *loudly.*) O'Neill!

O'NEILL (*with a start*). Yes!

KEARNEY. O'Neill, I used to sit that way thinking about Ellen, now I do it over the accounts for boots and shoes. Where's Dan Dolan's agreement?

O'NEILL (*producing it from his coat pocket*). There you are.

MARTIN (*knocking, and entering hurriedly*). Beg pardon, sir, but Mr Cossacks is wanted below.

GOSUKI. Eh, me?

MARTIN. Yes, you, sir. (*To* MOORE.) It's the boss, sir. Just back from

199

the races. He's in the greatest form I ever seen . . . has all the bookies broke. Some one from Dublin at Ballyhaunis told him the little Japanese gentleman was coming down, so he went and backed The Chinky at fifty to one in the Trader's Plate and it galloped home. He says it's all due to Mr Cossacks. (*Turning to* GOSUKI.) If you don't come down, sir, he'll be sure up and you'll get no more business done to-day. I'll engage to get you free in half-an-hour.

GOSUKI (*with a smile*). All ri'.

MARTIN. Follow me, sir.

(MARTIN *and* GOSUKI *go out.*)

KEARNEY. Good night! No more study land problem for Japan to-night!

MOORE (*rapidly scanning the agreement*). Forty acres. Twenty pounds. No use telling that to Dolan. He'll want it at ten! Bring him up, Kearney.

KEARNEY. Righto!

(*Exit.*)

O'NEILL. Who's the little man?

MOORE. Jap taking notes on the land question.

O'NEILL. Oh!

MOORE. Like to go out there?

O'NEILL. If they paid me.

MOORE. Hm! Is the pay all the interest you have in work?

O'NEILL. Why shouldn't it interest me?

MOORE. If you want to move, why not? (O'NEILL *does not answer.* MOORE *eyes him keenly.*) You came home by Killasolan?

O'NEILL. Yes.

MOORE. By O'Flaherty's pub?

O'NEILL. Yes.

MOORE. I see.

O'NEILL. Anything wrong?

(*Conversation is interrupted by* DAN DOLAN *and* KEARNEY'S *entrance.* DAN DOLAN *is a shrewd-looking old peasant farmer of small stature and strong physique. He carries an ashplant.*)

KEARNEY. Dan Dolan of Addergoole, Mr Moore.

MOORE. Nice day, Dan.

DAN. Yes.

MOORE. Sit down. (DAN *does so.*) Well, you saw the new holding?

DAN. Yes.

MOORE. And walked all the land?

DAN. Yes.

MOORE. And were told the acreage?

DAN. Yes.

MOORE. Forty statute or twenty-five Irish.

DAN. Yes.

MOORE. And saw the new house and out-office on it?

DAN. Yes.

MOORE. And refused?

DAN. Yes.

MOORE. Why? (*A pause.*) Well, Dan?

DAN. I want a pig-house.

MOORE. What?

DAN. I want a pig-house.

KEARNEY. As well as the new house and the forty-foot out-office?

DAN. I want a pig-house.

KEARNEY. We don't include pig-houses.

DAN. I must have a pig-house.

MOORE. All right. Note that, O'Neill.

O'NEILL. Pig-house granted?

MOORE. Yes.

DAN. With a cement floor in it?

MOORE. With a cement floor in it.

(*A pause.* DAN DOLAN *looks meditatively at the ceiling.*)

DAN. Aye. A bad farm. The worst I ever seen. No meadow in it.

KEARNEY. There's fifteen Irish of arable.

DAN. I want them two fields next to the herd's house.

KEARNEY. You can't get them.

DAN. Is that true, Mr Moore?

MOORE. Yes.

DAN. Aye. The worst land I ever seen. Have yous no land elsewhere to show me? What about Fitzgormanstown over the River fornenst me?

MOORE. No. We won't get that until a new Land Act is passed and a new bridge built.

DOLAN. I'll wait for that so.

MOORE. And when that comes, no one will get land but the landless.

DAN. Aye. No land. How *is it* Mr Beckett of Taylor's Cross was transposed by yous to that grand new place he got at Naven? – in the county of Meath?

MOORE. He surrendered three hundred acres.

DAN. Aye. Oh, aye. There's always an explanation for everything yous does. Is it only the black Protestants that yous are going to take out of Connaught? Answer me that? Wasn't there a cry in

Maynouth again the way yous were tricking the true Church and its following? Nothing but Atheists and Freemasons getting the fat of the land and the likes of us that suffered seven hundred and fifty years of fruitless fighting gets nothing. I tell you things will come to an end some of these days. Why can't I get a holding in County Meath?

MOORE. We're not here to discuss any exchange to County Meath. We were ordered to show you a new holding in Ballyglass and we've done so.

DAN. And why should you be so set on me to come out? There's a dozen others could come as ready as me.

MOORE. Because your holding is the key to our work.

DAN. Would yous give any other key man that come out the same sort of a house?

MOORE. Depends on the man and his family. What family have you?

DAN. Eight boys and two girls.

KEARNEY. You've only three boys.

DAN. Yes – three at home.

MOORE. Where are the others?

DAN. There's one in America, one in Kilkelly in the County Mayo and one at the Curragh in the Free State Army.

MOORE. That's six accounted for. Where are the other two? (*The old man does not answer.*) Where are the other two?

DAN. There's one went wrong in the head in the troubles and is in Ballinasloe, and the other's in France, God rest him!

MOORE. In France?

DAN. Yes, your honour. He went out with Tom Kettle that's beyond in Stephen's Green. (*A pause.*) What's the rent on the holding, if you please, gentlemen?

MOORE (*with a glance at* KEARNEY). Twenty-six pounds.

DAN (*with a gasp*). Ah, Glory be to God! Twenty-six pounds! Where's my hat? I'll be going, gentlemen! Twenty-five acres – fifteen to twenty of it old, sour callows and cut away bog for twenty-six pounds! Are yous humbugging me, Mr Moore?

MOORE. No. Twenty-six. Remember we build your fences and dwelling-house and out-offices.

DAN. And a pig-house?

MOORE. And a pig-house with a cement floor in it.

DOLAN. Aye. And the meadow fields next the herd's house?

MOORE. No.

DAN. Well, yous may keep the holding, gentlemen. Leave my own little snug house, is it, with the best of arable and the spring water

202

and the callows and the bog? . . . aye . . . be damned but I was forgetting the bog. Where's the bog?

KEARNEY. You saw it over in the distance at Muckanagh to the west.

DAN. Muckanagh? Sure there's no way into it!

O'NEILL. The gangers are working at a new road to it.

DAN. Aye. Is the bog included in the rent?

MOORE. Yes.

DAN. Aye. So yous won't give me the meadow field?

KEARNEY. We can't, I tell you. Pat Morrisey, the herd, has already signed for it.

DAN. Aye. Twenty-six pounds and the worst land I ever saw. And full of disease, red water, fluke and murrain.

KEARNEY. No such thing. Don't mind what the blackguard of a herd told you. He wants the land for his brother.

DAN. Aye. That's the proper lad would answer for a neighbour. Aye. And them was two nice sour-looking gentlemen that wouldn't give you the time of day when we come out and found them talking to the shover. Begorras, good neighbours is worth a fortune to any man and between them people that we saw to-day and that rogue elephant of a herd and his brother, it's *cead mille failthe* to Dan Dolan of Addergoole down there, I'm thinking. (*Suddenly.*) Begor, I won't face it, Mr Kearney.

KEARNEY. It's hopeless, Moore. He has no courage.

DAN (*angrily*). Courage, is it? There never was a Dolan yet that wouldn't face a regiment of Satans—

(*The door opens noiselessly and the little Japanese looks in, smiling.*)

GOSUKI. Excuse, please. . . . (*He smiles.*) I have escape . . . on parole . . . from horse talk. (*He looks at* DOLAN.) Please to meet—

MOORE. Mr Dan Dolan of Addergoole. This is a Japanese T.D.,* Dan.

DAN. 'Morrow to your honour.

(*There is a knock at the door, then* MRS MORRISEY *opens it and enters.*)

MRS MORRISEY. Oh, excuse me. I think I left my umbrella here. I'm so sorry to disturb you. I think I was sitting over here and I might have left it beside me.

(*She makes a futile search, in which everybody but* DOLAN *joins.*)

GOSUKI. Please description give.

* Member of the Dail Eireann, the Congress of the Irish Free State.

MRS MORRISEY. It had a nice silver-mounted horn handle with a red silk tassel. (*To* DOLAN.) Excuse me. (*She gives him a hard look.*) I think I know this gentleman. From Addergoole he comes, if I'm not mistaken.

DAN. Yes. I'm Dan Dolan of Addergoole, And who might you be, ma'am, when you're at home?

MRS MORRISEY. Oh, Mr Moore there will tell you. From Ballyglass I come, where the land is that we're all expecting a share of soon, thanks to Mr Moore. Now, where could I have left it? Isn't that strange now? I'm always losing things when I get full of anxiety. Ah, dear! it's an anxious time for us all in Ballyglass. A great misfortune to be running about and leaving your home. I'd never leave my home, Mr Moore – never. (*Looking hard at* DOLAN.) There's always sorrow on them that leaves their homes. (*The* JAPANESE *chuckles.*) Ah well, it's well the little Chinese gentleman knows it. But I was tempted to come and see you, Mr Moore, and see what comes of it. My good silk and silver umbrella— (*With another look at* DOLAN.) There's never any luck comes to them that can't abide at home!

MARTIN (*opening the door*). I've searched the whole house for that umbrella of yours, Mrs Morrisey, and Kate is after telling me you had none when you came in.

MRS MORRISEY. Well, I declare! I must have left it down in Owen Kelly's. I did! I did! I'm so sorry, gentlemen. Indeed I am, to disturb you. Good-bye and thank you, Mr Moore. And don't forget it'll take all the land up there and twice over to satisfy the just claims of the Ballyglasses. Well, good-day, gentlemen, and thank you.

(*Exit, followed by* MARTIN.)

DAN (*with a movement of his ashplant after them*). Is that one to be a neighbour of mine?

KEARNEY. Yes.

DAN. Aye. A nice, friendly spoken woman!

KEARNEY. She's all that.

DAN. And more if she took the notion.

KEARNEY. She might take a notion to you, Dan.

DAN. Ah, God forbid! I've troubles enough as it is. She's strong on the home life, maurya! Begor, I never was in Kilrea yet I didn't see that one somewhere. She must spend a power of time looking for umbrellas. Aye. A champion for a neighbour. Aye. (*Meditatively.*) Aye. Twenty-five acres.

MOORE. Yes.

DAN. And a house and a forty-foot out-office?

MOORE. Yes.

DAN. And a pig-house?

MOORE. Yes.

DAN. And twenty-six pounds rent?

MOORE. Yes. Twenty-six.

DAN (*rising*). Well, yous can keep it.

KEARNEY. And a bog plot in Muckanagh.

DAN (*going toward the door*). And a bog plot in Muckanagh. And the best of neighbours. All nice friendly spoken people. (*He suddenly turns.*) Here! (*He spits on his hands.*) Sixteen pound rent and the meadow field in it!

MOORE (*ignoring him*). O'Neill!

O'NEILL. Yes?

MOORE. Make out a note there to Jennings of Esker to come in to-morrow and show him that holding. (*To* DOLAN.) Well, good-day, Dan. Sorry we couldn't come to any agreement.

DAN. Here! (*Holding out his hand.*) Seventeen, and leave out the meadow!

MOORE. Can't be. (*To* O'NEILL.) And put in the note we agree to his terms.

O'NEILL (*writing*). Yes.

DAN. Here! Mr Moore! (*Then addressing the* JAPANESE.) What do you say, Mr Cossacks? Damn it, we'll split the differ. Now that's a fair offer. What d'ye say?

GOSUKI (*entering into the spirit of the affair*). Ah! Good! (*To* MOORE.) Yes? No?

O'NEILL. I'll take this note out. It would just about catch the post.

KEARNEY. Hold on! Make it twenty for him, Moore.

GOSUKI. Ah! (*To* DOLAN.) Yes? (*To* MOORE.) No?

MOORE. No.

GOSUKI. Ah!

DAN. Here! Be damned but I'll take it at the twenty. Now, Mr Moore!

MOORE. All right. Where's the agreement?

KEARNEY. Here.

(*Hands it to* MOORE.)

MOORE. There you are, Dan. Take it to your solicitor and get it signed.

DAN. Ah, begor, I won't pay six and eightpence to any solicitor. I'm tight enough in money as it is. Give me the pen, Mr O'Neill, if you please, and I'll sign.

(*He sits down, fumbles for his glasses, puts them on, and starts*

205

to read the agreement.)

KEARNEY. I read it all out to you before, except the rent. Sign here.

DAN. There's nothing here about a house or out-offices or a pig-house.

MOORE. No. But aren't they all there on the holding bar the pig-house? (DAN *laboriously signs the agreement watched with interest by the* JAPANESE.) Well, you've a long way to go to Addergoole, Dan. Will you have a drop of whiskey?

DAN. Troth and it's a very odd time now I touch whiskey, your honour—

MOORE. Well. . . . (*He looks at* O'NEILL.) No – Kearney!

KEARNEY. Yes?

MOORE. Take Dan down with you and get him what he wants, to drink luck to the new holding, and take Mr Gosuki down with you and explain the procedure to him. I want to talk to O'Neill.

GOSUKI. Eh, so. Much interest new farm making—

(KEARNEY, DOLAN, *and* GOSUKI *go out talking. A pause.*)

O'NEILL. What do you want to talk to me about?

MOORE. How long are you down here now?

O'NEILL. About three years.

MOORE. Would you like to be over twenty at it?

O'NEILL. I don't know.

MOORE. You'll have to make up your mind soon.

O'NEILL. Why?

MOORE (*suddenly*). Because, like Dolan, you'll have to say either yes or no. Stick it or quit and get out. If you want to quit, quit now. What's your answer?

O'NEILL. What else could I do but stick on?

MOORE. You're young yet.

O'NEILL. Yes. I mightn't – I mightn't be stuck here all the time. I might get back up East some time.

MOORE. Do you know the old saying, O'Neill? "Once West of the Shannon, you never go back." Do you think Dan Dolan goes in to work his new holding with the same ideas as you? There's a transfer of staff to be carried out in this area, but I'm not going to touch it before I know that you're prepared to stay the course. If you're not inclined to stay the course, get out and go somewhere else. But I want your answer to-night.

O'NEILL. I'm staying.

MOORE. Very well. Come back here, then, at nine to-night.

O'NEILL. To-night?

MOORE. Yes. See what you can do re-arranging Addergoole. And let

me give you a tip. Don't get messed up with people like . . . like
. . . Barrington.

O'NEILL. Why?

MOORE. Some time or other we'll be in tangles about land with him.
So keep clear.

O'NEILL. Keep clear?

MOORE. Yes. You know what I'm driving at. Keep clear of them all.
The top and the bottom. And there's only one way. Work!

O'NEILL. And what about – about—?

MOORE. Next Sunday?

O'NEILL. Yes.

MOORE. I've given you my advice.

O'NEILL (*fiercely*). I won't! It's not fair! It's not just . . . out all day . . .
walking, arguing, fighting, wrangling, and then coming in at night
to start putting it all down again and sweating here with you to
midnight! (*With a flash of defiance.*) I won't!

MOORE. Ease up! You called at O'Flaherty's coming home?

O'NEILL. Yes, I did.

MOORE. The public house at Killasolan Cross?

O'NEILL. Yes.

MOORE. What did you want with O'Flaherty?

O'NEILL. To swap that ten-acre plot of his for a bit on the Blake
estate. I went into the whole thing with you before.

MOORE. I didn't think it was the publican.

O'NEILL. Yes. He's the owner now.

MOORE. I see. Were you in his back parlour?

O'NEILL. I don't know what you call the room.

MOORE. And had a drink or two?

O'NEILL. Yes. (*A silence.*) What else could I do?

MOORE. No. You wouldn't see any alternative.

O'NEILL. No. Not to get what you wanted. He wouldn't agree—

MOORE. Just so.

O'NEILL. It's all right to plan out things here in this room with you,
but it's different when you get hearing his side of it.

MOORE. Yes.

O'NEILL. I know well what you're thinking, Moore. That I drank his
whiskey and let him talk me round. Think it if you like. And if you
want to know what I was doing with him— (*He pulls a document
out of his pocket.*) There – there's his old Za. agreement. Agreed
to the swap. It took me two solid hours to get him. But I've got
him! Yes. And I had to stop and drink his rotten two-year-old
poteen . . . ugh! . . . but I got him. It's bizzing my head a bit, but it

gives me courage enough to say to you what I'd like to say to those fellows up in Dublin. Go to hell!

MOORE. Go home to bed, you silly young ass!

O'NEILL. No. I'm not going home, and I'm not going to bed either. I've fixed up the Blake estate that you and Kearney have been tangling at for the last twenty years, and I'm going down below to the bar, and I'm going to hit up this rockery to-night!

(*He blunders out angrily to the door, and barely avoids a collision as it opens suddenly and* MARTIN *appears.*)

MARTIN. Did you ring, gentlemen?

O'NEILL. No. But I'll wring your neck if you don't stand aside.

(*He pushes* MARTIN *angrily aside on to the sofa, and blunders down the stairs.*)

MARTIN (*looking after him, and then turning with a slow smile to* MOORE). He's powerful like yourself used to be in the old days, Mr Moore.

(CURTAIN.)

208

ACT II

The same Scene as Act I. A few days later. MOORE *and* KEARNEY *are engaged comparing a map and the relating schedule. It is late in the evening.*

MOORE. Plot 29?
    (*He pores over the map.*)
KEARNEY. Yes. Do you see it?
MOORE. Right! I see it.
KEARNEY. Sixteen acres, one rood. It goes to John Hennessy, who surrenders— (*He pauses to emphasise the Numbers and also to allow* MOORE *to follow him on the map.*) 16A . . . 16B . . . 16C . . . 16H . . . 16L . . . and the undivided 3/16ths of No. 18B.
MOORE (*laboriously following him*). 16C . . . 16H . . . 16L.
    (*The town clock strikes nine.* MOORE *is still intent on his map, but* KEARNEY *yawns and gets up.*)
KEARNEY. I say, Moore!
MOORE (*without much heed*). Yes?
KEARNEY. If you don't mind I'm chucking. It's gone nine.
MOORE. Yes.
    (*He continues examining the map.*)
KEARNEY (*loudly*). Moore!
MOORE. Yes?
KEARNEY. I want to get home, if you don't mind.
MOORE. All right! All right!
KEARNEY. Sorry to stop, but – it's Ellen. . . . She's got a bit fidgety lately. Always gets that way when the long nights begin.
MOORE. She should have got used to it by this time.
KEARNEY. No, she hasn't. It's a bit lonesome down there at Tubber Knockmore in the winter. Nothing but the kids and herself there, you know, the live-long day. I wonder what it'll be like when they grow up and go away!
MOORE. H'm! (*Looking at the map.*) Yes. It's not a bad bit of work. All right. We can have another go at this on Friday.

209

KEARNEY. Very well. (*A gust of wind and rain.*) Rotten night for the drive back. (*A pause.*) Any chance of a move up for me, Moore?

MOORE. Not yet.

KEARNEY. I say, Moore! Do you never want yourself, sometime, to move out of this?

MOORE. Not now.

KEARNEY. H'm! Content to spend your life dividing land – devising bridge heads to places you find you can't get, like Fitzgormanstown. I'd certainly like a change now and again if it was only to be taking the missus – if ever you have one – for a spin on the Bray Road of a summer's day out to Killiney or Greystones.

MOORE. No.

KEARNEY. Or a night like this going in to see the latest at the pictures or the theatres?

MOORE. No.

KEARNEY (*disgustedly*). Ach! I suppose I'm younger than you, but it's a rotten life. All right for some, maybe, but out there at Tubber – all hours of the day – and often at night . . . knock – knock – knock – someone at the door. "If yous don't repair the kish that was put down for the right of way at Ballindine Bog, we'll have a question asked in the floor of the Dail – the drain between O'Flaherty Pat and Mick Hennigan is choked and Jack Dempsey Red has the water stopped on them below – the big wind of Friday last week has stripped the slates off Mick Dolan's new house – Tim Casey has put on a jennet for grass where he had only the right of a donkey. . . ." I wonder do they ever think up in Dublin of all that we ever go through down here?

MOORE (*smiling*). Do you ever think of all that they go through up in Dublin?

KEARNEY (*pointing at the Schedule*). Sure that stuff there only represents one-tenth of what we go through. Even if you said no . . . no . . . no . . . you can't stop it. You haven't the heart to curse and damn them off your doorstep like the old agents did in the Seventies. And agents had offices. I've nothing but my miserable little home and the only decent room in it is given up to this Moloch. (*A pause.*) Sorry, Moore, to be grousing.

MOORE. Grouse away, old man. It does no harm even if it doesn't do any good. (*Pause.*) There's a lot more work come down.

KEARNEY. What side? Fitzgormanstown?

MOORE. No. That waits a new Land Act. Down Ballinasheeda way.

KEARNEY. Where McCartan used to be?

MOORE. Yes.

KEARNEY. Well, there are worse places than Tubber! And Ballinasheeda's one of them.

MOORE. You're not inclined to face it?

KEARNEY. Not me, thank you! (*With a sudden note of alarm in his voice.*) For God's sake, don't send me down there, Moore. It would kill her – Ellen, I mean. It drove McCartan mad. Those people down there, they all go over the water to work in the summer and come back to sleep in the winter, and they don't come back the better for what they learned across the water, I tell you.

MOORE. Well, someone's got to go there. Read this.

(*He extracts a memorandum from an envelope on the table and hands it to* KEARNEY.)

KEARNEY (*reading*). "Estates of O'Mara – Fitzgibbon – Estimates – now required – 700 tenantry – re-arrangement – of holdings . . . provision – of – new roads – housing." (*He hands it back to* MOORE.) Thanks. Pie for somebody!

MOORE. I suppose you wondered why I'd been giving you additional work lately?

KEARNEY. To tell you the truth, I thought it was about time you were handing a bit over to O'Neill.

MOORE. I've been deliberately easing off O'Neill.

KEARNEY. Why?

MOORE. You have the reason in your hand.

KEARNEY. This?

MOORE. Yes.

KEARNEY. You're sending O'Neill to Ballinasheeda! (*He laughs.*) He'll only go phut like McCartan.

MOORE. Well, we'll see.

KEARNEY. A bit tough on him Moore!

MOORE. It's come up to the time when he's got to be flung into the water to see if he can swim.

KEARNEY. Or drown!

MOORE. Maybe.

KEARNEY. Does he know?

MOORE. Not yet.

KEARNEY. Where is he?

MOORE. Out with the little Jap somewhere.

KEARNEY. Hm! I suppose somehow or other they'll manage to get Mount Nevin way!

MOORE. I don't quite follow that remark.

KEARNEY. You didn't hear anything lately?

MOORE. About O'Neill?

KEARNEY. Yes – and that Barrington girl.

MOORE. No.

KEARNEY. I met our Mrs Marcus Morrisey yesterday.

MOORE. Well?

KEARNEY. And she dropped a few remarks about the pair.

MOORE. Hm! (*Knocking at the door.*) Come in. (O'NEILL *enters.*) Hello! back safe?

O'NEILL. Yes.

KEARNEY. So our Japanese friend turned up again on his way back from Mayo?

MOORE. Yes – full of notes and notebooks on his way home to Dublin to-morrow.

KEARNEY. Where is he now?

O'NEILL. Talking below with Mooney.

KEARNEY (*with a glance at* MOORE). Was he out with you to-day?

O'NEILL. Yes. On Muckanagh Bog.

KEARNEY. Anywhere else?

O'NEILL. No.

KEARNEY. Thought you might have gone Mount Nevin way and seen Dan Dolan.

O'NEILL. I didn't.

KEARNEY. How's Dolan getting on out there? Didn't he move there this week?

O'NEILL. Yes.

KEARNEY. No opposition?

O'NEILL. No.

KEARNEY. You weren't talking much to anybody out there then?

O'NEILL. No, I wasn't.

(*A gentle knock, then* GOSUKI *appears.*)

GOSUKI. Excuse. Just now . . . man . . . not know . . . say . . . give this . . . (*he shows a letter*) Mr Moore . . . and . . . pouf! . . . he run . . . not wait . . . reply.

(*He hands the letter to* MOORE.)

MOORE (*opening it and reading*). Hm! (*He smiles grimly.*) Interest you perhaps, O'Neill.

(*He hands it to the latter.*)

O'NEILL (*reading*). "If Dolan the grabber does not leave Ballyglass by Sunday, himself and you will have the following ready for ye and O'Neill. Captain Moonlight."

KEARNEY (*to* O'NEILL). Show. (O'NEILL *hands it to him.*) Hm! Three coffins, labelled Moore, O'Neill and Dolan.

GOSUKI. Excuse. May I please?

 (*He stretches out for the letter which* KEARNEY *hands to him.*)

MOORE. Kearney!

GOSUKI (*studying the letter*). Eh! Much interest. Captain Moonlight
. . . is . . . name . . . for . . . not real name?

MOORE. Yes. It's only a joke.

GOSUKI. Eh! So. Irish peoples much fun and laughings make all times,
and merry! Ha! Ha! May I keep please? Example . . . curio . . .
humour of Irish peoples . . . for Japans to see!

MOORE (*aside to* KEARNEY). Damn you! (*To* GOSUKI.) All right. I'd
prefer you burned it.

GOSUKI. I thank. (*Looking critically at the letter.*) Irish peoples not
artist good. Japans peoples all artist good.

 (*There is a sudden knock on the door. Then* BARRINGTON,
 flushed and excited-looking, enters.)

BARRINGTON. Hello! Got you all in. Moore!

MOORE. You're late abroad to-night!

BARRINGTON. I am, and thanks to you. I've come to warn you. There
may be some trouble to-night. Some blackguards came in last
night when I was out and pinched my two guns.

MOORE. Nothing new about that, is there?

BARRINGTON. No. But as far as I can gather there was no official raid
about it. Damn the whole silly crowd of you! Have you no sense,
Moore?

MOORE. Depends on the point of view you take.

BARRINGTON. You know mine, anyway. You went and took up all
that home farm of mine and put outsiders on it. You've given the
last bit of it now to that little rascal of a Dolan, and he can thank
his stars if he doesn't get about fifty pickle of shot into him if he
doesn't slip out by Sunday. If he lives through it all, and you do, I
suppose the demesne will have to go next to satisfy them. (*A
pause.*) It's damned unfair, Moore, the way you people deal with
us. Go and take up the only bit of land we could make a profit on
to keep up the demesne. Then when we can't stock and work
what you've left us, and have to set it in con-acre and grazing, you
say we're not working it properly, and then seize what's left.
Damn you! Damn the whole lot of you! (*A pause.*) Sorry! I'm a
bit on edge, but if you had known what that old place was like
when I was a boy . . . a hive of industry, and see it now . . . grass
growing in the yards, and the roofs of the stables caving in,
because I've got no capital to work it with – the mortgagees took
every penny you paid us. (*Suddenly.*) Are you going to take

Mount Nevin?

MOORE. You'd be the first to get that information.

BARRINGTON. Oh, yes! But a lot depends on what you wrote about it.

MOORE. Barrington, I wonder could you ever detach yourself from the personal point of view and look at Mount Nevin, and the way the place is used, as a cold examiner bound to report the truth without prejudice or favour?

BARRINGTON. And that's the way you've done it?

MOORE. I have tried to tell the truth.

BARRINGTON. I see. (*A pause.*) I had no post for two or three days, so I sent in Morrisey to-day to get my letters. He called and got them all right, but went off East to see his cousin and left word he'd call this way coming back. More devilment, I suppose! And they tell me one letter was from the Land Commission. Did *you* write me, Moore?

MOORE. No.

BARRINGTON. Hm! Then it's from Dublin direct.

(*Knocking.* MOCKLER, *a big heavy man enters. He is flustered and excited.*)

MOCKLER. And how are you, Mr Moore? And it surprises me nothing to find you here, Mr Barrington. It only confirms my suspicions that there's more behind this business at Mount Nevin than the people think. We had a mass meeting out at Ballyglass to-day and it is my duty to convey to you, Mr Moore, the unanimous declaration of the people there protesting against the despicable methods adopted in the recent division of land in our parish.

GOSUKI. Excuse, please. You . . . policy of official . . . condemn as bad?

BARRINGTON. Damned bad! Couldn't be worse.

MOCKLER (*looking hard at him*). Eh? Are those your true opinions or are they assumed for the moment? We've had experience of your tactics before, Mr Barrington. You were quite willing to surrender the land in 1920, but when different times came you reneged and fought the case through every Court of Appeal you could take it into.

BARRINGTON. And why shouldn't I? My people were sent to Hell or Connaught, and out of Connaught I'm not going till I get my rights. Stick that in your pipe and smoke it, Mockler.

MOORE. You are under a misconception, Mockler. Barrington came here to object to our proceedings.

MOCKLER. I'd like to have some more proof of that. (*He turns to* O'NEILL.) Wasn't it you put Dolan in yesterday?

O'NEILL. Yes.

MOCKLER. Aye. And you were out at Mount Nevin the Sunday before. (*A silence.*) Hm! Aye. And company keeping since with Miss Barrington.

BARRINGTON. Keep my daughter's name out of this matter, please.

MOCKLER. Very well. But keep your back-door influence to yourself. The land at Ballyglass has always been regarded as the rightful and lawful property of the people of Ballyglass from time immemorial— You're out of it at last and I advise you to keep out of it.

BARRINGTON. Here! Enough of that—

MOORE. Ease up, Barrington!

MOCKLER. A man named Dolan, a complete outsider, and stranger, without the knowledge or consent of the people of Ballyglass, has been put in possession of land in that parish.

BARRINGTON. I agree—

MOCKLER. And I want to warn you all that any attempt on the part of any official here or in Dublin to over-ride and trample on the just claims of the people to land in their own locality will be met with all the fighting opposition that an united and determined people can offer.

GOSUKI. Excuse, please. You and artist of this – (*he produces the Moonlight letter*) – same?

MOCKLER (*waving it aside*). No, sir. I repudiate any connection with that sort of method. If I have anything to say, I say it openly and without resort to cowardice and threats. But it is an indication of the feelings of the people and if disregarded, the end can only be disorder and bloodshed. You have had your warning, Mr Moore.

MOORE. Am I to be told that as a threat?

MOCKLER. It follows your action as night the day.

BARRINGTON. I agree.

MOCKLER. You – I don't want your approval of what I say – I feel too strongly that any representations of the people have been and are over-ruled by the Junkers and Mussolini's at Headquarters.

GOSUKI. Ah! Mussolini . . . and . . . Italy . . . much interest! (*To MOCKLER.*) Have you study make of Italians people and . . . reclamations . . . please?

MOCKLER (*with a gesture of disgust*). Ach! (*To MOORE.*) What message am I to take back to the people of Ballyglass to-night? Is it peace or war?

(*A loud knock at the door. It opens suddenly and* DAN DOLAN *appears in the doorway. Regardless of the rest of the company,*

215

he makes his way at once towards MOORE.)

DOLAN (*with a wild lash of his ashplant on the table nearest to* MOORE). Damn ye, when are you going to put the cement floor in my pig-house?

MOORE. Is it not in yet?

DOLAN. The divil an in! It's there to this day the same as when this gentleman here – (*pointing at* O'NEILL) – seen it last Friday and promised me in front of the ganger and John Morrisey, would be put in that night. And the damn the shovel or spade was ever laid on it since.

MOCKLER. Ach! We're talking here about something more serious than pig-houses and cement floors.

DOLAN. Are ye? Well, yous can talk away till yous are all blue in the face about anything yous like, but short of getting fair play and justice done me, I'll—

(*He makes another lash at the table but* O'NEILL *intercepts and prevents him.*)

MOCKLER. That's enough, you little omadhaun! You aren't in Fogarty's public house.

DOLAN. And travelling I am since seven this morning to get a hoult of you, Mr Moore – for that ganger you have down there is nothing short of a common cheat and deceiver. Mark my words, says I to him, I'm off to Mooney's of Kilrea to the Commissioners, and I'll expose you, you big omadhaun of a gobhaun carpenter and a mason, that you're only a three-card trick man and a thimble rigging trick of the loop scut ye, cheating honest men out of what was promised them.

MOCKLER. That's the proper talk. Nothing but bribery and corruption from the highest to the lowest. You done well to come away from the place you should never have ventured into.

DOLAN. And I've come where I can get justice! (*With a resounding blow on the table.*) Damn ye! When are ye going to put the cement floor in my pig-house?

MOORE (*suddenly rising*). Here – a minute before you destroy that table altogether! Sit down. (DOLAN *does so.*) Put that stick on the table. And take off your hat. (DOLAN *sullenly obeys.*) Aren't you married?

DOLAN. Yes.

MOORE. And did you get your breakfast this morning?

DOLAN. Yes.

MOORE. Tell me! Is this the way you asked your wife for it? (*Suddenly seizing the ashplant and welting the table with it.*) Damn

216

ye! when will ye give me my breakfast?

MOCKLER. That's right, Mr Moore! Learn the little omadhaun some manners that he can go back where he comes from, and teach it to them in Addergoole—

DOLAN. I will – and if yous don't put that floor in my pig-house, I'll resign all to yous – house and lands and pig-house, and go back where I come from.

KEARNEY. Back to Addergoole?

DOLAN. Yes. Back to Addergoole, and it's black sorrow is on me since ever I left it—

MOORE. Back to the bog-garden and the dobey-house and the one room?

DOLAN. Yes. I'll resign all to yous and go back. Isn't it a laughing-stock yous have made of me for the whole countryside?

MOCKLER. That settles the matter. I'm glad to see there's some glimmerings of sense in you yet, Dolan.

GOSUKI. Excuse please . . . (*To* DOLAN.) Not land or breakfast annoy but house for pig, not cement of floor?

DOLAN. Yes. And all the arable I have is eight acres of cold blue stiff clay, full of sleeping water, and double that of old, sour, wet callows and cut away bog that's full of red water and murrain.

BARRINGTON. Hold on there! It's the best land in Connaught if it was properly worked.

DOLAN. Oh, glory be! The best land in—! Drains in it the size of the Suez Canal that lost me two ewes and their lambs, and a yearling heifer, and a cut-out strip of a brown bog that hasn't two spits of turf in it, and what I have to be dragging home on the ass's back a mile to the county road, and has all my childer perished – I'll resign all to yous gentlemen. I'm going back.

MOCKLER (*putting out his hand*). Lay it there, Dolan! I'm proud to meet you and to know you're vacating and surrendering land yous never should have got.

DOLAN (*ignoring him*). The divil a surrender till I get justice! No surrender, and damn the penny rent I'll pay yous!

MOCKLER. What kind of crooked little gnat are you? Are you refusing now to go out of it and back to Addergoole?

DOLAN. There's no man living will put me back to Addergoole till it's failed me to get justice.

MOCKLER (*maddened*). Ach! You're only a contrary little, sucking little, pigeen of a man! A little twisted gnat of an adder from Addergoole that would bite the hand of any decent man that ever handled ye! (DOLAN *makes to strike him, but it is restrained by*

217

O'NEILL.) And I tell you, it won't be many days or weeks either that you'll be worrying about cement on the floor of your pighouse, but the heat of the floor of the place you'll be standing in alongside of the boneens of Judas Iscariot! (*He goes to the door.*) Good-night to ye, gentlemen, and be sure you pack him off, and all his little boneens with him, back to Addergoole this night, and no need to be wasting good powder and shot. Bannach leat.

  (*Exit.*)

GOSUKI. Excuse . . . please . . . parish . . . name of place . . . where . . . only . . . Christian peoples is?

BARRINGTON. Yes. We're all Christians. I hope, in the parish of Ballyglass.

GOSUKI. Most difficult . . . understandings . . . for Japanese. Christian doctrines and peoples . . . not same. (*Pointing to* DOLAN.) Ah! small man's not Christian?

DOLAN. I'd like to see anyone calling me a heathen!

GOSUKI. So! But why angry because of house for pig? Pig in Ireland object of respects?

KEARNEY. Oh, the pig is a most important animal!

GOSUKI. Ah! So! In Japans . . . Inarisama . . . Fox . . . animal . . . symbol . . . cunning! Much venerations . . . all peoples . . . give and small temple . . . shrine . . . small . . . nice . . . house build. Also Nakosama . . . Cat . . . animal . . . symbol . . . wisdoms . . . venerations give. What symbol . . . venerations – please . . . Pig?

BARRINGTON. You don't know what a pig stands for?

GOSUKI. No. Please?

BARRINGTON. It's supposed to be the greediest animal alive.

GOSUKI. Ah! Now understand.

  (*He takes notes.*)

MOORE. Better get home, Kearney.

KEARNEY. You're right. Good-night, everybody.

  (*Exit.*)

DOLAN. Are yous Christian gentlemen going to do nothing for me?

MOORE. Look here, Dolan. The cement floor will be put in your pighouse. Get it put in to-morrow, O'Neill.

O'NEILL. Yes, sir.

DOLAN. A slip of a note now, Mr Moore, to Pat Burke that has the caretaking of the woods up at Muckanagh.

MOORE. For what?

DOLAN. For a few deal trees to be making half a score of rafters for a bit of a lean-to shed I'd be wanting next to the pig-house.

MOORE. We can't.

DOLAN. Aye. No orders. No timber. No cement floor. Would yous write me an order, if you please, for a couple of larch poles then, for the makings of an ass cart?

MOORE. No.

DOLAN. An order then for a larch tree for a sheepcock pole? Ah, bad cess to it, Mr Moore— Ah, damn it, Mr Moore, you wouldn't be refusing me that?

BARRINGTON. Don't be so hard on the little beggar, Moore, if he is going to be the idiot enough to stick to his holding. Ask him for plenty, Dolan. Ask him for plenty.

DOLAN. It's well I have a friend in one of the old gentry. And maybe the new kind of gentry we will have now will listen to me when you're in it, your honour. The old landlords, God rest them! were some of them blackguards, but there's none of them ever treated us like some of the upstarts we have now on top of us.

MOORE. That's done it! (*He sits down and writes.*) Here, take this note for the half-score of deal.

DOLAN. Long life to you, Mr Moore! (*Hesitatingly.*) There's a nearing between myself and that thief of a Morrisey would want a couple of stakes, and a few strands of wire—

BARRINGTON (*with a sudden burst of anger*). What! Wire! Wire, did you say? If I see as much as an inch of wire up in my country I'll shoot you at sight!

DOLAN. Shoot me, is it? Mind what you're saying now! Maybe it's yourself, and Mockler, and that old soupladler of a Morrisey is at the back of this divilment, Mr Moore. (*He fumbles in his pocket and produces a note.*) That's the second of its kind that Norah found stuck on the door of the pig-house. (*He hands it to* MOORE.) And it's well I know who put the fist to it.

MOORE (*critically examining it*). Hm! Same paper, same rotten drawing.

DOLAN. And I can tell you, Mr Barrington, as I told the Morriseys yesterday, and that ganger of yours, Mr O'Neill, that's in the swim, that I posted up a notice on Morrisey's new poultry house that he got by swindling the Department, that's none of your 'nonymous ones, but that's signed by me in full – Dan Dolan. That'll put the fear of God into that mean, yellow rent-warner and grabber.

BARRINGTON. Here! Keep a civil tongue in your head about the Morriseys. The best gamekeepers and faithfullest retainers the Barringtons and the old stock ever had—

DOLAN (*angrily*). Faithful to the Barringtons and the old stock, maurya! For every pheasant yous got, he sold two and ate one, and it's well everybody but yourself knows it. Presarving game, maurya! Presarving foxes for a covert that ates all the laying ducks, for no pay but the delight they has in annoying decent neighbours. Only that he got some job from yourself, Mr Barrington, to come in for letters this morning, I tell you I'd make that Morrisey sorrow for the day he ever put a fist to them papers. (*With a resounding whack of his ashplant on the table.*) That's the way I'll sign my signature on him when I sees him. Long life to you, Mr Moore! And no harm to Mr Barrington, but it was the great day for this country when Parnell, God rest him! swept away the whole of yous in '81!

> (*Exit.*)

BARRINGTON. There you are, Moore! What sort of an infliction is that you've blistered me up with at Mount Nevin? Well, there's not much use, I suppose, in discussing the matter further. Yourself and O'Neill and that little blackguard can face all the consequences.

MOORE. Yes.

BARRINGTON (*turning to* O'NEILL). I think you'll understand the situation, O'Neill, but for fear you didn't, I stayed to express it. I have no desire for further observations from Mr Mockler about my daughter's association with you. So let that end now, please. Is that clear enough?

O'NEILL (*bowing*). Yes.

BARRINGTON. Thank you. Good-night to you both.

> (*Goes out.*)

GOSUKI. Mr Moore! Excuse, please . . . may I . . . small mans of pig-house letter see? Please.

MOORE (*producing note* DOLAN *has left behind*). This?

GOSUKI. Yes, please. (*He takes it and then compares it critically with the previous one in his possession.*) One joke . . . but . . . two . . . not nice . . . not fun. (*He hands them both back to* MOORE.) Much interest . . . but . . . not . . . clean. (*He makes the gesture of washing his hands.*) Much interest but not keep. Much troubles all nations . . . land . . . (*Turning to* O'NEILL, *and smiling.*) But most troubles young peoples is . . . (*he smiles*) Love! Pardon . . . and excuse. Go men ma sai. . . . Good-nights.

MOORE. Good-night. (*Exit* GOSUKI.) I suppose you understand what Barrington meant?

O'NEILL. Yes.

MOORE. I'm very glad. I thought—

(*He stops short.*)

O'NEILL. Yes. What did you think?

(MOORE *makes no reply, but sits down quietly and takes up the map he had been working at with* KEARNEY.)

MOORE. That's not a bad scheme of Kearney's by any means.

O'NEILL (*after an uneasy silence*). What did you think?

MOORE. Oh! (*He does not look up, but continues to examine the map.*) I thought – (*he suddenly lifts his head and looks straight over at* O'NEILL) – that you were fond of the girl.

O'NEILL (*with an effort*). No. (*His voice trembles slightly.*) Not a bit.

MOORE. Well, that will make things easier then. Take Kearney's schedule there, and call out the numbers of those plots till I have a view of this. We stopped at the sixteens. John Hennessy.

O'NEILL (*sitting down*). John Hennessey!

MOORE. Yes. See it? 16L. Next.

O'NEILL. 16M . . . 16N.

(*A long pause.*)

O'NEILL (*trying to restrain himself and then losing control*). 16 . . . 16 . . . 16. . . . I'm lying to you, Moore! I'm mad . . . about her . . . I can't eat – I can't sleep – I can't . . . I can't . . . (*He suddenly pulls himself together.*) Forget it. 16N . . . 16N . . . 16N . . . (*Despairingly.*) I'm sorry.

MOORE. Better have a drink.

(*He goes over and rings.*)

O'NEILL. No, thanks.

MOORE. Oh! When did you go on the wagon?

O'NEILL. Since that night you spoke to me.

MOORE. Excuse me, O'Neill, if I don't believe you – I mean, that it was due to anything I said. I'm only judging by the way you took it that evening—

O'NEILL. I'm sorry. I apologise. But I didn't hit up the rockery that night. (*A pause.*) I met her—

MOORE. Miss Barrington?

O'NEILL. Yes.

(*Knocking.*)

MOORE. Come in.

MARTIN (*opening the door*). You ring, sir?

MOORE. Sorry, Martin. I meant to order a drink, but changed my mind.

MARTIN. Yes, sir. Great gas below, sir.

MOORE. Eh?

MARTIN. Mr Mockler and the little Addergoole fellow is after having a hell of a set in the yard, and only for the little Japanese gentleman there might have been some bloody business done. He jeejoojed Mr Mockler. Will yous want anything before the bar closes, sir?

MOORE. No, thanks.

(MARTIN *goes out.*)

O'NEILL. I pity that poor little devil going his way home all alone to that country.

MOORE. Yes. Enough to make all of us feel ashamed. If we have to put up with a lot of things we don't like – abuse, misrepresentations – criticisms – what's that compared to all that little warrior's got to go through? Hell for a couple or three years, maybe.

O'NEILL. I'll make him a happier man to-morrow.

MOORE. How?

O'NEILL. Putting in the cement floor of the temple of the pig, as our Japanese friend would call it.

MOORE. Leave that to the ganger— I want you for something else to-morrow. It'll be your turn to play the migrant, O'Neill.

O'NEILL. I don't quite follow—

MOORE. Did you know McCartan?

O'NEILL. Yes. I was with him once stripping bog, years ago.

MOORE. At Ballinasheeda?

O'NEILL. Yes.

MOORE. You know Ballinasheeda, then?

O'NEILL. Yes. A God-forsaken hole!

MOORE. It is.

O'NEILL. I heard he went wrong afterwards.

MOORE. Yes. He was dismissed.

O'NEILL. What happened?

MOORE. If you want to know the real reason – he was a damned bad migrant.

O'NEILL. It would take some courage to stick out life in that place.

MOORE (*grimly*). It would. It was a mistake to put McCartan there. I don't like making mistakes, and I may be making another one, but I've no option. (*Suddenly.*) O'Neill, you said you weren't a quitter!

O'NEILL. I'm not.

MOORE. Well— You're going to-morrow to Ballinasheeda.

O'NEILL. To – to Ballinasheeda!

MOORE. Yes.

O'NEILL. To – to Ballinasheeda! Moore! you don't – you can't mean it! Did you ever see McCartan's digs?

222

MOORE. Yes. I lived in them before McCartan.

O'NEILL. But . . . Moore – I can't understand . . . what have I done?

MOORE. Nothing. It's not a punishment.

O'NEILL. What other way could I see it?

MOORE. Do you want to know what it is?

O'NEILL (*without heeding him, and despairingly*). It's miles and miles away.

MOORE. Yes. Miles and miles away in one sense. But it's not miles and miles away from the one big thing—

O'NEILL. What's that?

MOORE. The work.

O'NEILL. The work! There's any amount of work – you know there is – round here. Why would you do this on me – why? Why? (*He stops suddenly and looks in a queer way at* MOORE.) It's surely not because of—?

MOORE. Some time later you'll ask that question of yourself and you'll be able to answer it.

(*The door opens gently, and* DOLAN *puts his head in.*)

DOLAN. Would you give me an order for a sheep-cock pole, if you please, sir?

MOORE. Write one out for him there, O'Neill. How are you getting home, Dolan?

DOLAN. Walking, sir.

MOORE. Walking! This night!

DOLAN. Yes, sir.

MOORE. It's fifteen miles and more!

DOLAN. Yes, sir.

(MOORE, *without further remark, leaves the room abruptly.*)

DOLAN (*going over slowly to* O'NEILL). Could you be pleased to make it a double when you're at it, Mr O'Neill? Sure, one more or less would make no matter. (*Confidentially.*) She's in the town!

O'NEILL. Who?

DOLAN. Her!

O'NEILL. Who's her?

DOLAN. That one.

O'NEILL. Which one?

DOLAN. Your one.

(MOORE *enters. He is dressed in his waterproof coat and sou'wester hat.*)

MOORE. Dolan!

DOLAN. Yes, sir?

MOORE. I'll give you a lift home.

DOLAN. To Ballyglass?

MOORE. Yes.

DOLAN. God spare your honour the health, but I wouldn't be putting that labour on yourself.

MOORE. Anybody else come in with you?

DOLAN. No, sir.

MOORE. Come on then. You come, O'Neill?

DOLAN. He can't. He has some business that I made for him.

MOORE. Eh? (*He looks very sharply at* O'NEILL.) Very well, O'Neill!

O'NEILL. Yes?

MOORE (*going to a bundle of large bulky envelopes and bringing them over to the table beside* O'NEILL). Have a look over some of this stuff. It's the work you'll be taking charge of, out there.

(*He goes out, followed by* DOLAN. O'NEILL *goes to the window and looks out. A burst of rain and wind lashes at the window. He shrugs his shoulders despondently and sits down, takes up some notepaper and hastily writes, puts it in an envelope, addresses and seals it. The door opens gently and he looks up with astonishment to see* CECILY BARRINGTON.)

O'NEILL. Why, it's you, Cecily!

CECILY. Yes. I met Kearney and he said – said you were going away. Is it true?

O'NEILL. Yes. To-morrow.

CECILY. To-morrow! Where are you going?

O'NEILL. A place called Ballinasheeda.

CECILY. Where's that?

O'NEILL. A long way west of this.

CECILY. So that I'll hardly ever see you again?

O'NEILL. I don't suppose you will.

CECILY. How long will you be there?

O'NEILL. A very long time.

CECILY. Years, maybe? (O'NEILL *nods.*) I see. So they made this arrangement between them! They must have!

O'NEILL. Who?

CECILY. Moore and father. I saw them talking in the lounge as I came past. (*She suddenly catches sight of the letter.*) You were writing to me?

O'NEILL. Yes. (*He picks up the letter.*) I thought I wouldn't have the chance of seeing you again before I left.

CECILY. What have you written in it?

O'NEILL. Nothing of any consequence. Only a – a few lines.

CECILY. To say good-bye?

O'NEILL. Yes.

CECILY. And is that all?

O'NEILL. No. But the rest doesn't matter.

CECILY. Let me read it, please!

O'NEILL. No. (*He suddenly tears the letter in pieces.*) The rest of the letter was – it was only— (*He looks hard at her and trembles.*) There . . . I can't help telling you . . . what good is it going to do, I don't know, but it's the truth, Cecily . . . I love you!

CECILY. And what reply did you expect?

O'NEILL. I didn't ask for any.

CECILY. So this is the end then! I suppose – (*she hesitates and then holds out her hand*) – we'll have to say good-bye?

O'NEILL. Good-bye?

(*He takes her hand, and then turns away.*)

CECILY. And neither of us really cared? . . . (*She comes closer and looks up into his face.*) Say that you never really cared?

O'NEILL. *You* never cared.

CECILY (*with sudden and passionate anguish in her voice*). I do care. (*He takes her in his arms.*) Oh, believe me. I only want – want you!

(*The door opens and MOORE stands on the threshold in his oilskins and sou'wester.*)

MOORE. (*suddenly entering*). I'm sorry, Miss Barrington. – Your father is below – asking for you. (*He pauses.*) I'm afraid that he's got rather bad news.

CECILY. Did he get the letter he was looking for?

MOORE. Yes. His demesne has been declared.

CECILY. Oh! (*She trembles, and vainly tries to keep back her tears.*) Poor darling old daddy! (*With a despairing cry to O'NEILL.*) You – you didn't do it, anyway. You had no part in this.

(*The door swings open and BARRINGTON appears. He is trembling with excitement.*)

BARRINGTON. Cecily! What are you doing here?

CECILY. I came to see Hugh.

BARRINGTON. Have they told you what has happened?

CECILY. Yes!

BARRINGTON. I see. So it has come to this end for the Barringtons! My lands gone – my house gone! Cecily!

(*He looks at her as if she too were lost to him.*)

CECILY. No! No!

BARRINGTON (*looking at* O'NEILL). Make your lot with him, if you wish, with these servants in the Temple of the Pig – for that's the

God they serve, and well they know it, both of them. Good-night, Moore. Good-night, young man. I suppose you are both satisfied with your work.

(*He goes out slowly like a broken man.*)

CECILY (*looking imploringly at* O'NEILL). I can't – I can't – leave him like this.

(*They all stand silent.* CECILY *makes a despairing gesture and walks out. A pause.* O'NEILL *makes a movement to follow.* MOORE *stops him with a commanding gesture.*)

MOORE. Let him get his agony over alone. (*A pause.*) "Servants in the Temple of the Pig." . . . I don't wonder he feels bitter to-night. (*He moves over to the window, looks out, and calls.*) Dolan! Is that you?

DOLAN'S VOICE (*from below*). Yes, sir.

MOORE. Wait there a moment – I'll be down directly. (*He turns round.*) You needn't stay up for me, O'Neill. I'll be calling on the way back with Mockler.

O'NEILL. With Mockler?

MOORE. Yes. To tell him we're standing by that little fighting devil. He's not afraid to face them. A migrant in a thousand! And let you, boy, have the same courage where you're going.

O'NEILL. I?

MOORE. Yes. You're my migrant to Ballinasheeda.

(*The door opens and* GOSUKI *appears.*)

GOSUKI. Excuse, please. I to-morrow . . . Dublin . . . Japan go. Galway . . . Roscommon . . . Mayo . . . have seen. Thousands of new house . . . new farm . . . migrants. Most impress. Pardon . . . one mistake . . . policy. When Government . . . eh . . . state . . . land give to people . . . eh . . . control and ownership should keep. My view. (*He takes a small parcel from his pocket and presents it to* MOORE.) Little token . . . present . . . small fan of remembrance to Moore Sama. I salute and thank. I, inscription on it have made, "Remembrance gracious to Moore Sama. Officer of Great Department of State, Ireland." Sayonara.

(*Exit.*)

O'NEILL (*cynically*). This great department of the State!

MOORE (*roused*). Yes. This great department of the State that is slowly wiping out the wrongs of centuries of oppression. And if an older man's advice can avail you anything, be proud to serve this great department of the State that gives us power for good or evil, reaching beyond the grave of this generation.

O'NEILL (*with a cold cynicism that gradually works itself at the end to vehemence.*) Did you hear the Japanese with his houses and his temples of the Fox and of the Cat? I tell you, Moore, Barrington was right. You and I serve in the Temple of the Pig. And the floors of it, and the walls of it, are the floors and the walls of a shambles.

MOORE (*slowly*). A shambles? I used to think like you once. Years ago. But I do know this. That by this work we carry out, what was once a shambles and a house of greed may yet become—

(*He pauses, and, as if hesitant to complete his words, moves towards the door.*)

O'NEILL (*wonderingly*). Yes?

MOORE (*turning towards the door and speaking as if reluctant to confess outwardly*). A Temple – of the Living God.

(*There is the sound of a brisk fusillade of revolver shots outside in the Square. The two men stand still in a shocked, motionless silence.*)

O'NEILL (*looking over at* MOORE *with a grim smile*). A shambles or a Temple of the Living God – which is it, Moore?

(CURTAIN.)

227

ACT III

The same scene from some twelve years later. There is but little change in the furniture, and it is only by the alterations of the curtains, and perhaps the wallpaper, that any indication of the lapse of time is conveyed. The little Japanese fan still remains like a forgotten relic on the mantelpiece. The room, however, has been tidied up; all the array and litter of documents, maps, etc., have been cleared away. A couple of rucksacks and an old portmanteau lie labelled and ready for removal.

MOORE, *now an old man, is seated, asleep, in one of the armchairs. Outside can be heard the faint notes of a flute playing the air of the "Gentle Maiden." It is still daylight, though evening is rapidly approaching.*

(*A knock at the door, then it is opened and* MARTIN, *the boots, comes in, carrying a tray with decanter, syphon and glasses.*)

MARTIN. Beg pardon, Mr Moore! (*He places the tray on one of the tables.*) Asleep! (*He goes over to examine the baggage and looks at the labels inquisitively and reads*): "Stephen Moore. Passenger to—" (*He looks up.*) Begor, the ould gentleman didn't finish writing them! Where's he going now at the end of his days, I wonder?

(*The flute stops.*)

MOORE (*wakening*). Yes, yes! I heard you! Yes, yes! I'm coming! Oh! It's you, Martin! Time to go, is it?

MARTIN. No, sir. You've another three-quarters of an hour before the bus goes to the station.

MOORE. Very good. I was asleep, Martin.

MARTIN. Yes, sir. I see yous are all packed and ready.

(*The music outside recommences.*)

MOORE. Stop that music. Too mournful.

MARTIN. Yes, sir. (*He goes to the window.*) Hi there, Packy!

VOICE (*outside*). Yes?

MARTIN. Stop that one!

VOICE. Right!

(*There is the sound of an altercation, and the music abruptly ceases.*)

MOORE. Thanks. (*He suddenly sees the tray.*) What's all this array for?

MARTIN. Boss sent it up with his compliments. He'd like to see you before you go, sir.

MOORE. Of course. I'll see him. Thank him for me, Martin.

MARTIN. Are ye sure you've got everything packed up, sir?

MOORE. Yes.

MARTIN. You have no address on them labels, sir.

MOORE. No. (*A pause.*) Has the down mail come from Dublin yet?

MARTIN. No, sir. Were you expecting somebody?

MOORE. Yes.

MARTIN. Is it a new man from Dublin is coming to take your place, sir?

MOORE. No.

MARTIN. Miss Mooney got a note this morning from somebody called Watersley.

MOORE. Oh yes, yes – Watersley!

MARTIN. Is he the gentleman that's going to be after you here?

MOORE. Not at all. Watersley is one of the new juniors.

MARTIN. I see. Another colt to be broke in. That'll be three now I've seen in my days. Have you all your papers gathered?

MOORE. I think so, Martin.

MARTIN. Will you want the Japanese gentleman's fan, sir?

(*He lifts it carelessly from the mantelpiece.*)

MOORE. Leave it there for the present.

MARTIN. Right, sir! (*He replaces the fan and begins to examine the chest of drawers.*) Nothing here. . . . Except the top drawer. It's locked, sir.

MOORE. 'Pon my word, now you mention it, Martin, I didn't look in it. (*Fumbling in his pockets and producing a key.*) Give the key to Mr Mooney when you've cleared it out. I was nearly going off with it.

MARTIN. Yes, sir. (*He opens the drawer and examines it.*) Here's something! Photy of a new house. (*He turns it over and reads from an inscription on the back.*) "Plan of Migrant's House. Dan Dolan, Ballyglass."

MOORE. Oh, that be damned! Burn it.

MARTIN. Yes, sir. (*He throws it carelessly aside.*) Here's another.

MOORE. What's it?

MARTIN (*after a scrutiny*). "The Rose Garden, Mount Nevin."

229

MOORE. How did that get there? (*After a pause.*) Burn it.

MARTIN. I'll stick it up here. It's nicer nor Danny Dolan's house's photy.

(*He puts it on the mantelpiece.*)

MOORE. As you like. (*Musingly.*) Poor Barrington! (*With a sudden note of tragic apology.*) "Thou canst not say I did it."

MARTIN (*astonished*). Not at all! No one could blame you. The will of God, sir. A decent old gentleman, Mr Barrington. He done well to clear out of that place. All gone and divided now, sir.

MOORE. Yes. Wiped out. As we all will be some day or another, Martin. What's the rest of that stuff you've got?

MARTIN (*extracting, as he talks, from the drawer*). An old map. (*He throws it carelessly on the table.*) Doesn't look much importance whatever. Here's the last. (*He looks casually at an old diary he has pulled out.*) That's all that's in it. An ould diary of yours, sir. Nineteen hundred and – ach! it's years old. (*He hands it over to* MOORE, *who begins to look carelessly through it.*) Beg pardon, sir. Aren't you sixty-five now, sir?

MOORE. Yes – and two more on that.

MARTIN. There! that's what I told Mr Mooney yesterday. Sure, says I, Mr Moore got took on two years longer than the rest of them, in order, says I, to finish up the Kilrea country—

MOORE (*smiling*). Finish up the Kilrea country! Do you know, Martin, there were old fools like me here in Kilrea who thought the same thing three hundred years ago. And I suppose they, too, kept official diaries like this, and divided the land, and gave some to the Barringtons, some to the Burkes, and some to the Blakes—

MARTIN. Divil a sod they gave my ancestors, anyway. (*With a final look into the drawer; then locking it carefully and pocketing the key.*) I'll call you when it's time, sir.

MOORE. Thanks, Martin. (*Exit* MARTIN.) Hm! (*He continues looking casually through the diary.*) I suppose when I was scribbling this twelve years ago I thought it most important data. (*As he carelessly turns the pages, his attention is suddenly arrested by an entry. He looks carefully at it, and then, intensely interested, begins to read aloud:*) "December 14th. Went Ballinasheeda. O'Neil absent without leave. No information whereabouts. Work in order." "December 15th. Ballinasheeda. Found O'Neill at Lisnashee." (*He peers closer at the page.*) "Formed impression he was—" Hm! Something stroked out. . . . I remember. Poor devil! . . . admitted offence – signed statement . . . sent report Dublin. . . . "December 30th. Severely reprimanded and reduced. Gave word

of honour if allowed remain at work in Ballinasheeda he would—
" (*Slowly, and then with a sudden vehemence.*) And, by God,
O'Neill, you kept it! (*He rises and goes over to the table, and his
attention is suddenly drawn to the map which* MARTIN *has
discovered. He lays down the diary, takes up the map, and begins
to examine it.*) Fitzgormanstown! The Bridge Head! My old
draught map of twenty years ago!

(*Knocking.*)

MARTIN (*appearing*). Mr Mockler to see you, sir.

(MOORE *folds up the map and puts it into his pocket.*)

MOCKLER (*entering smiling*). Mr Moore, and how are you? And I've
someone else with me. (*Speaking towards door.*) He's here. Come
on in, Mrs Morrisey.

MRS MORRISEY. Well, an' I'm glad to see you, Mr Moore. And how
are you? (*She looks at the baggage.*) And all your little belongings
packed and ready. Well, well, but this is the saddest day we've had
in Kilrea this many a year.

MOCKLER. We both just came to pay our last respects, Mr Moore.
And to wish you the best of the best, wherever you're going.

MRS MORRISEY. Indeed, we all wish him the best of the best. Yes,
indeed. (*To* MARTIN.) You can tell my son to come up. He's
waiting in the hall below.

MARTIN (*to* MOORE), Shall I, sir?

MOORE. Yes.

(*Exit* MARTIN.)

MRS MORRISEY. And it's to-day you're going, is it?

MOORE. Yes.

MOCKLER. We had some great arguments in the past, Mr Moore, but
sure there was bound to be disagreements occasionally, and on
the whole you done fair between man and man.

MRS MORRISEY. Indeed he did. And sure if he didn't do what we
thought was justice, there'll be great chances now with that big
place of Fitzgormanstown coming.

MOCKLER. Yes. Thousands of acres in it. Room for everybody.
Launawallia for the landless and twice over.

MRS MORRISEY (*looking through the door*). Ah! Here's my son now.
Come on in, Michael. This is my youngest, Mr Moore.

(MICHAEL, *a rather surly-looking man of thirty years of age or
thereabouts, comes in.*)

MICHAEL (*nodding to* MOORE). Brave day!

MOORE. Yes.

MICHAEL. I hear you're leaving, Mr Moore?

231

MOORE. Yes.

MICHAEL. I suppose there'll be a new man coming?

MOORE. Yes.

MRS MORRISEY. I wonder now who it might be!

MOORE. Don't know.

MRS MORRISEY. I thought they'd have had a matter like that settled long ago?

(MOORE *does not answer.*)

MOCKLER. Begor, this life is nothing but changes!

MICHAEL. Well, I'm not sorry for one. I'm not afraid to repeat what I wrote up to your office as Secretary of our Committee, that we look on the whole of yous as little short of tricksters.

MOORE. Yes. I read that letter.

MICHAEL. I wanted to come in here to-day and see who your successor was, because from this out we want fair play given. No more hole and corner secret dodging, but square play. And before you divide one perch of Fitzgormanstown we want to have the say to them that's to get land in it. Who's your successor, Mr Moore?

MOORE. I've already told you I don't know.

MICHAEL. Well, I want to see him when he comes. You done my mother and me here out of land in Ballyglass that was ours by right years ago, but things is going to be different now, I can tell you. Well, seeing the new man isn't here, I'll be saying good-bye.

(*He moves off.*)

MRS MORRISEY. Michael! Michael! Won't you wish the old gentleman good luck?

MOORE. He needn't waste his time, Mrs Morrisey. I cannot say I'm glad to have met you, young man, on my last day in Kilrea, but I can tell you this to your face, that if you and our mother had got the land that time you were looking for it, it would have been the damnedest scandal in Kilrea. (*With a burst of indignation.*) Go out, and be damned to you!

MOCKLER (*motioning to* MICHAEL). That'll do now, go on down. (*Exit* MICHAEL.) Don't mind the youngster, Mr Moore. Sure we were all like that once. (*To* MRS MORRISEY.) He has no right to be writing stuff like that up to them in Dublin.

MRS MORRISEY. Didn't yourself read it over before he sent it, and you told him it was a grand letter!

MOCKLER (*somewhat taken aback*). Aye. Well. (*He quickly recovers.*) Ach! Mr Moore knows well the kind of balderdash them young fellows be's at. Balderdash! Nothing in it!

MRS MORRISEY. Ach! Never mind the young people. They're always at that sort of thing. Kicking out the old ones. Now, land apart and away, here's my hand, Mr Moore, and sure you and I haven't long to be going, but there's no bad feeling between us.

(*She shakes it with emotion, and then, apparently overcome, she leaves the room.*)

MOORE (*reluctantly taking her hand*). I will believe you then, if so you say.

MOCKLER. She means it, the creature – for the time being! Sure we all means well, sometime or another. It mightn't last, but sure we all mean it while it's on us. Here. (*He goes closer to* MOORE.) Would you like to know the real reason I cam' up to see you? I was sent up by Mooney. Aye. Now not another word about it, but maybe there'll be a little pleasant surprise for you yet, Mr Moore. Just a few of us below in the parlour— (*Knocking.*) Come in.

(KEARNEY *enters. He is of course, older and bent, but little changed otherwise.*)

KEARNEY. Ah – hello, Moore!

MOCKLER. Ah! So you've come, Mr Kearney. Did you see the boss?

KEARNEY. Yes. He's waiting on you below.

MOCKLER. Right. I'll see you again, Mr Moore, below. For the present, slan leat.

(*Exit.*)

KEARNEY. Well, well! So the day's come at last! Der Tag! Eh, well you're the great old soldier. (*Noticing the bags.*) Packed and ready?

MOORE. Yes.

KEARNEY. Of course you're waiting for the – well – you know . . .

MOORE. Waiting for the what?

KEARNEY. Oh, well, it's nothing much. Just a little token. . . . I shouldn't have mentioned it, perhaps.

MOORE. Look here, Kearney. I want to leave this place just as I came into it twenty-five years ago. None of your fussing.

KEARNEY. Like the old Scriptures, eh? "Now lettest thou thy servant depart in peace."

MOORE. But that's part of a burial service, damn you! I'm not dead yet.

KEARNEY. Where are you going? (MOORE *murmurs an indistinct reply.*) What? Not going home to your friends?

MOORE. Friends?

KEARNEY. Yes. Your own people?

MOORE. My own people! (*With a faint smile and gesture.*) They're all – all—

KEARNEY. Any news who your successor is likely to be?

MOORE. No.

KEARNEY. Strange, word hasn't come yet.

MOORE. It is.

KEARNEY. I suppose, Moore, I'd hardly get it, would I?

MOORE. Kearney – I couldn't tell you.

KEARNEY. There's a huge pile of new stuff coming down.

MOORE. Yes. And I used to think – God help me, Kearney! I used to think we were winding up.

KEARNEY. Winding up! We're only just begun. Did O'Neill come up from Ballinasheeda?

MOORE. O'Neill! (*He carefully puts the diary away into one of his pockets.*) Yes, O'Neill . . . O'Neill . . . !

KEARNEY. What about O'Neill?

MOORE. Nothing. (*He looks round the room.*) Do you know, Kearney, it gives me a bit of a wrench to part company with this – this old what-you-call-it – sweating chamber. (*He goes over to the decanter.*) Old Mooney sent this up. Decent of the old man. He's down there in his parlour like a great, big, rheumatic spider unable to do anything but send out messages to the bookies. (*He fills up drinks.*) Cheerio, old comrade!

KEARNEY. Cheerio, old commander! (*He turns away to avoid showing any emotion, and suddenly sees the photograph* MARTIN *has left lying carelessly on the mantelpiece.*) Hm! The Rose Garden, Mount Nevin! Do you remember the rows we had long ago at Ballyglass – old Barrington? His Rose Garden! (*He laughs.*) It's growing the finest of early Rose of Arran spuds for the Morriseys now! My God, what fools we mortals be! What? What? Idiots! What?

(*The door opens slightly and* DAN DOLAN *peeps in.*)

DAN. Mr Moore in?

KEARNEY. Who are you?

DAN. Is Mr Moore in?

MOORE. Yes – I'm here. What is it?

(DOLAN *comes slowly in. His left coat sleeve is empty, for he has lost that arm, and he is bent with age and hard work.*)

DOLAN. D'ye not remember me, Mr Moore? Yourself drove me to hospital the wild bad night they shattered my arm outside that window there.

MOORE (*slowly*). Dan Dolan from Addergoole!

DOLAN. Yes, your honour. Dan Dolan from Addergoole that yous migrated.

234

MOORE. Yes, yes. I know you now.

DOLAN. Well, did the lady call with yous yet?

MOORE. What lady?

DOLAN. There was a lady out at Mount Nevin to-day, and she told me she was coming in to see the Commissioners about a graveyard.

KEARNEY. A graveyard!

DOLAN. Yes, your honour. There's a kind of wild old small place there, on the last bit that yous give me extra at Mount Nevin was once an ould graveyard, for it has broke tombstones in it. She says it's hers.

KEARNEY. Who . . . what she?

DOLAN. Begor now, 'twas Miss Barrington, but she didn't stay no time much, and then she walked up to where the hall steps used to be, and looked kind of bewildered and crying like, as if she couldn't make out what would have been the front and the back of it. Hard for her, when all the stones of the big house had been sold and drew off for the County Council stone-breaker of seven years ago.

MOORE. It would hardly be Cecily Barrington!

KEARNEY. 'Twas a ghost you saw, man! You'll never see a Barrington back in this country again.

DOLAN. Oh, bedad, this was no ghost! Heck! it's a quare ghost that puts you into her car and brings you in along with her. She told me to go ahead of her while she went in to see the Canon.

(*Knocking.*)

MOORE. Come in.

MARTIN (*at door*). Mr Mooney would like to see you, sir, and Mr Kearney, if you'd be pleased to come. He's waiting below in the parlour.

KEARNEY. Right! You'll have to come down, Moore.

MOORE. All right, Martin. (*Exit* MARTIN.) One moment! (*He thinks hard.*) Graveyard! Mount Nevin! Kearney, there was to have been a reservation to the Barringtons of a graveyard plot. There's a copy of the map somewhere in that pile over there. (*He goes over to it and searches.*) Yes. (*Extracts a map.*) There it is. (KEARNEY *and he examine it.*) That small plot there in the north-east corner. I can't see very well, but there's something written in pencil on it.

KEARNEY (*taking up map and scanning it*). Yes. (*Reading.*) "Vendor originally asked for reservation of this plot but took no final steps to have it excluded. Included in parcel 10A. Dan Dolan, allottee."

DOLAN. That would be right, your honour. She said she would call here about it.

235

MARTIN (*again at door*). Boss is waiting, gentlemen.

MOORE. Here – sit down, Dolan. (*He pours out a drink.*) Take a drink, and wait a minute or two and have a look at this map. We'll be back directly.

DAN. Right, your honour.

> (MOORE *and* KEARNEY *go out.* DOLAN *seats himself and sips his drink, while he closely examines the map.* MARTIN *eyes him curiously. There is a short pause.*)

MARTIN. Have you took to maps or to drink, Dolan?

DOLAN. Would you mind, if you please, looking after your own business?

MARTIN. I might as well be telling you the truth. You'll never answer the job you're looking!

DOLAN. What job?

MARTIN. Mr Moore's. There's a new man coming from Dublin, so you can go home and give up this mapping business.

DOLAN. Here, young man! If you had something was nothing much to yourself but was worth a power to someone else was mad to get it, what would you charge them for it?

MARTIN (*with a grin*). You're not going to get made a Commissioner by stealing my brains!

> (*Exit.*)
>
> (DOLAN *resumes his seat at the table and continues his study of the map, and meditatively sips his drink. A knock at the door. It opens and* O'NEILL *looks in. He is still young, but his face is lined and careworn.*)

O'NEILL. Where's Mr Moore?

DOLAN (*with a sharp look at him*). He'll be back presently.

O'NEILL. I'll wait for him here then.

> (*He sits down at the table opposite to* DOLAN.)

DOLAN (*taking a long survey of him*). Be the powers, but it's surely the same!

O'NEILL (*returning his look*). Well, have you sized me up yet?

DOLAN. Begging your honour's pardon, but you're the great likeness of a young man that had hard battling since I seen him here the time I was moving to Ballyglass.

O'NEILL. Ballyglass!

DOLAN. Yes. It's convenient to a place there that went by the name of Mount Nevin. (O'NEILL *gives him a sharp, startled look, but remains silent. The daylight grows dimmer.*) 'Tis easy enough to remember a place by custom, but begor, they all changes. Faces and places. And I seen another face to-day – begor, I wonder

236

would you be remembering it? You'd have more reason than myself for the same, I'm thinking.

O'NEILL (*angrily*). What are you saying?

DOLAN. I mind it well now. This very room. . . . A wild bad night it was. . . . Twelve years ago. . . . And I went over to you and told you she was in the town.

(*He suits the action to the words, and as if in a dream, the scene between the two men unconsciously repeats itself.*)

O'NEILL. Who?

DOLAN. Her.

O'NEILL. Who's her?

DOLAN. That one.

O'NEILL. Which one?

DOLAN. Your one.

(*A silence. It is now dim twilight. A sudden burst of the strains of "For He's a Jolly Good Fellow" comes up from* MOONEY'S *parlour somewhere below. As it gradually dies down, the door opens and* WATERSLEY *enters, followed by* MARTIN, WATERSLEY, *a young, well-dressed youth in tweeds, carries a small portmanteau and despatch bag, and* MARTIN *follows him with a golf-bag, luggage, and a bundle of large brown paper official envelopes.* MARTIN *switches on the light after depositing his burden.*)

WATERSLEY. Hello!

O'NEILL. Hello!

WATERSLEY. Is this the room?

MARTIN. Yes, sir. You can leave these things in here for the present till you gets fixed up. (*Placing the baggage, and then looking hard at* O'NEILL.) You waiting to see anybody, sir? (*Suddenly recognising him.*) Ah, begor, I'm glad to see you again! And how are you, sir?

O'NEILL. I'm well, thank you, Martin. Don't worry anybody. I want to see Mr Moore when he's free.

MARTIN. All right, sir. The boss says you're to have Mr Moore's room, sir . . . in there. I'll put your bags in it presently. (*Nodding towards* DOLAN.) The boss wants him down there as a representative of the migratory gentlemen to say something. Come on, Dolan – you can bring that map with you.

(*He guides* DOLAN *out and shuts the door.*)

(*The strains of "Auld Lang Syne" are heard, with sundry yells of enthusiasm.*)

WATERSLEY. What's all the racket?

O'NEILL. Farewell going on.

WATERSLEY. Funny! I had mine last night.

O'NEILL. Indeed!

(*The singing ceases abruptly.*)

WATERSLEY. Yes. Some of our chaps gave me a bit of a beano last night. (*He points to the golf-bag.*) Gave me that presentation golf-bag there. Jolly decent, wasn't it?

O'NEILL. Very.

WATERSLEY. I won the Captain's Prize this year at Milltown; they took me down three strokes. Any links here?

O'NEILL. I don't know.

(*Sound of applause.*)

WATERSLEY. Hm! Who's getting all the laurel wreaths below?

O'NEILL. Old Stephen Moore.

WATERSLEY. Oh yes – the old chap in charge who's leaving?

O'NEILL. Yes.

WATERSLEY. Jolly glad I got here in time to catch him before he went. I've some letters for him. They should have been posted yesterday, but as I was coming down they made me bring them. I gave them to the boots to deliver. Hell of a journey from Dublin! Took damned near five hours on the train!

O'NEILL. It would.

WATERSLEY. I'd no idea this place was such a beastly distance from Dublin. I say, there wouldn't be much chance of getting back for the week-end, would there?

O'NEILL. Not an earthly.

WATERSLEY. That's a bit tough! You're one of Moore's old squad down here, perhaps?

O'NEILL. Yes.

WATERSLEY. Who's taking his place, I wonder? I hope it's some sporty chap. I heard old Moore was a bit of a Tartar, and gave some of you chaps a bit of a gruelling.

O'NEILL. Yes. What did you hear?

WATERSLEY. Not quite sure what it was all about, but there was something about a girl that one of the chaps got a bit potty about. . . . It wasn't you, by the way, was it? No? . . . Well, the girl jilted him, it appears, and the beau went off the deep end.

O'NEILL. Did he?

WATERSLEY. Yes. And old Moore gave him no end of beans – nearly got him sacked. No fear of me getting sappy like that on girls! It's a proper mug's game. Sport's my line of country. Any chance of a bit of dry fly stuff down here? I brought a rod on the off chance.

238

Do you live here?

O'NEILL. No. I'm at Ballinasheeda.

WATERSLEY. Ballinasheeda! Where's that?

O'NEILL (*beginning to take an interest in the unconscious youngster*). About fifty miles further west by car – sixty by rail.

WATERSLEY. Great Scott! Dublin must be a complete washout for you anyway?

O'NEILL (*laughing in spite of himself*). It is, surely.

WATERSLEY. Hope I'm not stuck there. Where's the nearest links?

O'NEILL. At Lahinch.

WATERSLEY. Jove! That's great! I've often heard of it. How far is it from here?

O'NEILL. About sixty.

WATERSLEY (*dejectedly*). Gosh! I say, does old Moore golf?

O'NEILL. No.

WATERSLEY. Or fish?

O'NEILL. No.

WATERSLEY. Do you?

O'NEILL. No.

WATERSLEY (*alarmed*). And what the hell do you do?
   (*The door opens and* MARTIN *enters carrying a further consignment of envelopes and baggage, which he deposits.*)

WATERSLEY. Oh! I must see where my fishing tackle got to.
   (*Exit.*)

MARTIN. Power of stuff addressed for you here, Mr O'Neill, whatever— Something to occupy that young gentleman in his spare time! (MOORE *enters.*) I'll be taking your baggage down now, Mr Moore. The bus will be round in a couple of minutes.
   (*He takes up* MOORE'S *baggage and goes out.*)

MOORE. Hello, O'Neill! Glad to see you again. So you got my wire?
   (*They shake hands.*)

O'NEILL. Yes. What did you want me for?

MOORE. Because I was anticipating this. (*He hands* O'NEILL *a letter.*) It came by hand to-day from Dublin. (O'NEILL *reads it slowly.*) Seems to have got delayed somehow. It is quite clear?

O'NEILL. Yes. (*Slowly.*) I'm to be . . . your successor in Kilrea.

MOORE. Yes. They followed an old precedent. Took the man from Ballinasheeda.

O'NEILL. Thanks, Moore.

MOORE. You won't be sorry to leave it?

O'NEILL (*with a slow smile*). Were you?

MOORE. No. (*A pause.*) There's someone you and I knew long ago is

239

back again in this place to-day, and you'll have to meet her as my successor and help her.

O'NEILL. Who?

MOORE. Dermot Barrington is dying and has sent – his daughter down about the burial ground at Mount Nevin. I ceased to be an official yesterday – according to that letter you have – so I can't help, but you can. . . . It's not much, only a formal approval.

O'NEILL. Of what?

MOORE. Giving back to the Barringtons their burial ground.

O'NEILL. Burial ground?

MOORE. Yes. Strange world! One time her people had 40,000 acres and 900 tenantry. Now all they hold is barely a rood of burial ground and that by the grace of Dan Dolan – a stranger like ourselves. Dan Dolan . . . twice that old man has given land to us for the same purpose – for a bridge head.

O'NEILL. I didn't follow you, Moore.

MOORE. He gave land years ago as a bridge head for the living. To-day he gives land as a bridge head for the dead . . . for Dermot Barrington, so he can cross over to his own folk!

O'NEILL. Moore – I can't! I – suppose you know. . . . It was he compelled her to write me – and break it all off between us . . . twelve years ago . . . and I buried her at Ballinasheeda.

(KEARNEY *enters.*)

MOORE. O'Neill, I've already told Kearney the news.

KEARNEY (*shaking hands with* O'NEILL). And congratulations, O'Neill. I thought it might have come my way, but I'll try not to grouse, though I know Ellen will. You've had a long tarry at Ballinasheeda and done a powerful lot of work.

O'NEILL (*looking at* MOORE *appealingly.*) Couldn't . . . Kearney?

MOORE. No. It's your responsibility.

(WATERSLEY *enters.*)

KEARNEY. What's this?

WATERSLEY. My name's Watersley. It was I that brought down the good news.

KEARNEY. The what?

WATERSLEY. The good news. They mugged up things a bit in the office, and I was to have come down yesterday, but instead I caught the mail this morning.

MOORE. I see. So you're our new recruit! Have you met O'Neill?

O'NEILL (*smiling*). Yes. I know a fair amount about him already.

(DAN DOLAN *and* MOCKLER *enter.* MOCKLER *is expansive and hilarious with drink.*)

240

MOCKLER. Hurroo! What d'ye think, gentlemen? Look at him! Dan Dolan! . . . The Duke of Addergoole! . . . The man that's after agreeing to sign, convey and assign land free, gratis, and for nothing, to oblige the remains of an ancient ould family. More power to you, Daniel! (*He slaps the latter on the back.*) But weren't you the greatest old omadhaun in the world that didn't wait on the great news that's come down by the Deputy – the new Land Act is through and Fitzgormanstown Ranch will be for the people. (*He laughs uproariously.*) And you! (*He thumps* DOLAN.) You left your holding at Addergoole and faced murder and loss of limb, and if you'd only had the sense of a mouse and waited, you'd have had the grandest and the greatest holding for the asking! The Duke of Addergoole! (*As he talks he drifts nearer the decanter and tray.*) The only bit o' land that they can put a bridge across to get into it, and you sold it for what you got in Ballyglass! Begorras! and there's idiots still walking the earth and you're one of them. But a gentleman, Daniel – you were always a gentleman!

(*He commences filling out drinks from the decanter.*)

(*The mention of Fitzgormanstown has made* MOORE *suddenly recollect the map in his pocket. He takes it out and shows it to* O'NEILL *as* MOCKLER *ceases talking.*)

MOORE. If it's true about Fitzgormanstown, this old map of mine might be some use to you, O'Neill. Take it, and welcome.

(*He hands it over.*)

MOCKLER. And now, gentlemen, I'm only after leaving our good host Mr Mooney below, and says he to me, "Mockler, will you go up and make sure that the company above take advantage of what I sent up, and drink a dock-an-dorus to Mr Moore" (*Turning to the decanter and tray.*) And he told me to take no refusals.

MARTIN (*at door*). The bus is waiting, Mr Moore.

MOCKLER. Here! (*Catching him.*) Make yourself attentive. Give me a hand with this. Give everybody something. (*Approaching* WATERSLEY *with a drink.*) So you're the young one that's come down?

WATERSLEY Yes. (*He makes a gesture of disapproval.*) No, thanks. No, thanks. Don't drink.

MOCKLER (*astonished*). You what!

WATERSLEY. Don't touch. Knocks you off form.

MOCKLER. Knocks you off what?

WATERSLEY. Off form. No, thanks. Don't touch.

MOCKLER. And what d'ye do?

WATERSLEY. Well, I hope – I hope it's no harm: I'm fond of a bit of

241

sport.

MOCKLER (*effectively and delightedly*). Good boy! The Curragh, maybe – or The Galway Plate?

WATERSLEY. Oh, no, no. Golf!

MOCKLER (*as if he hadn't heard aright*). Golf!

O'NEILL. Yes – he golfs.

WATERSLEY. Yes. (MOCKLER *suddenly sees the golf-bag and inspects it.*) That's my presentation bag.

MOCKLER (*with a gesture of surprised explanation towards the company present*). He golfs!

WATERSLEY. Yes.

MOCKLER. Anything else?

WATERSLEY. Yes, I – fish. Dry fly.

MOCKLER (*to the company*). Fishes! Dry fly!

WATERSLEY. Yes.

DOLAN (*waking up suddenly from a contemplative silence, during which he has regarded* MOCKLER *with growing resentment*). So I'm . . . I'm the Duke of Addergoole to-day, is it, Mockler?

MOCKLER (*delighted at having roused the old man*).Yes, Daniel. The Duke of Addergoole, and well named.

DOLAN. Aye. And the greatest old omadhaun in the world! Aye! That didn't wait on the great news and the great new Land Act. Aye. A walking idiot with no sense that could have had the greatest and the grandest holding in Fitzgormanstown for the asking, Mr Mockler?

MOCKLER. You could—

DOLAN. Whist! Is it golf sticks (*he points to* WATERSLEY) or O'Neill or the Commissioners? Or is it yourself and young Morrisey and your committee? Half-a-crown down and register for land! Twopence on the postage, fourpence on the station'ry, a shilling on the Secretary, and the rest – on the crown and feathers! Two-and-sixpence for the greatest and the grandest holding in Fitzgormanstown for the asking! Live horse and get registered for grass! (*With passionate anger.*) I asked all I'll ever ask, and I got all I'll ever get from one man here (*he points to Moore*) and the damn the Committee, Commissioners, Morrisey or Mockler will ever get me to surrender one perch of what I got, for the hundred best acres in Connaught. (*He goes over to* MOORE *and takes his hand.*) Long life to you, Mr Moore, and good-bye. You always treated me decent. (*He makes his way towards the door.*) And may the great God be ever wondering at the luck you'd be having – and good-bye.

242

(*Exit.*)

(*A loud motor-horn blows impatiently.*)

MARTIN (*suddenly*). Oh, glory be to God – the bus, sir! The bus! Time to be off.

(*Exit* MOCKLER.)

MOORE. Well, I must say good-bye, boys. (*He goes over to* WATERSLEY *and looks quizzically at him.*) Good-bye, my boy. I don't know whether to laugh at you or cry. . . . I think I'll laugh. . . . Fishing! (*He looks over smiling at* O'NEILL *and* KEARNEY. *Then he begins to laugh.*) Golfing! (*The whole company burst into laughter.*) Good-bye!

(KEARNEY *and* O'NEILL *precede* MOORE *through the door. As the latter is on the point of going out he catches sight of the little Japanese fan that* GOSUKI *had presented. He takes it, glances at it, and then quietly throws it into the fireplace and passes out.*)

(*A silence. Then the strains of "Auld Lang Syne" are heard from below.* WATERSLEY *goes over to the window as if to watch the farewell. The sound of the bus departing; the singing stops.* WATERSLEY, *going over towards the baggage, glances carelessly at the photograph of the Rose Garden, then picks up the fan, and reads the inscription on it.*)

WATERSLEY. "Remembrance gracious to Moore Sama, Officer of the Great Department of State, Ireland."

(*He drops it carelessly back in the fireplace, goes over to his golf-bag, extracts the putter, and begins practising assiduously with an imaginary ball. He is fully occupied doing so when somebody approaches the door, which has been left open, hesitates, and knocks.* WATERSLEY, *too intent on what he is doing, does not hear. The somebody comes in. It is* CECILY BARRINGTON.)

CECILY. I beg your pardon!

WATERSLEY. Oh, not at all! Do you want to see anybody?

CECILY. Yes. I have a document here – a form of some kind of consent. (*She produces it.*) I was to get it signed by the officer in charge.

WATERSLEY. Oh! Are you in a hurry?

CECILY. Yes. I am going on by car immediately I get it completed. It was to have been signed by Mr Moore, but I understand he's gone.

WATERSLEY. Yes – gone for good. Didn't you hear all the hooley that was going on? "Auld Lang Syne" and all the rest of it? Have a seat while I go down and see if I can get the new man for you.

(*He hurriedly goes out, having given her a chair.* CECILY *sits nervously fingering the document she has brought. She suddenly rises as her eyes catch sight of the little picture post-card of the Rose Garden, and involuntarily she goes over, takes it in her hand and examines it.*)

CECILY (*slowly reading from the card*). "The Rose Garden, Mount Nevin. From C. B."

(*She replaces the card and slowly goes back to her seat. Then overcome, gives way to her tears.* WATERSLEY *re-enters. She hurriedly tries to regain her composure.*)

WATERSLEY. They're just gone off on the bus to the station. Be back in a jiffy.

(*He begins unconsciously to resume practising his putter.*)

CECILY. Thank you. (*A pause.*) Are you one of the staff here now?

WATERSLEY. Yes. But as a matter of fact, I only came down to-day to join up.

CECILY. Oh! And what are you going to do down here?

WATERSLEY. Between you and me, I'm going to try and wrangle a few games with this (*waving the putter*) if I can.

CECILY. Will you be doing anything else?

WATERSLEY. Oh Lord, yes! Work, I suppose.

CECILY. What sort of work?

WATERSLEY. Oh – the usual sort of stuff . . . you know, taking up land from people and giving it out to people.

CECILY. Do you ever take land from people and give it back to them again?

WATERSLEY. No! Never heard of such a case – did you?

CECILY. No. It's rarely done, I suppose.

WATERSLEY. I should say so. Did they take up land from you?

CECILY. Yes. They took all we had.

WATERSLEY. Oh! And you're wanting some back?

CECILY. Yes.

WATERSLEY. I wouldn't ask if I were you. It'll only mean trouble.

CECILY. It's only a very small plot.

WATERSLEY. Doesn't matter – small or large – same thing! I've seen a man murder another over a few perches of street. They might be different down here, but I doubt it.

CECILY. Will this work of yours ever come to an end?

WATERSLEY. Don't know. I suppose we'll go on dividing to Tibbs' Eve!

CECILY. Until Ireland is all one great sea of small holdings?

244

WATERSLEY. Yes.

CECILY. Nothing but little cottages and little farms?

WATERSLEY. Yes. Millions of them! The old demesne and those places, they'll all go phut!

CECILY. And no one will ever remember the people who lived in them once?

WATERSLEY. I say—(*He gives her a suspicious stare.*) No! Sorry, but I can't discuss things like that. Against the regulations. You see, we're forbidden to discuss politics.

CECILY. But we might be talking economics?

WATERSLEY. Same thing. No, thanks. One of our chaps got into the – beg pardon! – he got into the devil's own row last week down in Kildare because he was blathering about rates on a bog. . . . So I'm taking no chances. Talk nothing but golf now. Safer! (*He makes a few strokes with his club, then stops and takes a long look at her.*) Do you belong this side of the country?

CECILY. Yes. We once had a place out here.

WATERSLEY. Oh! What did you call it?

CECILY. Mount Nevin. I came down here to-day to see if I could get – well, just a little bit of it back again.

WATERSLEY. I know, yes. Site for a bungalow or something like that?

CECILY. No. A place where my people are buried.

WATERSLEY (*abashed*). Oh! Sorry! I'm really sorry. (*There is a noise outside.*) Here they are now.

(MARTIN *and* O'NEILL *enter.* MARTIN *is carrying baggage.*)

MARTIN. In here, Mr O'Neill. This way to Mr Moore's old room.

(MARTIN *crosses over to the door to left and goes in.* O'NEILL *is following him when he suddenly sees* CECILY *and stops.*)

WATERSLEY. This lady is waiting to see you, sir – about – a – plot . . . land up at Mount Nevin.

O'NEILL. Oh, yes. (*He bows formally.*) Moore told me. I'm sorry to hear the reason. . . . Have you . . . the form?

CECILY. Yes. (*She produces it.*) Dolan has already signed it and I understand all that's required is formal approval by you, subject to consent in Dublin.

O'NEILL. Yes. (*He looks over the form.*) Would you mind signing here – on that line. (CECILY *does so. He examines her signature.*) "Cecily Travers!" . . . married woman?

CECILY. Yes.

O'NEILL. Then add wife of— and put your husband's name.

(*She does so.* O'NEILL *witnesses her signature in silence, blots, and then hands over the form.* MARTIN *passes silently through*

245

the room and goes out.)

CECILY. Might I ask a small favour?

O'NEILL. I would be glad to grant it if I can.

CECILY. If I may, I would like to take that photograph there of the Rose Garden.

O'NEILL. I – I think it belongs to Moore.

CECILY. No. I sent it to you. (*He goes over to get it for her.*) It was the only one I had. May I take it with me?

O'NEILL (*after a glance at it*). Yes. I've lost all title . . . to anything of yours long ago.

CECILY. But did you want to keep it?

O'NEILL. I lost it – as I did something . . . more important years ago. And to-day's the first time I've seen . . . either of them again.

(MARTIN *suddenly appears at door.*)

MARTIN. The car is ready, ma'am.

CECILY. Thank you. (*Exit* MARTIN.) It's strange to be back in this same room . . . and to see you . . . again . . . after all these years. Where have you been ever since?

O'NEILL. At Ballinasheeda.

CECILY. All those years? Ever since—?

O'NEILL. Yes.

CECILY. Are you going back there?

O'NEILL. No. I'm here as Moore's successor.

CECILY. To carry on his work?

O'NEILL. Yes, if I can.

CECILY. If you can. Do you believe in it?

O'NEILL. He did.

CECILY. Do you?

O'NEILL. Yes. (*He stops.*) Pardon me. . . . (*He rises abruptly.*) It was the only thing at Ballinasheeda – I could believe in. . . .

(*He goes off abruptly to his room and closes the door.*)

(CECILY *stands irresolutely silent. Then she sees* WATERSLEY, *who has remained a silent spectator.*)

CECILY. Will you give him a message from me? That I . . . I . . . I shall come back again to thank him . . . I'm . . . I'm very grateful to all of you – to him . . . and to Dan Dolan . . . and to Moore.

WATERSLEY. Yes. But Moore's gone.

(*Exit.*)

(WATERSLEY *looks after her for a second or so. Then, with a sudden gesture of dismay, he hurriedly starts to search in his despatch case and extracts some documents. He looks at them, and then goes over and knocks at* O'NEILL'S *door.*)

246

CECILY. I don't think he's gone. Good-bye.

WATERSLEY. I say! O'Neill! O'Neill! (O'NEILL *comes out.*) She's gone— Never mind— Said she'd come back again soon. But look here . . . I'm damned sorry! They told me to be sure to give you this first thing. Urgent and most important. (*He hands the document over.*) And I put it away so carefully that I lost sight of the damned thing!

O'NEILL (*looking through the file, then with a start*). Watersley! What do you think this is?

WATERSLEY. Haven't the foggiest!

O'NEILL. And the old man hardly gone! It's an order to inspect at 10 a.m. to-morrow. . . . (*Reading.*) "Owner has been already notified direct to meet you at Fitzgormanstown."

WATERSLEY. Where's that?

O'NEILL. I forgot. Of course you wouldn't know. They say here they've sent blank sheets and a schedule from the Valuation Commissioner's records. The schedule is here. Where are the sheets?

WATERSLEY. Over there. That bundle Martin brought up.

O'NEILL. Open them out. Quick! (WATERSLEY *unrolls them on the table.*) Wait! Wait a moment! The old man gave me his map! (*He extracts it.*) Take those sheets and Moore's map, and compare them and edge off the boundaries in pencil and tick off the town-lands, while I read out the schedule. (WATERSLEY *arranges the maps, and begins to work as directed.*) Ready?

WATERSLEY. Yes.

O'NEILL. Fitzgormanstown Eighter. One thousand, two hundred and six acres, no roods, ten perches.

WATERSLEY. . . . ten perches. Right! Got 'em!

O'NEILL. Fitzgormanstown Oughter. Two thousand, one hundred and fifteen acres, three roods, six perches.

WATERSLEY (*after a pause*). Right! Got 'em!

O'NEILL. Cloonascragh. Five hundred and nine acres, two roods and fifteen perches.

WATERSLEY. Cloonascragh – can't see it. Cloonascragh . . . now where the hell is Cloonascragh? Ah! that's where my Irish comes in. The cows' meadow – meadow land – that should be near a river. Right . . . the river Shivna runs all round the place . . . except to the south, and that's all swamp and bog. How on earth will you ever get into this place? Cloonascragh! (*He studies the map carefully.*) Hallo! There's roads here on this old map and not a sign of them on the new sheets! New holdings and fences and

247

plantations, and sites for houses . . . and more roads . . . and not a trace of them on the new sheets. And here's a – a – bridge. (*Reading from map.*) "Old holding of Dan Dolan. Road to be reserved for" . . . marked in big letters . . . "Bridge Head."

O'NEILL. Dan Dolan's land! "Bridge Head!" "He gave land years ago as a bridge head for the living. To-day he gives land as a bridge for the dead. . . ." And she *is* dead. I buried her in Ballinasheeda years ago.

WATERSLEY (*interested and intent on his map*). Eh? There's no Ballinasheeda here. Ah! Here I've got Cloonascragh! Right! Sorry. Go on, please. My Scott! but there's whales of land here. And new holdings . . . ten . . . fifteen . . . thirty . . . thirty-five . . . by Jove! . . . one-hundred-and-sixty new holdings. Phew! Go on, O'Neill. Next, please. . . . I've got Cloonascragh. Next, please. Go on. Next. (*He suddenly looks up aghast at* O'NEILL, *who is gazing at him with a blank stare.*) I say – what's up? What are you staring at me like that for, O'Neill?

O'NEILL. My God! (*With a sudden spasm of relief.*) It is *you,* Watersley!

WATERSLEY. Yes. Why, who else would I be?

O'NEILL. You could be – and you were – and you might yet be what I saw in your chair a second ago.

WATERSLEY. Who?

O'NEILL. Something that was old Stephen Moore.

(CURTAIN.)

BIBLIOGRAPHICAL CHECKLIST

Plays
The Turn of the Road, Maunsel, Dublin, 1907.
The Troth, Maunsel, Dublin, 1909.
The Drone, Maunsel, Dublin 1909; Luce, Boston, 1912.
Red Turf, in *The Drone and Other Plays*, Maunsel, Dublin, 1912.
Evening, in *The Lady of the House*, Christmas 1913, pp. 43–44.
Phantoms, in *Dublin Magazine*, I, 5 (first series), December, 1923, pp. 382–391.
A Prologue, in *Dublin Magazine*, II, 11 (first series), June 1925, pp. 723–725.
Bridge Head, in *Plays of Changing Ireland*, ed. Curtis Canfield, Macmillan, New York, 1936, pp. 405–71. (Canfield supplies introductory comment on pp. 198–99.)
Published separately: Constable, London, and Macmillan of Canada, Toronto, 1939
Peter, Duffy, Dublin, 1944; revised version, Duffy, Dublin, 1964.

Collections
The Drone and Other Plays (containing *The Drone, The Turn of the Road, Red Turf, The Troth*), Maunsel, Dublin, 1912; Little Brown, Boston, 1917.
Selected Plays (containing *The Drone, Peter, Bridge Head*), ed. John Killen, Institute of Irish Studies, Queen's University of Belfast, Belfast, 1997.

Translations
a) Irish
Fé Bhrigh Na Mionn (The Troth) trs. Liam O'Domnaill, Comor-cluici Leabhar, Dublin, 1927; Official Publications Office, Dublin, 1932.
An Liúdramán (The Drone), trs. Eoghan Ó Neachtain, Stationery Office, Dublin, 1932.
Peadar (Peter) trs. Seán Mac Maoláin, Stationery Office, Dublin, 1945.
b) Swedish
Där vägen kröker (The Turn of the Road) trs. Rudolf Verne, Lagerström, Stockholm, 1911.

First Productions of Plays

Unless otherwise stated all were first performed by the Ulster Literary Theatre.

The Turn of the Road, privately, 4 December 1906, at the Examination Hall of the Queen's University, Belfast; publicly, 17 December 1906, at the Ulster Minor Hall, Belfast.

The Drone, two-act version: 24 April 1908, at the Abbey Theatre, Dublin; three-act version, probably sometime during 17–22 May 1909, at the Grand Opera House, Belfast.

The Troth, 31 October 1908, by William Mollison's Company at the Crown Theatre, Peckham, London.

The Gomeril, 29 April 1909, by the Theatre of Ireland at the Large Concert Hall, the Rotunda, Dublin.

The following plays were all first performed at the Grand Opera House, Belfast:

Captain of the Hosts, 8 March 1910

Red Turf, 5 December 1911

If!, 25 November 1913

Evening, 2 March 1914

Neil Gallina (revised version of *Captain of the Hosts*), 13 December 1916

Industry, 6 December 1917

Phantoms, 28 November 1923, Gaiety Theatre, Dublin

Peter, 28 January 1930, Abbey Theatre Company, Abbey Theatre, Dublin

Bridge Head (then called *Bridgehead*), 18 June 1934, Abbey Theatre Company, Abbey Theatre, Dublin.

Prose

'The Freeholder' in *The Irish Review* (Dublin), I, 1, November 1911, pp. 432–434.

'Gerald MacNamara', in *The Dublin Magazine*, XIII, 2 (second series), April 1938, pp. 53– 56.

'The Theatre' (on Lennox Robinson's *Forget-Me-Not* and Sean O'Casey's *The Plough and the Stars*), in *The Bell*, IV, 1, April 1942, pp. 47–54.

'The Theatre – Two Opinions' (the first: on Paul Vincent Carroll's *The Strings are False*), in *The Bell*, IV, 2, May 1942, pp. 145–46.

'The Best Books on Ulster' in *The Bell*, IV, 4, November 1942, p. 252.

'F. J. McCormick', in *The Capuchin Annual*, 1948, p. 171.

'The Ulster Literary Theatre', in *The Dublin Magazine*, XXX, 2 (second series), April–June 1955, pp.15–21.

Selected Biographical Sources and Criticism

Sam Hanna Bell, *The Theatre in Ulster,* Gill & Macmillan, Dublin, 1972, *passim.*

'The Bellman' (pseud. of Larry Morrow), 'Meet Rutherford Mayne', in *The Bell*, IV, 2, November 1942, pp. 241–48.

D. Felicitas Corrigan, *Helen Waddell. A Biography*, Victor Gollancz, London, 1986, *passim*.

John Killen, '"Rutherford Mayne Re-assessed": an exhibition at the Linen Hall Library, 11 November–27 November 1993', in *The Linen Hall Review*, X, 2, Autumn 1993, pp. 12–13. (With two Grace Plunkett illustrations.)

John Killen, 'Introduction' to Rutherford Mayne, *Selected Plays*, Institute of Irish Studies, Belfast, 1997, pp. 1–18.

Margaret McHenry, *The Ulster Theatre in Ireland*, 'A Thesis in English Literature presented to the Faculty of the Graduate School in Partial Fulfillment of the Requirements for the Degree of Doctor of Philosophy', Westbrook Publishing Company, Philadelphia, PA, 1931, *passim*.

Cornelius Weygandt, 'Mr. Rutherford Mayne', in *Irish Plays and Playwrights*, Houghton Mifflin Company, Boston & New York, 1913, facsimile reprint Greenwood Press, Westport CT, 1979, pp. 233–39.

IRISH DRAMA SELECTIONS

ISSN 0260–7962

1. SELECTED PLAYS OF LENNOX ROBINSON
Chosen and introduced by Christopher Murray
Contains *Patriots, The Whiteheaded Boy, Crabbed Youth and Age, The Big House, Drama at Inish, Church Street*, Bibliographical Checklist.

2. SELECTED PLAYS OF DENIS JOHNSTON
Chosen and introduced by Joseph Ronsley
Contains *The Old Lady Says 'No!'*, (with Curtis Canfield's list of poems used in the Prologue), *The Moon in the Yellow River, The Golden Cuckoo, The Dreaming Dust, The Scythe and the Sunset*, with Johnston's prose introductions and essays on the plays, Bibliographical Checklist.

3. SELECTED PLAYS OF LADY GREGORY
Foreword Sean O'Casey
Chosen and introduced by Mary Fitzgerald
Contains *The Travelling Man, Spreading the News, Kincora, Hyacinth Halvey, The Doctor In Spite of Himself, The Goal Gate, The Rising of the Moon, Dervorgilla, The Workhouse Ward, Grania, The Golden Apple, The Story Brought by Brigit, Dave*, Lady Gregory on Playwriting and her Plays, Bibliographical Checklist.

4. SELECTED PLAYS OF DION BOUCICAULT
Chosen and introduced by Andrew Parkin
Contains *London Assurance, The Corsican Brothers, The Octoroon, The Colleen Bawn, The Shaughraun, Robert Emmet*, Bibliographical Checklist.

5. SELECTED PLAYS OF ST JOHN ERVINE
Chosen and introduced by John Cronin
Contains *Mixed Marriage, Jane Clegg, John Ferguson, Boyd's Shop, Friends and Relations*, prose extracts, Bibliographical Checklist.

6. SELECTED PLAYS OF BRIAN FRIEL
   Chosen and introduced by Seamus Deane
   Contains *Philadelphia, Here I Come, Translations, The Freedom of the City, Living Quarters, Faith Healer, Aristocrats*, Bibliographical Checklist.
   This title is only for sale in North America (by Catholic University of America Press).

7. SELECTED PLAYS OF DOUGLAS HYDE
   Chosen and introduced by Janet Egleson Dunleavy and Gareth Dunleavy
   Contains *The Twisting of the Rope, The Marriage, The Lost Saint, The Nativity, King James, The Bursting of the Bubble, The Tinker and the Sheeog, The Matchmaking, The Schoolmaster*, Bibliographical Checklist. This volume publishes the original Irish language texts with Lady Gregory's translations.

8. SELECTED PLAYS OF GEORGE MOORE
   AND EDWARD MARTYN
   Chosen and introduced by David B. Eakin and Michael Case
   Contains Moore's *The Strike at Arlingford, The Bending of the Bough, The Coming of Gabrielle, The Passing of the Essenes;* and Martyn's *The Heather Field, Maeve, The Tale of a Town*. Bibliographical Checklist.

9. SELECTED PLAYS OF HUGH LEONARD
   Chosen and introduced by S. F. Gallagher
   Contains *The Au Pair Man, The Patrick Pearse Motel, Da, Summer, A Life, Kill*. Bibliographical Checklist.

10. SELECTED PLAYS OF T. C. MURRAY
    Chosen and introduced by Richard Allen Cave
    Contains *Sovereign Love, Birthright, Maurice Harte, The Briery Gap, Autumn Fire, The Pipe in the Fields*, the hitherto unpublished *Illumination*, and his essay 'George Shiels, Brinsley MacNamara, Etc.' Bibliographical Checklist.

11. SELECTED PLAYS OF MICHEÁL mac LIAMMÓIR
    Chosen and introduced by John Barrett
    Contains *Where Stars Walk, Ill Met by Moonlight, The Mountains Look Different, The Liar, Prelude in Kazbek Street*, Selected writings on Plays and Players, Bibliographical Checklist.

12. SELECTED PLAYS OF M. J. MOLLOY
Chosen and introduced by Robert O'Driscoll
Contains *The King of Friday's Men*, *The Paddy Pedlar*, *The Wood of the Whispering*, *Daughter from Over the Water*, *Petticoat Loose*, and the previously unpublished *The Bachelor's Daughter*. Bibliographical Checklist.

13. SELECTED PLAYS OF RUTHERFORD MAYNE
Chosen and introduced by Wolfgang Zach
Contains *The Turn of the Road*, *The Drone*, *Red Turf*, *The Troth*, *Phantoms*, *Bridge Head*, *Peter*, 'The Ulster Literary Theatre' and 'Meet Rutherford Mayne', Bibliographical Checklist.

14. SELECTED PLAYS OF AUSTIN CLARKE
Chosen and introduced by Mary Shine Thompson
Includes *The Son of Learning*, *The Flame*, *Black Fast*, *The Kiss*, *As the Crow Flies*, *The Viscount of Blarney*, *The Second Kiss*, *Liberty Lane*, and the hitherto unpublished *The Frenzy of Sweeney*, and *St Patrick's Purgatory* (a translation of Calderón's play), 'Verse Speaking and Verse Drama', Bibliographical Checklist.